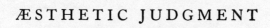

ÆSTHETIC JUDGMENT

ÆSTHETIC JUDGMENT

D. W. PRALL

Introduction by Ralph Ross

"No intelligent man will ever be so bold as to put into language those things which his reason has contemplated, especially not into a form that is unalterable,—which must be the case with what is expressed in written symbols."
—PLATO.

THOMAS Y. CROWELL COMPANY
NEW YORK

PREFACE

This book makes no claim to being a substantive contribution to æsthetic theory. It was written primarily for the use of college students, and its purpose is to offer with some degree of adequacy and system a survey of the field. No one who has even glanced at recent books on the subject will be likely to think more than this possible in a general treatment. There are too many open questions, too many well-grounded and at the same time widely differing views of the field itself, and too many obvious holes in our knowledge of the arts and of our relation to them. A text-book in æsthetics is after all only an essay. But it is surely not absurd to try to put into writing such relevant information as seems reliable in the light of constant illustration, and to bring this matter together under a few general conceptions and in an order that may throw light upon it.

The substance of many of the chapters is therefore that of usual discussions, and it would have been mere pedantry constantly to acknowledge indebtedness for ideas which are for the most part the common property of those at all instructed in æsthetic theory. On the other hand, I have not thought that anything less than the most I could suppose I knew, or had grounds for thinking reasonable or relevantly interesting, either in the way of general ideas or of particular opinions, would be best to offer to students. Consequently I have written as I should write for any one else, and I hope that there may be something in the book that is of value to mature minds interested in æsthetic theory or in the fine arts.

PREFACE

What seems to me more or less my own in the volume may be pointed out briefly to such readers of this preface as do not care to waste time on the succeeding pages. I have treated æsthetic judgments as records of æsthetic experience and tried to indicate the nature of such experience, primarily as occurring in everyday life, by inquiring into the meaning of these records. I have distinguished the beauty of strictly æsthetic surface from the beauty of art, and analyzed the more narrowly æsthetic sensuous field in accordance with the usual division into auditory and visual elements. In these I have distinguished the types of order intrinsic to the elements as such from the imposed orders used in composition in the arts; and in a somewhat lengthy account of rhythm I have indicated the nature of one of the most fundamental kinds of imposed order. I have also tried to do justice to the data of the "lower" senses in emphasizing the elementary but definitely æsthetic character of smells and tastes and vital feelings. In surveying the fine arts as conscious expression externalized upon æsthetic surfaces I have followed the usual list; but I have tried to indicate the significant difference between the comparative immediacy of music at one extreme and the largely non-æsthetic beauty of poetry at the other. In treating of prose as one of the combined arts, and of expression in nature and symbolism in art, I have gone a little further to justify this distinction.

The chapter on primitive art is merely illustrative, but it furnishes solid ground for taking æsthetic surface in the thinner sense, and the analysis of this surface in ordinary experience, as significant for any theory of beauty. The chapter on criticism is an attempt to make out, in the light of modern value-theory, the relation of critical judgment and appreciation to more strictly æsthetic judgment, and to indicate briefly but definitely the nature of standards, the types of criticism, and the function of critics. The last chapter relates æsthetic judgment and æsthetic theory to knowledge in general and suggests that pluralism is as necessary to sound thinking in the regions of art as Mr. Dewey has found it to be in social and political thinking. The logic that is the ground of such a view is not Mr. Dewey's; but in any case it could hardly be defended in an essay in æsthetics; its only possible sanction here lies not in the authority on which it rests, high as that authority is, but in the theory it has engendered. What value that has, either in clarity or in comprehensiveness, must be left to the judgment of readers who will go further than a preface.

The illustrations, in so far as the reproductions are successful, are simply concrete instances, specific beauties, to remind the reader, when the author fails to do so, of the actual subject-matter under discussion.

I have had so much help from so many friendly experts by way of careful criticism of these chapters that particular acknowledgments would make the book appear a collaborative enterprise. Since my collaborators are not to blame, however, for the weakness of my efforts or the inadequacy of my results, I shall name no names and think the protection thus given better thanks than printed expressions of gratitude. The book was finished in the early fall of 1927, but this preface is dated February, 1929.

CONTENTS

CONTENTS

CONTENTS

CONTENTS

INTRODUCTION

ALTHOUGH his academic career gave no signs of it, David Wight Prall had in him the qualities of a revolutionist. Like Josiah Royce he first taught English, was on the faculty at Berkeley, California, and then moved to Harvard. He never pushed his ideas systematically in Royce's fashion, but at the time of his death he was expanding some papers in epistemology and may have glimpsed the final form of his own philosophy.

Prall started his work in the theory of value, the subject of his dissertation and of an exchange with John Dewey, and then wrote two books on one branch of value-theory, æsthetics. *Æsthetic Judgment* came first and was the broader of the two; *Æsthetic Analysis,* his second book, started from some of the more technical ideas in *Æsthetic Judgment* and developed them further. Many people who quote Prall seem to have read only one of the two. Susanne Langer accepts Prall's analyses of the arts in *Æsthetic Analysis* as impeccable, but finds him too narrow, accusing him of neglecting subjects which in fact he treated carefully in *Æsthetic Judgment.* Other philosophers consider Prall to be the author only of *Æsthetic Judgment* and make curious evaluations of him, unjustified even by this one book. Paul Weiss, for example, finds Prall a positivist, but that is perhaps only another way of treating him, as Mrs. Langer does, as too narrow.

More recently, Prall has been disappearing from anthologies of æsthetics in favor of philosophers stating a more contemporary theme. He is absent from those books in name only, of course, because he influences the entire subject of æsthetics, in part because of his "narrowness." He taught a generation or two how to analyze each of the arts, how they differed from each other, and how knowledge of technique and detail influenced our very perception of works of art. If the New Critics did not read him, and I suspect few of them did, they were nonetheless responsive to his implicit demands that art be looked at freshly, and that its history and influence be secondary to perception and analysis of individual works. They learned very well something else Prall taught—that hallowed principles of æsthetic should never be applied simply or mechanically to any object of art. Think of the nonsense that would result from applying Aristotle's principle of unity to post-classical drama: *Hamlet* would emerge a shambles.

But what I have been saying has to do with Prall's ambience and influence, not with the revolutionary theme he uttered, that has not been developed in subsequent philosophy. In *Æsthetic Analysis* Prall shifted the burden of the revolution to Dewey, whose massive American reputation at the time could carry any burden, saying "Mr. Dewey has shown us" that "art is necessarily the nearest approach to anything like adequate communication." In *Æsthetic Judgment* he was bolder, at least in this respect, and went farther, announcing "that the arts express deeply and broadly, but always determinately and uniquely, the very point of life, that they are the most precisely drawn lineaments of men's souls that we know." And then he condemned "intellectual persons" who minimize the precision of artistic statement and prefer discourse, by adding, "A still further limitation or degeneracy of mind is that which deals in these linguistic symbols alone, failing to recognize through them those ultimate sensuous data or essences, to refer to which they were invented, and which are themselves the only targets that the shafts of discourse can actually hit."

Prall was implying, I suppose, that language on the level of intension was inevitably circular, as dictionaries attest. A disembodied intelligence might memorize the entire dictionary in any and all languages and still not understand what one word meant, because words in a dictionary are defined only by other words. It is not intelligence alone that enables us to grasp meaning, but the body, too, with its sensations and internal network. The reason it takes body-and-mind to deal with meaning is that linguistic symbols refer *basically* not to other linguistic symbols but to elements of experience, Prall's "targets." Of course, some words are about words, as are the rules of grammar, but their usefulness is predicated on the relation of most words to experience. Science, too, may deal with its own procedures and hypothetical structures, as grammar deals with relations among words, but the fundamental condition that makes this kind of scientific work intelligible and useful is that in the end science is anchored in observation.

Scientific observation is undoubtedly more than glancing in front of our noses; one needs training before his observation is trustworthy. So, for Prall, one needs training in all observation, training of all the senses to perceive and discriminate exactly the data of experience. In *Æsthetic Analysis* he says, ". . . the difference between perceiving clearly and understanding distinctly is not the great difference that we are sometimes led to think it." And in *Æsthetic Judgment* he intimates that adequate perception includes perception of meanings. Many philosophers would think that Prall confused his account of meaning by writing such things as "... not even language can do more than refer to meanings." In the usual account, what is meant is not itself a meaning (with some exceptions), but a thing, an event, a relation, an idea. But to take Prall literally, as he insisted on being taken, linguistic symbols refer to "ultimate sensuous data or essences." And if language can only refer to meanings, then sense-experience contains meanings, and they are understood as they are perceived.

Some of this argument is a conclusion from Santayana's metaphysic—and it is Santayana, whom Prall seldom mentioned, who exerted the great influence on his thought. To talk of "sensuous data or essences" is to talk Santayana's language by identifying the elements of sense-experience with essences. Essences, of course, are ordinarily thought of as abstractions that contain, or are, the meanings of particulars: thus, "horse" is the word we use for what all particular horses have in common; and it is "horse" we define, not individual horses which, like all individuals, can be described but not defined.

But Prall is using Santayana's terms and moving in his universe. And in that universe things or objects are not immediately apparent to sense; they are products of consciousness and are hard to come by. What are immediately apparent to sense are qualities (the characteristics of things) like red, round, smooth, tart, fragrant. Things are conceived to be groupings of qualities, and in *experience* they are never more than such groupings. What is left of an apple if it loses its redness, roundness, hardness, and sweetness? What happens to the dance when the dancer stops? We may have to attribute to the apple an underlying substance, or matter, in which its qualities inhere, but we never perceive the substance itself, only the qualities.

Any particular sight of yellow may be called an instance of "yellow," or yellowness, if we appeal to the abstractions, or universals, in which, traditionally, the meaning of particular qualities consists. But to Santayana "yellowness is only some sensation of yellow raised to the cognitive power and employed as the symbol for its own specific essence." And yellow, like any quality but unlike particular things, cannot even be described; it can only be experienced and recognized. This is not to deny that yellow can be defined in terms of the spectrum or of wave frequency, but to do that is simply to state the relation of yellow to other colors or to specify a physical condition for its occurrence. Neither definition tells us what yellow is, as a color seen. And yellowness is finally defined as the quality of being yellow, which is so circular it is useless. The only definition of yellowness is in extension: it is a word that stands for all possible instances of yellow; it is the idea of yellow.

Things, as we conceive them, come into being and pass away. Horses are born, they age, and they die; but the idea of horse remains untouched by time. Qualities are not things. And the idea of a quality differs from the idea of a thing in the manner of its definition. The idea of yellow (again as the idea of a seen color) can only be defined by pointing out yellows. And that cannot be done for a disembodied intelligence, but only for a being with eyes and color vision. The idea of yellow is nearly indistinguishable from the perceived quality, yellow, and is thus dissimilar to the idea of horse, which is quite different from the things it refers to: stallions and mares, sorrels and roans and bays. And the idea of yellow is equally dissimilar to, say, the idea of justice, which is itself very different from the particular instances of just conduct to which it refers.

To put this hypothetical argument in another way, the *idea* of yellow is not itself yellow, as the idea of horse cannot run and as the idea of justice is not just. But the meaning of "yellow," which is the linguistic symbol of yellowness or the idea of yellow, has no content save yellow, a color seen. And that is quite different from "horse" or "justice," which have elaborate intensional or dictionary meanings, in addition to their extensional reference to actual and potential horses, and to instances of human conduct. So an instance of yellow, every time we see it, may be conceived as a meaning, or an essence, and no particular horse or example of justice could possibly be conceived in that way. Since words ultimately refer to sensuous data, which are the elements in the perceived surface of the world, it follows that they refer to qualities or essences. With such an argument implicit in his thought, Prall could speak legitimately of "sensuous data or essences," and of language referring to meanings.

Even in science, observation is at its best when it is first articulated in sentences like "there is a red line in front of of a green square." Statement of what was seen as one or more objects comes later, because it is interpretation. And the first articulation is the ultimate articulation, for science must by its very nature move from its most dizzying abstractions to practical test in the form of observation of sensuous data.

What I have been saying is within Santayana's universe as Prall inhabited it. It has used as evidence Prall's statements of the revolutionary doctrine, revolutionary at least for philosophy, that art is the most adequate form of communication and expresses the very point of life. But it is only a hypothetical construct of a philosophy perhaps implicit in Prall's writings, and it is incomplete because I have barely introduced science, to argue that its language could be shown, in Prall's terms, to refer in the end to the meanings present in sensuous data. One could develop, I think, an impressive philosophy that would hold that sensuous data are meanings, that adequate perception of them *is* understanding, and that all forms of human creation in art, philosophy, and science must treat those data as the origin and end of thought. The data would thus be understood as the occasion for problems which provoked hypotheses that finally were tested by, or measured against, such data. And that would imply that human thought started and ended with perceived meanings. Art would be the most adequate way of dealing with sensuous data in terms of value, man's ultimate concern. Prall did in fact believe that æsthetic analysis could bring us, not just to handsomer and more functional cities, but to a better life and to social justice. Yet he never expanded the philosophy that would support his belief. So it is enough—perhaps more than enough—to show where such a philosophy might go; it would be folly to develop it in detail, unless one believed it.

As for Prall's "narrowness," which Mrs. Langer understands as a refusal to think of all art as symbolic and which Mr. Weiss identifies as positivism, it is a stubborn concern for the work of art seen in its detailed relationships. Æsthetics had been very much more general before Prall. The relations of colors, the order of tones, the movements of the lips in reading poetry were not the common fare of philosophers. Nor had they urged, as Prall did, that one learn to play the violin if his musical taste seemed inadequate. There was large talk about art, some of it very good talk indeed, but not with such an intense focus on the exact detail which made for beauty.

I suspect it was Prall's precise technical analysis of basic elements in the arts—his real innovation—that made *Æsthetic Judgment* a classic so quickly. The radical extension of Santayana was, so far as I know, unnoticed, although Dewey shrewdly perceived that Prall's criticism of him relied on Santayana's metaphysic. But although Prall never developed his comments on art and society, or on the role of art in history, *Æsthetic Judgment* was treated as a great work. The review of it in *The New York Times* said, ". . . it is a worthy successor to Santayana's 'Sense of Beauty,' and is, standing beside it, the most important work on æsthetic theory to come out of America." The review continued by saying that *Æsthetic Judgment* "must undoubtedly take precedence" over Croce's *Æsthetic*. And it culminated its appraisal of the book by asserting, ". . . Dr. Prall has made an original synthesis of the poles represented by the central æsthetic idea of each of the above philosophers. This new view is much more close to the reality of æsthetic experience, and thus supersedes both the others." High praise indeed!

Much of Croce's æsthetic was accepted by Prall, who believed with Croce that what we intuit, what is present to the senses or the mind, is expressive and so contains feeling; and that, as Croce put it, "the æsthetic fact . . . is form." The *Times* reviewer was right, too, that Prall made a kind of synthesis of Croce and Santayana, holding with Santayana that what we intuit contains our own responses which we have objectified, that is, read back into the object of intuition. Just as the color of an object is in reality our own response to the frequency of light waves that strike the eye, but is projected by us onto the surface that confronts us, so the beauty of the object is our own response projected to the object. Yet the synthesis of Croce and Santayana in Prall is neither complete nor fully consistent, and it is not quite the philosophy, I believe, that Prall would have written had he lived to do so.

What made Prall important to at least one generation of Americans was his direct approach to the arts. For that approach, it scarcely mattered what his more general philosophy was. Just as one's metaphysic is, in the end, irrelevant to his political theory, it is equally irrelevant to æsthetic analysis. And whether the experienced world is entirely in our minds, or on the contrary is identical with a real world independent of our sense and thought, what we say about it scientifically is not changed one iota.

The reason for the title "Æsthetic Judgment," and for Prall's concern with the idea, was that his real subject, æsthetic experience, is private and fleeting. Criticism, of course, is public and relatively enduring, but criticism was not basic to Prall's interest. Æsthetic judgment is the record of æsthetic experience. The problems of substituting the record for the experience are enormous (although Prall seems not to notice them), for the record is necessarily verbal, and the experience is not. But if one is going to write about art, and if objects of art are to be treated as experiences, then he is committed to verbalizing and might as well verbalize the experiences themselves. In that way the subject of analysis at least becomes public and stable.

It is natural beauty that Prall deals with first, moving

to art by careful steps. The region of æsthetic experience is "the intuited surface of our world." There are other ways of dealing with that surface: one may seek its relations to other surfaces, ask what underlies it, be concerned with its place in nature or in the economy of life. But if we put aside such things and all matters of why, where, and for what purpose, we can attend to intuited surfaces æsthetically. We can, that is, contemplate or regard them in themselves, noticing—or being struck by—the specific qualities before us, the roar of the sea or the city, the rise and dip of flight.

"Æsthetic surface" is clearly an important concept in Prall's æsthetics, but he never defines it precisely. I take it æsthetic surface is an idea related to Santayana's belief that things are discriminated later than qualities. Prall prefers to talk of qualities as intuited, rather than perceived, as though perception were more complicated than intuition, and we intuited qualities but perceived objects. In that case, the qualities we intuit make up æsthetic surface. But the æsthetic attitude then differs from others, such as the cognitive attitude, by bringing us to focus on the æsthetic surface itself with all our powers, seeing relations in it, grasping the nature of the surface, discriminating its elements. It does not take us where other attitudes might: to classification, understanding, moral evaluation. The æsthetic attitude does not even take us to the objects whose surfaces we intuit, except insofar as we can treat the objects themselves as surfaces. In a crude analogy, the æsthetic surface of the "Mona Lisa" is its design. And writers like Roger Fry and Clive Bell seem to find the specifically æsthetic values of the painting in just that.

Æsthetic activity is indispensable to æsthetic experience.

Without it there are only the rudimentary experiences of daydreams, rest, and relaxation. With it we may intuit the æsthetic surface in its specific and discriminated detail. That detail distinguishes it from other surfaces and may provide a sense of unity, which in simple forms can be a striking characteristic to which all else is subordinated. Æsthetic activity is alert and sensitive attention, an ability that can be more and more highly trained.

Tastes, odors, touch, sights, and sounds may all be contemplated, discriminated, and enjoyed æsthetically. A superb dinner or an overwhelming fragrance may bring delight, which is heightened by attention and discrimination. But they are not, and cannot become, art. Art demands order, like the spectrum of colors or scales of pitch, and there is no such order of tastes, smells, and touch. Art can exist only in a medium in which we can compose, and sight and sound are the only senses that provide such a medium.

But although sight and sound have natural orders which we can manipulate to our own ends, and so can compose and create art, a beautiful æsthetic surface is not in itself art, except perhaps in music. The arts all require an æsthetic surface, but that surface is only a necessary condition for visual and literary art. If one classifies the arts in terms of their æsthetic surfaces, music is at one end of the continuum, being entirely or almost entirely a matter of the perfection of sensuous content, the visual arts are in the middle, and the literary arts are at the other end. The medium of literature is words, and so is entirely referential. Literature's "perfection and success lie in such control of this medium as succeeds in making meanings themselves beautiful. . . ."

I am not so sure as Prall that music is almost entirely a matter of surface or sensuous content. It is at least as convincing to argue that music states actual and possible emotional patterns and that "a musical idea" is more than a technical device. And Prall in some passages does speak of music as an externalization of feeling. On his account of it, anyhow, the same continuum of the arts from music to literature could be duplicated on the basis of cognitive content. In either case, whether we employed æsthetic surface or cognitive content as the principle of our arrangement, visual art would be in the middle, for it is more a matter of æsthetic surface than literature and more cognitive or referential than music. Thus Prall opposes the purists from Roger Fry to today who treat visual art as a matter of surface only. Representation is delightful, he insists, and it is foolish to limit the delight in art.

Prall's classification of the arts, it seems to me, is not nearly so important as his implicit distinction between natural beauty and the beauty of art. I say "implicit" only because Prall never completed the distinction by carrying the argument to its conclusion. Natural beauty is æsthetic only, he thought; art is more than æsthetic. "Æsthetic" here is a characteristic of surfaces. Art is composed; it orders its materials so that they convey, or are, expressions. Since "it is a work of the human spirit, a work of art functions also in expressing that spirit's feelings and emotions of desire and satisfaction." And, Prall insists, although it is technique that brings art into being, it is expressiveness that gives it interest and vitality.

I think Prall's argument, given his distinction between nature and art, should have been based on meaning and communication, not on expressiveness. And he should not have insisted that art is more than æsthetic, for it is not clear how it is. Prall had learned too well from Croce that intuition is expressive, and there is one obvious sense in which that is so. If it is true that we objectify our feelings and values, projecting them onto qualities and objects, then red is warm and green cool, and the tiger's snarl is menacing. Prall did think in terms of objectification and so he found all æsthetic surface expressive. The difference in expressiveness between nature and art, then, becomes only one of degree. Still, Prall could argue that the complexity of the human spirit expressed in art is far from the relative simplicity of a natural surface.

If Prall had used meaning and communication, instead of expressiveness, as the basis of his distinction between beauty in nature and beauty in art, he could have found differences in kind, not just in degree. When we seek significance in nature, we discover either what we project into it or else causal, or functional, relationships. To the latter we sometimes assign the word "meaning." So there is the warmth of red, which is a human response objectified, and there is the relationship between dark clouds and rain, which we sometimes describe by saying "dark clouds mean rain." The former is, in Prall's sense, expressive; the latter is symbolic or referential. Perhaps the point is made better by using the same natural phenomenon for both examples. "Dark clouds are threatening" is expressive; "dark clouds mean rain" is referential.

In neither of the two cases above does any communication take place. Expression and meaning are found in (or read into) nature, but no one arranged the clouds to threaten or to mean rain. There was no other person, in addition to the recipient of meaning, no person who meant, or intended, or communicated. We experience what can be contemplated or regarded æsthetically, the threatening character of the clouds. And we understand—we can think of this scientifically—that since there are dark clouds now, there will probably be rain soon. We do what Prall believed could always be done with perceived surfaces. We attend to their qualities in the first instance, and we go beyond them to other matters in the second instance. Our first response can be treated as perception of expression, our second as grasp of meaning.

Art, unlike nature, is an instance of communication. I have never liked the word "communication" in connection with art, because it minimizes the value of the medium and seems to imply, erroneously, that the work of art is like a symbol in discourse. But the word is useful for the symmetry of this argument about nature and art. Where there is a work of art, there is, or was, an artist. And the meanings in a work of art are there because the artist put them there. I raise no question of conscious intent on the artist's part; he made the work. Our task in viewing, or hearing, or reading the work is in part to discover its meanings. A proper æsthetic response does not include projecting our own meanings into the work.

How, on Prall's understanding of artistic creation, is the artist able to embody meaning in his work? By the same ordering of elements into form which he regards as sufficient for expressing "feelings and emotions of desire and satisfaction." Prall does talk of meanings on occasion, but his great concern with music and his scanty technical treatment of literature insofar as it is more than æsthetic surface lead him to concentrate on expression. And as

INTRODUCTION

might be expected of a man deeply rooted in music, it is
verse, not fiction, that Prall can deal with at all effectively
in literature. If he had attended more to meaning in art,
Prall could have used more impressively his distinction
between the elements of æsthetic surface that delight us in
nature and the ordering of elements that makes art. The
elements in both cases are expressive: they have "meaning"
only metaphorically, in the way individual words have
meaning. Literally, individual words have reference. Literally, meaning is conveyed by sentences. Words can be
thought or contemplated, and they have a quality of feeling,
as colors do. But in isolation from each other, words convey neither idea nor information. And in confused and
ungrammatical array, words in combination are still literally meaningless. Meaning comes when words are in
the grammatical and logical order proper to sentences.

So, Prall could have maintained, there is an analogy of
words and sentences to the elements of æsthetic surface and
the kinds of order that make genuine art. The threatening
cloud can appear on a canvas that makes a powerful comment on man's relation to nature. Wonderful as the cloud
is in itself, in Giorgione's "The Tempest" it is not only
an important element in relation to the rest of the canvas,
but it bears a significance it could not have in isolation,
either in nature or in art. It is like the central or most
operative word or phrase or image in a poem, which
shapes the meanings of the other words.

The conclusion Prall might have come to is that æsthetic
surface is expressive in nature and in art, but that the
æsthetic attitude precludes meaning on nature's æsthetic
surfaces. Works of art, however, contain or embody mean-

ing. That meaning derives from the artist and alters the expressiveness of art's æsthetic surface by concentrating attention in one way and not another. Whether expressiveness is an objectification of human response or the result of a transaction between the senses and natural phenomena, it is at least partly the viewer's or hearer's. When the surface is that of a work of art, it is controlled by the maker. And that surface is the medium which contains his meanings, not ours. It is correct to say, as we sometimes do, that once a work is finished it is public, and belongs to everyone who wants it. It is also usually the case that the artist cannot tell us in expository prose what his work means. And, of course, no work of art can be completely paraphrased. But it does not follow that we can do better than try to discover what meanings are actually in the work.

The vital points of this argument are that the very elements of æsthetic surface are expressive, that the artist can alter, contract, or expand the expressiveness of the elements in a created æsthetic surface by the way he orders those elements, and that the great difference between natural beauty and a work of art is the meaning embodied in the work by the artist.

We have all learned much about expressiveness from Prall, but we have not learned much from anyone about meaning in art. Contemporary æsthetics, perhaps for this reason, has emphasized the difficulty of resolving æsthetic disagreement by any appeal to fact. It has become skeptical that the very words we employ to describe things in the arts have the same meaning each time they are used. What is needed is an adequate theory of æsthetic meaning, which would include value. Perhaps we cannot advance much from where we are until a philosopher develops such a theory with the precision and detail Prall gave to his discussions of surface and expressiveness.

RALPH ROSS
Claremont, California

CHAPTER I

THE EXPERIENCE RECORDED IN ÆSTHETIC JUDGMENT

1. The available but limited data for æsthetic theory indicated in æsthetic judgments. 2. Such judgments record beauties directly felt. 3. Beauties as supervening upon transactions in nature. 4. Æsthetic experience distinguished by its disinterested absorption in determinate qualities and forms.

§ 1

WHEN the places in the world are not merely within a radius of thirty-three hours but immediately to be reached by light-wave transportation or perfected instruments of distance vision; when all the problems connected with having the fare to pay for these instantaneous journeys are completely solved; when there are no more wars or national rivalries or passports or customs regulations to complicate the overcoming of natural barriers by the raising of artificial ones; when men have full knowledge of their bodily mechanisms and their health—or the cure for death—and when, alive, they shall have found out how to live together in society:—when all this is accomplished, if we are not to sit down and wish for the return of our practical difficulties to give us occupation, or for death to relieve our boredom, æsthetic matters will have to be taken seriously. For the present the subject matter is to be studied in those accidental or lucky developments that have come about in spite of men's other preoccupations. In our own present world there are two main regions at our disposal. There are first the rudimentary æsthetic data to be found in tired moments of stopping to glance at the surrounding commotion or in turning to more or less violent relaxation in popular games. The one gives us æsthetic contemplation as we all know it best, perhaps; the other gives us an intimation of creative activity or artistic expression. The second source for information and available data on the subject is to be found in those less popular, though no doubt most select and sometimes esoteric cases of æsthetic contemplation and artistic activity that are so labeled.

We may thus survey our subject matter either in primitive manifestations where it is difficult to differentiate contemplation from mere daze or stupor, or pleased infantile wonder, and where free expert activity appears rather in the guise of truancy; or we may turn to its abnormal aspects, such appreciation as is typical of concerts and museum tours and such activity as is to be found in the seclusion of studios and art schools. Not having a very healthy, mature social world we have not even the conditions for normal æsthetic expression either contemplative or creative. But the crude rudimentary aspects of a subject exhibit some of its fundamentals, and its esoteric and abnormal aspects often reveal with startling clearness not only its aberrations but its purest possibilities. Insanity teaches us much of the mind, and it is possible that rats and apes offer us examples of processes common to all the thinking that goes on in connection with animal bodies. Our limited æsthetic data need not then lead us altogether astray.

Besides these disabilities æsthetics suffers further from our lack of knowledge in many fields. What perception is exactly we do not know, nor what judgment is. We do not know too much even about sounds and colors, and we know still less of words and language as pure meaning. Since most æsthetic experience is a matter of the very surface of our world, whether we are creating it or enjoying it, and since this surface is almost all perceived as sound and color, we are greatly hampered. But with all these difficulties there remains the genuine and natural human concern with happiness and beauty, and by noticing our limitations and taking a point of departure honestly, even though it be scarcely scientific, we may clear our minds of some confusion and perhaps indicate some of the regions to be scientifically explored in the future.

We noticed that æsthetics begins where mechanics and physics and biology, economics and politics and ethics, end, where most of what we know of life is perfected into habit or even cessation. But we should remember too that at any stage of any activity the æsthetic aspect is likely to be present, perhaps indeed that it is always necessarily present. And the treatment of it by itself is only justified because it is so important as coloring and toning all the aspects of the world we live in. A mechanism may be beautiful; and so perhaps may social institutions be, if not in their clumsy irrational structures, at least in some of the personal human activities and relations involved in them. But since we have so little of science to guide us in all this, we may as well turn to a simpler investigation and begin at the point where we should conclude. All of us say now and then in some determinate way or other that something is beautiful. Beautiful may not be our word; we use fine, often, or grand or capital or jolly; and we say attractive or pretty or charming or lovely more appropriately and less self-consciously than we say beautiful. But any one of these more or less determinate expressions means in a loose, easy way, or in a simple, direct way what beautiful means more vaguely and abstractly or more solemnly or dogmatically; and all of us suppose that we know what we mean when we use them.

Lacking then any full knowledge of the subject matter of æsthetics, we may profit by examining the meaning of our own æsthetic judgments, an analysis which should supposedly tell us what that meaning is. If we knew completely what we meant by the judgment, *this is beautiful*, as we use it in any given case, and if we further knew exactly what it meant in all cases, we should know so much more of æsthetics than is at present known that in an attempt at finding out this meaning, unscientific as such an attempt may appear to be, we can hardly be wasting time.

In other words we are noticing frankly that in method our study is not to be strictly or narrowly scientific but general and philosophical. But this is not to be confused with being either vague or fruitless. For the method need not be uncritical or lacking in rigor; and if we keep firmly in mind what facts are available, we need not lose ourselves in arbitrary theorizing. We may comfort ourselves too, if we like, that we are not running the supposed risks of scientific method itself, which in this field is far from having any comprehensive generalizations that offer very much control over the subject matter. And we need not at all neglect the principles that have so far been suggested or formulated. But we are to begin the other way round; the æsthetic judgment is to be taken for granted as significant, and with the judgment itself as our starting point we are to investigate its meaning.

§ 2

At once then we need to be clear as to what æsthetic judgment is. It is not of course æsthetic experience as such,

4

about which psychology and psychological æsthetics have had so much to say. Nor is it criticism, which is occupied largely with assessing and analyzing relative æsthetic values in a scale of value or placing a given example under some familiar rubric, as when we notice that a play is a farce or a college building pseudo-Gothic. Æsthetic judgment is distinguished from æsthetic experience as such by the simple fact that it follows and records such experience after the experience has been had and with reference to what was experienced. And it is distinguished from criticism equally clearly by the fact that it is content with simply making this record explicit. It makes no attempt at first to say that one thing is better than another, nor to explain on what grounds it is so, nor to say just what class of things it belongs to, nor to explain it in any sense, nor yet to reproduce in an account of the thing some of its quality of beauty so that a reader of the criticism may re-enact a similar æsthetic moment of more or less derivative appreciation.

Positively, æsthetic judgment is easier to point to than to describe or define. But it is always a record of direct æsthetic experience, of the fact that in the presence of some object that object's beauty has been felt. Perhaps indeed feeling is the best word, even technically, to use here; but for the present we are safe in using it only in its most general sense, in which it applies as well to feeling that we were right to run away or stay behind as to feeling a thrill of emotion. The word is commonly used of the process or act of appreciation, as when we say that we feel the exquisite grace of flowers or, less probably, of the vase they are in; but in more pronounced cases, as when a young man encounters a young woman whose appearance stirs his enthusiasm, the word is more likely to be striking. One is always struck by great beauty, the feeling is called forth suddenly by a blow upon the senses. Instead of saying that we feel something, we say that something makes us feel, that something strikes us. It is shocks of this sort that we record in æsthetic judgment.

And one more distinction. If you are struck by the beauty of something in your experience and record that fact to me, I may accept your judgment and repeat your statement in sincere belief. But here the judgment is taken merely as recording one fact among others, and to know its meaning accurately and fully I should have to have the experience myself. So that it is as well to keep to direct judgments, records of an experience had by the person making the statement. If we take other judgments to examine, statements that are merely accepted and repeated on authority, they may mean no more to us than any memorized phrase, or mere verbal formula, such as that a certain dye is an amido-compound, or that carcinoma is sometimes of epithelial tissue or that democracy is equality of opportunity. It is in this latter way that we may all believe and assert that the Parthenon is beautiful, and we should learn little of æsthetics by attempting to go deeper into that judgment, since for most of us it has no depth, scarcely even a meaning of any sort.

§ 3

Before we turn to examples, their kinds and their various sorts of meaning, we should also be a little clear as to one further characteristic of æsthetic experience and hence of the meaning of any æsthetic judgment that records it. This characteristic is named variously, rapture, aloofness, disinterestedness, indolence, uselessness, and all these expressions have some genuine applicability from some point of view.

6

But there are many misunderstandings involved in them, as in a dozen other equally common descriptions,—the innocence of the artist or his perversity, the parasitical nature of art or the divineness of it, its freedom from ulterior motive or its exclusiveness and pretense.

All these follow from one simple fact. Both the creation and the contemplative appreciation of beauty, the blazing red of geraniums, the intense equilibrium of a pianist, these are events that go on in the world. The geranium reflects light to an eye which perceives its color; the pianist acts upon his instrument, and if he is quite perfect, he and the instrument, so far as both produce sound, are parts of one activity, one process, one group of coördinated movements. So of the eye and the blazing red geranium in the sun. Now process and movement are extended both through time and in space, and all qualities, pitches, colors, as well as variations or changes in pitch or color, occur only along with such extended processes and motions. Nature is not static, and we are not outside nature looking on; but all things, all human beings among them, act and react in a continuum of moving reality both spatial and temporal. Not only the physical world but all life is a flux. Beauty, if it is seen or heard or felt, is recognized as a quality supervening upon this flux in some particular situation. And situations are marked for human minds by these supervening qualities and by nothing else. But the quality itself has an identity. We know red when we see it, whether it gleams proudly as a broad stripe or glows in the ashes or incarnadines the waves or spots the table linen in strawberry season. If we are to see it at all, and if it is to be at all, something must happen; very special transactions among chromatic mechanisms of the eye, and very special microscopic movements in reflecting surfaces.

Now as redness occurs only in a transaction as the quality there, so does beauty, and the mechanics of the transaction in the case of beauty are apparently complicated and certainly very little understood. They involve not only light transmission from surfaces, sound transmissions through air, nervous activities in organs of perception, brain activities, muscular movements, coördinating responses and so on and on, but also the processes involved in such perception, or such feeling, as finds more than color and sound and shape, namely, the beauties of these.

But here we are noticing what is common to all qualities, beauty included. The process, whatever it is, in connection with which quality is present, has no end. If it were the process itself that were beauty, beauty would never be felt or known at all, since every process runs into other processes forever and through all space. Any single process is but one mode of the moving reality of nature. But such processes as involve certain bodily functions are marked for us by the presence of what we call qualities, defined simply and uniquely in their own immediacy as the qualities or natures they happen to be. Beauties of all sorts are among determinate qualities. Hence, while beauty is obviously transitory in its occurrence, it is also a defined nature, a specific sort of being; and every particular beauty is permanently the selfsame determinate nature or quality that it is, no matter how or when it appears as the quality of this or that object. Every beauty is eternally itself, eternal, not as lasting through time, but as in its own nature what it is regardless of time, eternal in the simple familiar sense in which a geometrical meaning is eternal, independent as to its nature or character of the exigencies of time and space, held to no date and no place to be what it is, as triangularity needs no place to occupy and no time to fill in order to be what it means anywhere at any time. It simply is what it means, and when and where it is embodied makes no difference to this meaning, nor whether it is ever embodied at all. Its own nature is exhausted in its definition as itself, and the truth of any situation that happens to embody or reveal it is that this situation exemplifies triangularity and all that can be said of triangularity as such.

So of any determinate beauty. A beautiful vision that has occurred cannot literally occur again; only another vision may come to take its place, and perhaps another of the same form. For the beauty of the first vision is what it is exactly, whatever the time or place of its occurrence, and whether or not any one ever sees it again. There is no recurrence of any event, for events pass; what we call recurrence of events or situations, is the identity of their apparent character or quality. It is not specific beauties that may properly be said to occur or pass away, but rather what bears these beauties upon its surface. For mind the flux of events is arrested in recognizable forms, which have thus their own permanent identity. Of course the actual material works of men's hands may change so slowly that these forms seem also permanently embodied. The pyramids are pyramidal still to our living eyes. The precise shape they once had, however, is no longer to be seen upon their physical existent masses. But that shape, identical as present to the mind of their ancient architects with what we mean when we speak even now of their original shape, is forever the same, possessed of its own identical nature, which is all that we mean when we refer to it.

So of all qualities and so of all beauties. It is because any particular beauty is thus identically what it is in its own self-defining nature or being that it is nothing else, but solely and separately its purely qualitative and unique self.

Of course then æsthetic experience, while it is an activity, a transaction in the flux of nature, culminates and has its characteristic point in an absolute static quality or determinate beauty, no more subject to the contingencies of existence, and no more in danger of destruction, than the meanings of geometrical definitions or the logical principles of implication. Its occurrence, its happening to appear, is a passing event. Its being or nature, its qualitatively defined specific character, is independent, and hence aloof from the contingency of existing things, as logical meanings or æsthetic qualities in general are aloof by being the meanings or qualities of things, not things or events themselves. But this is not to say that these qualities are separated off by distance into a special realm of their own. That would be making of them the spatial and temporal substances that they are not, instead of realizing that their whole being is quality or form, and that they appear constantly as the very surface of our perceived world everywhere.

§ 4

In æsthetic experience attention is focussed on this qualitative identity, this permanence of form, so that such experience is the antithesis of practical activity, moral or economic. The artist, however busy his hands, is absorbed in a form, an appearance felt specifically as the object and aim of his effort, perhaps even fully delineated in his imagination, a form which is to be embodied by the expert manipulation of intimately known materials, and made present to others, who may in their turn become absorbed in the contemplation of it. And we need not keep to such terms as these to illustrate so familiar a phenomenon. If a waiter in a restaurant folds a napkin expertly and carefully, laying it beside a plate in precise and intended relation to the silver and the glasses, a prospective patron and diner may view with pleasure the neatness of the table, without perhaps being at all aware of the specific details of form that constitute this satisfying appearance. But it is this form, intended by the waiter, that the napkin and the glasses and the silver embody, and it is this form that may strike an attentive or discriminating guest, as it was also this form, this particular appearance, that the waiter had in mind, as we say, all along.

As it is only expert trained attention that discriminates and feels in all its fullness and precision of detail the effect of a well-set table, so the seeing of the quality and point of a complex work of art involves not only previous training, often of years, but full attentive activity summoning the most elaborate nerve and brain and muscle processes to its aid, processes which for most of us are not even available on the spur of the moment. We may appreciate quite adequately a neat, clean table; but we are not so competent in the matter of subtle designs on plaster walls or foreign fabrics. We miss the accuracy or the vagueness of an orchestra conductor's beat, and we may fail altogether to distinguish such discriminable and defining character in works of art as gives them their chief value or even their sole significance. Æsthetic experience, full and complete, not only requires tremendous training beforehand but intense activity at the time, so great that living through the exciting complexity of an elaborate musical composition, or grasping the intricate intellectual form and detail of a fine building, produces exhaustion. It does not tire our legs, perhaps, like mountain climbing or bicycle racing, but the mere fact that the activity involved is not gross in the anatomical sense is not a ground for calling it indolence or passivity.

But as the expert wine-taster consumes no wine at all, takes none of it into his internal metabolic economy and uses up only so much of the available supply as will excite his organs of taste and be spat out again, so artistic activity and æsthetic contemplation in general, having their consummation in the presence to minds of specific forms, do not contribute to the interested practical and social activities of men. If indolence is thus hardly justified as the description even of æsthetic contemplation, for practical purposes uselessness, of course, is; and since artists use up materials, and those who even stop to contemplate qualities use up time and energy in doing so, there is some sense in saying that æsthetic activity is at least an expense to the world and a luxury in it. Moreover, since the form achieved is the end in view, it is clear enough that other more practical ends are neglected. While beauties are mere qualities, not substantial things, and hence permanent in their being, and independent, in their own defined nature, of mere events and physical objects, still their occurrence upon objects and their presence, to men, involve materials and activities. Artists and those who cherish art or contemplate beauty are human beings, consuming goods and in dependent contact and relation with other men, and they are subject to all the regulations of law and morals, as well as to physical and biological and economic necessities.

Since æsthetic qualities occur as the characters of things which are the products of long labor; since also the perception of these qualities is usually contingent on time-absorbing training, and the enjoyment of them always takes time and energy, æsthetic and artistic activity may be judged critically as costing human energy and exhausting materials. And so far it seems also to be condemned, since it serves no practical purpose beyond itself. But this is a very incomplete account. For when we look for the justification of any activity, we find it at last in some human satisfaction; and if æsthetic activity is itself directly satisfactory, instead of seeking ulterior justification, it is in the clear position of needing none. It is in fact the very type of the only sort of thing that ever justifies anything else. But this will appear more clearly later. For the present all we need to notice is the plain fact that æsthetic experience, recorded in æsthetic judgments, is aloof not in indolence, but in the intense activity of full contemplation, and aloof because what such experience takes as its object is not existing things but their essential qualities, not events but appearing essences or forms immediately and satisfyingly present to us, whether as embodied externally in things or in imagination. It is this sort of aloofness, common to all disinterested attention, that is mistaken sometimes for inattention or idle day-dreaming or sophisticated pretense. As if all attention to anything were not also inattention to the rest of the world, or as if direct, absorbed, satisfied activity were not necessarily the neglect of other activities, and necessarily without pretense. As to indolence, it is said to have been Descartes' early morning "indolence" that invented analytical geometry; and in general it may be fair to think that a little fruitful "indolent" contemplation would make our world less frivolous and more humane.

The present chapter has simply presented very generally the subject matter of æsthetics, the starting point and the method of our study, and a description of the characteristic disinterestedness of æsthetic experience. We have next to follow through some examples of æsthetic judgment, so as to set before ourselves in some intelligible order the more specific and detailed aspects of what we are attempting to survey as the meaning of all such judgments.

CHAPTER II

THE TRANSACTION INVOLVED IN ÆSTHETIC EXPERIENCE

1. Though preference is vital to the apprehension of beauties, these lie objectively upon the surface of the experienced world. 2. Conflict in æsthetic judgment therefore not anomalous; an object may vary in beauty even for the same person. 3. Sensuous and bodily resonance a condition of the fullest beauty.

§ 1

BEFORE we turn to varieties of æsthetic judgment and their meanings, it is worth while specifying the character of æsthetic judgment in general as distinguished from other kinds of judgment bordering closely upon it. We may take as critical the case of disagreement in æsthetic judgment where in other judgments there is admitted agreement, and in finding just the point of the disagreement find also just that which is the specifically æsthetic nature of the judgment and its meaning. There is nothing more regularly disagreed upon, I suppose, than the beauty of women, and in such cases there is often no disagreement as to the facts. If we say, How lovely she is,—such eyes, such hair, such skin! we may be answered, Yes, just such eyes, just such hair and skin, but not lovely at all. And such regular features, we add. But what if one prefers to regularity of features sensitive and intelligent mobility? As soon as the question of beauty comes clear of the rest, it turns into preference, apparently. And since this is typical of æsthetic differences of opinion, we may stop at once to notice not merely that it is typical, but that it is the heart of the matter.

Not that beauty is what I prefer as against what you prefer, but that we never make the direct judgment that this or that was beautiful, with regard to what we have ourselves seen, unless what we judged about satisfied or pleased or charmed or attracted us, suited our preferences in the matter. The question then comes to be whether æsthetic judgment is merely a record of our having preferred something to something else, or of having liked something or other. That it is not this alone is obvious at once. King James liked his old friends best because they were like comfortable old shoes, and I suppose that even King James hardly thought his old shoes beautiful. So of much that we prefer or like or even love; we should never think of calling it beautiful, whether it is oysters to eat, or old friends to see, or old shoes to wear. We are not speaking simply or mainly of affections, or of our likes or dislikes or preferences in general when we call things beautiful. How then does it happen that in disagreements in æsthetic judgment, likes and dislikes are so sure to be the end of the argument? How does it happen that, even when one party to the disagreement is willing finally to concede beauty where he does not discern it, he adds, as the fundamentally important point, that, while the object in question *may* be beautiful, though he can't see that it is, he really doesn't like it?

At least it must be admitted that no mere statement by others is in the matter of beauty acceptable. We are willing enough to admit another man's record of the dimensions of a rug or an estate, often without verification; but whether the rug is beautiful or ugly, whether the gardens or the buildings are fine to look at, we can only tell by looking ourselves. And once we do look and see them, if they delight us by their physical appearance, we have the experience necessary for making the judgment that they are beautiful, or for agreeing with or verifying this judgment as communicated to us by some one else.

And æsthetic judgments are peculiar in this respect. If we doubt that a baby weighs thirteen pounds, we can be assured of it by inspecting the scales with the baby's weight on them and finding that the weight reported was correct. If we doubt the fact that carnations are sometimes green or that a locomotive will run ninety miles an hour, the tests of these judgments, while they sometimes involve complicated processes of measurement, are sure to satisfy us if they are carefully and accurately made by any merely rational human observer. If the green is not the shade of green expected, or if the locomotive runs eighty-nine and nine-tenths miles, the statements are verified at least approximately. Not so of statements as to beauty. If we attempt to verify such a statement as that something or some one is beautiful, we must see that some one or something ourselves. And it often happens that in the very presence of a friend whose experience completely verifies the judgment, our own experience as completely fails to. Our informant, pointing to the beautiful object before us both, asks us to agree that his judgment is correct, and instead we disagree; we find the object not beautiful or even positively ugly.

Since the object and its qualities, its shade of color, its shape, its dimensions, do not vary, it would seem clear that the variation which is to account for the difference, and hence for the conflict of judgments, lies in the person having it. And this would accord with what we have already noticed.

If qualities occur as qualities of objects only in certain active transactions, and if beauty is a quality present to you when you look at a building but not to me when I look, it must simply be a different transaction that goes on between me and the building from what goes on in your case. That such a difference is possible is shown by the parallel case of what are called the secondary qualities. If I have eyes sufficiently different from other eyes to be partially color-blind, I may on a trial choose what is red when I am asked to pick out the green; and when a quality is such that it is received through one sense and one sort of sense organ, there is no mystery in such a mistake nor in the mistaken judgment that would express it, nor yet in a conflict between two judgments ostensibly upon the same thing, since these are records of different experiences through different kinds of eyes. A defective or abnormal sense organ cannot furnish the same experience that a normal one does in the same circumstances; or rather, the circumstances are not the same in a transaction between a colored surface and a defective eye as in a transaction involving the same surface and a normal eye. And the possessors of the two differing eyes, since they are not capable of being in the same ocular circumstances, the same perspective relation to objects, cannot have the same visual experiences. Their records of what they experience will thus conflict if they are taken to be, as of course they are not, merely two distinct records of the experiencing of identical permanent qualities.

It would seem reasonable to suppose that a parallel explanation is adequate in the case of conflicting or contradictory æsthetic judgments. Unfortunately for our knowledge here, we do not know what exactly is involved in our experiencing the beauty of an object, except that it seems to be a very great deal that goes on in our bodies, including at least, beyond the apprehension of the ordinary qualities, the apprehension of the beauty either of these qualities themselves or of the object possessing them in apprehension. And since this apprehension is not merely that of the qualities as such—for these we may agree on and still disagree as to the beauty—it seems clear enough, provided that our recording judgments are honest and ingenuous, that they are a clear indication of the difference between us in what goes on at our end of the transaction that constitutes our looking at things æsthetically. Since disagreement is so common between æsthetic judgments, it would appear also that the processes of apprehension in the case of beauty differ from person to person much more widely, whether because of native endowment or by acquisition through training, than the processes of ordinary sense perception of ordinary sense qualities.

This apprehension of beauty, whatever it is fully and analytically, however many processes internal to our bodies and brains and nerves and muscles and our very blood it may involve, is characterized roughly by the delight we feel or fail to feel in apprehending objects. Our part of the transaction, the whole of which is our apprehension of the beauty of anything or the manifestation of that thing's beauty to us, seems then to be the delight in the object as directly apprehended, with no reference beyond this apprehended form or appearance. Thus æsthetic experience is an experience of an object as apprehended delightfully, primarily too, as so apprehended directly through the senses. This is what is properly signified by the term æsthetic in the first place, and it is the primary meaning, never to be neglected in the analysis of æsthetic experience. Such experience is, no matter how much of ourselves it involves, the experience of the surface of our world directly apprehended, and this surface is always, it would seem, to some degree pleasant or unpleasant to sense in immediate perception. But the use of the word perception here may too strongly suggest more than any immediacy. An act of perception may look beyond the surface and fill in our immediate data with the content of previous perceptions or similar ones. We may perceive solidity through a mere surface area, a substantial round orange where for bare sense apprehension there is perhaps only a spot of orange color. Of the delight that is apprehended beauty it is better to say not that it is perceived but that it is intuited. For it is characteristic of æsthetic apprehension that the surface fully present to sense is the total object of apprehension. We do not so much perceive an object as intuit its appearance, and as we leave this surface in our attention, to go deeper into meanings or more broadly into connections and relations, we depart from the typically æsthetic attitude.

Thus the ordinary conflicts of æsthetic judgment reveal at once various important points. First of all, in our apprehending beauty or in beauty's being manifested to us, the character of the transaction depends as clearly on the apprehending process as upon the other main term in the transaction, that is, the object; and while the object may remain the same, persons differ greatly by nature and training with respect to this apprehending activity. If beauty has not actually been apprehended, the æsthetic judgment purporting to record its presence is either false or meaningless; false if we are pretending to record such beauty on our own authority as discoverer or observer of it, meaningless, or at least purely formal and empty, if we accept and repeat an æsthetic judgment verbally given by another whose experience we have not had and perhaps are not capable of having. This is not to say that there is no beauty where we ourselves experience no delight in apprehending an object; but it is at least certain that some one must be so constituted as to experience this delight in apprehension, if æsthetic judgment is ever to have any meaning for any human mind.

If all æsthetic judgments were empty of such specific meaning, it seems impossible that any of them would ever have been pronounced, or that beauty would ever have been discovered. As we shall see later, there is even ground for supposing that beauty is constituted in the very transaction that is this pleasurable apprehension, and that it is therefore properly called a tertiary quality, since for its manifestation it requires not merely sense perception as of color or shape, but such further processes as are in themselves pleasurable. But being processes of apprehension and not mere bodily feelings like pains in the eye or comfortable warmth in the interior bodily regions, their delight must be taken as the quality of what is apprehended, the only term in the transaction to which we can attach them, the only visible or sensible object to be found in the experience, the only object present at all. Not seeing the light transmissions or the nervous currents running about or the brain processes going on, but being conscious of delight in what *is* happening, and needing to have this attributed to something —since it is qualitative and all qualities are by us attributed to something, quality meaning attribute, of course—we attribute beauty to all that there is present to consciousness in the case, namely, the so-called external object entering into this elaborate transaction. And we call the object beautiful no more figuratively or less literally than we call it red or round or solid or external or objective, since after all the object is continuous in nature with everything else as an event within related events. Its beauty, however, is not an event, but the character of one, the specific quality which it literally has in relation to a human organism apprehending it, in the only sense in which any event or any object has qualities at all which are present to minds.

Thus our example of a conflict in æsthetic judgment reveals also the sense in which beauty, although it is the quality only of an occurrence in a transaction in which human organic activity is an essential, functioning element, is a quality of the object apprehended. If it is properly only a tertiary quality so-called, in distinction from qualities involving merely the processes of factual perception, it is still an objective quality just as truly as any other—shape or size or redness. Only, since all qualities of all objects are present to minds solely by virtue of transactions with bodily nervous organisms, it follows that in an organism lacking in certain training and resultant habits of mind, or defective or otherwise abnormal in more or less hypothetical internal structures and modes of functioning, the transaction which characterizes an object as delightful in some minds, will not result in such characterization of the object for other minds, since it will not be the same transaction. As a blind man misses colors, an æsthetically deficient man misses beauty. As a lazy man misses the exhilaration of physical activity or an unskilled worker the feeling of skillfulness in doing his work, so a man who has not exercised his perceptive powers to discriminate fine differences, or a man who has not learned a given technique, is simply incapable, in the presence of objects or events of certain sorts, of responding in the particular and complex dynamic response that is one part of the event upon which beauty supervenes before him as an objective quality upon, and of, the object or event apprehended. We do not apprehend the full process or event going on. For apprehension there is only the form, the unified group of qualities which signifies for us an object. To this our attention is directed, and to this we attribute the felt delight as the beauty it possesses in its own right.

§ 2

Thus to admit genuine conflicts in æsthetic judgments, conflicts which may be full contradictions as they stand, is in the first place to admit that the meanings borne by such judgments are also contradictory. While one thing delights you with its beauty, there may be in it as experienced by me no beauty at all. It *is* beautiful in relation to your trained apprehension or your instinctively good taste; in relation to my untrained faculties and my lacking taste it is not beautiful. But this involves no contradiction in the account of what happens in nature. There goes on in you, when you see it, a process which presents a delight necessarily attributed to what you experience, to all that there is for your conscious experience, namely, the object itself. And as we saw, beauty always is just felt. If it strikes you and you are struck by it, the blow is upon your feeling capacities through the senses, not merely upon the external senses themselves operating only so far as to apprehend the so-called primary and secondary qualities of the object, its shape and color, say. It is the object as one unified and unitary apprehended form that has the beauty that you feel. When I see the object, the same things do not happen; there is no such intense feeling to be attributed to the object, and I do not feel a great beauty, because the process giving rise to its occurrence is not called forth in me by the object. We are both judging the same object. We define it alike, we test its qualities and properties by the same modes of verification; but the beauty of it cannot come fully into being when it strikes my senses, simply because my organic structure has not been trained, or is not naturally gifted, so to respond as to set up the processes giving intense delight and felt as the beauty of the object. Thus our contradictory judgments involve no contradictions in the statements about the actual situation as fully made out. There are simply two different situations to which the same external object is common. As gasoline under certain conditions is an active part of the event that is the smooth running of an engine, and under others is part of the event which is the storing of gasoline in a tank, so one object may be a term in the apprehension of beauty by one organism and a merely present object, not beautiful at all, in connection with another human organism.

Two further points follow here at once. As the same engine sometimes runs smoothly in transactions with gasoline and sometimes does not run at all, refuses to enter into transactions with gasoline; and as we do not say either that it is not the same engine or that the gasoline has changed its nature, but only that something is wrong; so with the same subject in the presence of the same object at different times. What is apprehended at both times is, say, the prospect from a certain point of vantage in this sort of light. It is the same prospect that I saw yesterday, and I am the same person for all the purposes that require identity of name and personal responsibility. But today the beauty is not present as it was yesterday. Am I to say that the prospect is no longer beautiful? Literally I am. Or rather,

I am to say that I do not now directly feel the beauty of the apprehended prospect, not because it is there and I fail to see it, but because without my response it is absent, unconstituted. In other words, the processes that bring about delight in an object are not going on in the transaction, between me and the prospect, which is my present apprehension and recognition of it as what I have seen once before, then as beautiful, now not so.

It has often been urged by theorists that I am then not perceiving the same object. It would be rather more to the point to say that I am not the same person. But neither statement is warranted for intelligible and practically efficacious discourse. Since no objects are anything but the forms of changing events, and no organisms anything but events either, and since, roughly, identity is established in any such slowly passing event as an animal body or a physical object, it seems more to the purpose to say that what is missing when I do not see the beauty is so much of the transaction as depends on or is constituted by my functioning in a particular fashion. Since such functioning is actually necessary to any beauty at all, just as necessary as the relatively permanent properties of the prospect, it also seems reasonable to say that the same object perceived by the same person may at one time be beautiful and at another time not, according as those transactions are or are not carried through, without which no beauty is ever present. What it would mean to have beauty present in the absence of these processes is the same sort of thing that is meant by the presence of determinate size without an agreed upon unit of measure or standard of comparison, or of sound when there are no hearing mechanisms. Both are entirely relative matters, which means that they are constituted in a relation both terms of which must be present as conditions of *their* presence. In the case of beauty the term on the human side is not mere perceptual processes, but those accompanying functional activities, perhaps deeper or more voluminous, occurring in certain apprehending relations established between the person and the object apprehended; activities that on some occasions fail to be set going, or else do not occur intensively enough to be felt and consciously recognized as beauty even in connection with the same perceived object.

§ 3

But it should follow that if it is apprehension that involves the feeling of beauty, all apprehension whatever, bare perception itself of length or breadth, may have some degree of delight in it. And hence all objects should have some degree of beauty. Then the same human being could not possibly sometimes in the presence of a certain object experience its beauty and sometimes not. And this is to be taken into account. But to do so is a simple matter. The two cases of seeing a prospect as beautiful and seeing it as not beautiful are most probably cases of the relative intensity or volume of the processes going on. But at a sufficiently low degree of intensity, due to any of a thousand causes, such as indigestion, or a very low temperature, which may absorb energy or distract attention, or sorrow, which sometimes reduces all vitality nearly to coma, and so on and on—at such a low intensity the feeling is almost nil and the beauty has faded or quite vanished. In extreme cases, of course, the processes of apprehension may be actually unpleasant on account of other concurrent bodily processes, and the object which was delightful may now be directly offensive to sight.

We are often reminded that logicians and mathematicians have æsthetic pleasure in their own specialized logical and mathematical objects. And this too is a clear possibility on our view, although it is also clear why other men miss these beauties, and why the appreciation of them is not primarily and typically illustrative of æsthetic contemplation. Usually the attention of intellectual endeavor is focussed ahead, in the perception of spreading relations from a point rather than in the intuition of forms present and static. Only enough of this attention is given to the stage reached at any point in calculation to grasp the possibilities for future operations. But if a mathematician stops at all, if his attention even for a moment rests entirely on the form of what is before him, he of course may and no doubt usually does have æsthetic pleasure in it. And if he completes a demonstration or a great scheme of operations in which are comprehended formally vast numbers of meanings in relation, he may easily dwell upon this form itself. In other words, as soon as he stops his mathematical operations and notices their form, he is a contemplating subject with precisely the sort of absorbing object of attention that is typical of all æsthetic experience. Only, since pure symbolic forms lack color and sound and richness of sensuous content in general, even the purest mathematical æsthetic contemplation, disinterested and intense as it may be, lacks volume. It occupies less of sense apprehension, less of those accompanying processes stirred into action by the senses that resound in felt delight. If it is the purest and most elevated æsthetic pleasure, it is at any rate also the thinnest and most meagre. It is frugal if not ascetic.

Our two added points, then, are that all apprehension may be tinged with æsthetic feeling, touched with beauty, but that it is the full sensuous resonance of the process that is typical, in cases where we stop at intuition of form or quality instead of moving on to perception of relations and connections and further meanings in general. And second, that since this resonance of sensuous volume may or may not be stirred by the same object at different times, even the same object may be perceived by the same person as beautiful at one time and not at another and still remain the same perceived object.

All that we have been taking account of in the present chapter reinforces the view that actual beauty is present upon objects only in connection with processes involving more than the properties of the so-called external objects which enter into them. While these processes terminate for conscious attention in the form of the object, they involve within human bodies, which thus enter into transactions with these objects, little known, but, we may suppose, elaborate activities that extend further than those involved in the perception of sense-qualities as such. In fact, if attention is characteristically perceptive and not intuitive, these further processes remain largely in abeyance, as when in musical dictation one hears so well as to write out accurately what was perceived through the ears and the sense for rhythm, without in the least feeling the formal or sensuous or expressive beauty of the dictated passage.

Experience is genuinely and characteristically æsthetic only as it occurs in transactions with external objects of sense or with the objects of sensuous imagination held clearly before the mind in intuition; and the beauty attributed to objects in æsthetic judgments, while it is objectively theirs, just as any quality is, is like all other qualities the essence or form attended to by directed feeling, dependent for its nature as well as its manifestation upon human organic activities just as truly as upon the objects felt to be beautiful and afterwards recorded as beautiful in æsthetic judgment.

CHAPTER III

THE DISCRIMINATION OF SURFACE QUALITIES AND THE INTUITION OF SPECIFIC BEAUTIES

1. Characteristic æsthetic judgments indicate that sense discrimination is the primary condition of æsthetic experience. 2. Risks involved in the neglect of discriminable surface qualities. 3. Æsthetic vitality as evidenced in attention to the surface of everyday life.

§ 1

WHILE conflict in æsthetic judgment indicates the kind of situation necessary to æsthetic experience, the merely general account of this situation is of little interest after all. No one doubts that we differ in our tastes as expressed in judgments, and no one doubts that this is to be explained by the true account of the æsthetic experience. But the account here given is at the best in very general terms, and if it appears to be consistent in itself and not to neglect the facts, that is a minimum to be demanded of it. If it is to give any real light on the subject, it must accord with those typical descriptions of beauty that have been made out by theorists and recognized by all of us as relevant. Further than this it must give us a basis on which to explore and systematize in our minds the whole region of æsthetic experience, the intuited surface of our world, and that special part of its surface made by man, both the arts in general and the objects of fine art. It is of course the last that have been most discussed in books and in talk, but it is the æsthetic aspect of our more general experience of the world that would seem more appropriate to begin with, because it is with this surface that we are familiarly faced in daily living.

If æsthetic judgment in this field is not so characteristically expressed nor so clearly different at first sight from other sorts of judgment, the lack of emphasis on its distinctive nature is compensated perhaps by its familiarity, and we shall do well to begin with these milder, less characteristic, but better known beauties, and by clearing our minds as to the function and meaning of æsthetic judgment here, come to some realization not only of its specific nature but also of its common occurrence. This too may make it plain that the surface of all of our experience is æsthetic, that everywhere and at all times the surface that our senses come upon may be dwelt on for what it is in direct intuition. If it is dwelt upon only momentarily for the most part, even so it may be dwelt upon with a degree of pleasure, and often of course it becomes the object of intense and relatively lasting contemplative delight. It will be easy to cite examples to indicate this, as well as to mark off the meaning of these judgments from that of other kinds of judgment, and so to characterize a little more specifically the æsthetic aspect of experience recorded in them.

We have already said that the most accessible æsthetic data are to be found in casual truant glances at our surroundings, when the pressing occupations of practical effort either tire us or leave us for a moment to our own devices, as when in the absorbing business of driving at forty or fifty miles an hour along a highway to get to a destination, the tourist on his holiday glances at the trees or the hills or the ocean, or when, in sheer exhaustion, from a desk covered with letters to answer, or accounts to disentangle or invoices or contracts to check over, we look away and instead of turning to the clock to see when we must stop to meet an appointment, or when we may stop without prejudice to our wages, we turn instead, perhaps only for a moment, to the commotion about us, listen to the vast city noises roaring outside, notice the worried look of a face bent over another desk, the odd self-confident tone of a voice giving instructions, the monotonous repetition in the cadence of the telephone operator's answers and calls, the expertness of her manipulation of the switch-board, the rattle of the typewriters, the banging of the surface-cars, the smoky shafts of light striking through dull window-panes, the enveloping odor like hot glue that comes from the packing-house nearer the river, or even the image of the opaque river itself, swirling in oily patches under the bridge past the embankment.

All of these glances at our surroundings or into our remembered images, all these day-dreams that let attention rest simply on what is presented to it in sounds and colors and smells, are recorded, if they are recorded at all, in simple judgments using such terms as we have used already in citing them. The city is noisy; the voice sounds self-confident; the telephone girl is expert; the river looks thick and solid. And these sound like ordinary judgments of fact, the reports of observation, the direct perception of the nature of our surroundings. There is nothing in their form to differentiate them as æsthetic, and any one of them might be, instead of the record of a dream or of the mere ingenuous contemplation of the surface of experience, part of a practical and entirely unæsthetic report. The self-confidence heard in the voice, for example, may be recorded as part of the suitableness of the office-manager for his position, or one of the many signs that have been taken as evidence of his competence and character in the eyes of whoever put him in charge of an office. The noise is one of the conditions taken into account in deciding that the office should be moved to the other side of the building facing the slip. The smell of the packing-house is noted as the unavoidable disadvantage of the location, possibly part of the reason for a rent that is not prohibitive. There is nothing in the worded form of these recording judgments to tell us that they are records of anything but the most practical matters.

But if our glance is aside, and not in the direction of our main efforts, nor towards some ulterior purpose in the interest of future activities or plans, the recording judgments are not practical at all, much less for the purposes of information or of science. That the city roars about us is a fact in isolation from all the busy activities that cause the sound we hear, a sound that takes our attention, strikes us, and holds us. And if we remain attentive to this sound, or oblivious to the rest of the world and oblivious to our business in it, inevitably the sound becomes for us characterized simply by its own heard nature, which we take satisfaction in, or else try to blot out by other more vivid or more tolerable impressions. When we looked up from work, the noise had been merely a dull sense of being called away from what we were doing by something pressing in upon us vaguely. Now, when we give ourselves to it in complete attention, it is our own work that not only becomes irrelevant but is altogether put out of mind. The sound we are listening to is our sole object, simply as the specific sound it happens to be. That we do dwell on it for a moment is a clear enough indication that it is holding us, that we are enjoying it in contemplation. If not, we turn to something else before it even becomes fully characterized and defined in our ears. Thus quite evidently our judgment here that the city roars with noise, in this case of glancing aside from practical concerns to a sense object that strikes us, if this judgment goes into the least detail as to the nature of the experience simply as it is and with no reference to other matters, is not practical and factual primarily, but æsthetic. It records the æsthetic nature of the object discovered by dwelling in the satisfied contemplation of it, taken in isolation as the focus of attention and held to for its own sake simply so long as it satisfies us or until it bores or exhausts us.

This matter of being struck by something, and the dwelling on that something by itself, is the elementary necessity that has, in more complicated and highly developed cases of æsthetic appreciation, been erected into a canon of critical theory. In our elementary example it is the obvious fact that if we contemplate at all we contemplate that which is before us, the single object that has struck us and that we choose to dwell upon. Even if this object is the mere diffused sounds about us, it is the single characterized blur of noise that we attend to. As judgment is always about something or other which must be singled out, and which is commonly named in the grammatical or the logical subject of the statement, so æsthetic experience of the most meagre or even crude elementary sort does require unity, the unity involved in there being that which strikes us and takes our attention, that single thing on which we let our minds or senses dwell in a lingering glance or perhaps in the full absorbed activity of contemplation, properly so called.

But what is interesting and characteristic, what is in the first place striking, and what holds our interested attention, is not this oneness of the object, a character common to all objects that are distinguishable as such and capable of being experienced or judged about. What strikes us and keeps our attention is not there being a discriminated single object, but the specific discriminated nature of that object. Moreover, there must be detail in this object to be further discriminated, or its own special character as a whole must be sufficiently striking to distinguish and differentiate it. Lacking such specific and differentiated character it will not hold our attention satisfied and lost for the time to practical concerns, or to other objects ready to enter our sense perception, to strike upon our organs, call our attention to their own special qualities, and in their turn occupy our absorbed contemplation. It is objects as of specific discriminated character, and in their variety of detail, that most fully satisfy us. And the discriminating of such absolutely specific natures and of such internal character, as distinguished from noticing that an object is of some general kind, conveniently named, or the following out of relations to other objects or to interests and purposes, is the very heart of æsthetic activity. Without such specific discrimination, continuous and more and more refined, æsthetic experience remains *mere* day-dreams, mere relaxation or truancy, a rest perhaps, but not a refreshment and delight in perception. The lack of active, ever-developing powers of more and more sensitive and alert discrimination, playing upon the sensuous forms that occupy attention directly on the surface of our experienced world—this lack is the lack of the essential condition of having full æsthetic experience at all, and it involves in the end complete ignorance of the meaning of any but the most undeveloped æsthetic judgments.

§ 2

An adult may like bright colors as well as a child or a savage. A child may appropriately say pretty lady, whether he is faced with a Siennese madonna, or a portrait of a smart Parisian, or with a Carmencita, or a Royal Academy personage with coronet and pearls and sweeping train. But when a grown man, except in the affectation of modesty in such matters, makes the equally indiscriminate comment, *jolly portrait*, or *glorious beauty*, in the face of such varied objects of sense experience, whatever else we may think of him, we must admit either that he has no means of expressing his experience and so is deficient in articulation, or else that so far as æsthetic judgment goes he is in the savage or infantile stage. In our world such stunted ignorance is common, of course. Public men, or men in the highest positions in universities, who would be ashamed to misspell a word or use a conventionally incorrect salutation in a letter are quite content in matters of sounds and colors and shapes, architecture and music and art, not only to fail in the most elementary discrimination, but to reveal their ignorance blatantly and offensively in a thousand ways, in public utterances, and in their sanction of charlatans in the arts and of commonplace stupidity or dullness in almost any strictly æsthetic matter. All of which reveals in them a lack of judgment in such matters resting on sheer lack of acquaintance and of trained discrimination.

While the ignorance resulting from such lack of æsthetic discrimination may possibly be unimportant for many highly practical social purposes, it can hardly be said to be less than primarily relevant to education, especially if it turns out that only such discrimination can give men any full or lasting satisfaction in the world they live in as directly and accurately experienced. Women, of course, have traditionally had some leisure from practical achievement. In dress they have taken a natural interest, and cultivated it highly. And in general they have noticed what the world is as actually present to our eyes and ears, and our noses and our mouths,—how infinitely varied and often how ugly or tasteless. But men even take pride in the neglect of sensuous discrimination, as if paying attention to the satisfactoriness of the world as it appears about us were a weakness of character, instead of being the only way to avoid the actual stunting of the mind and the loss of full satisfaction in that world as it is actually and really present. This would do for a primitive Christian, of course; but if life is lived here on earth and not mainly in heaven afterwards, it is obviously in a modern mind the neglect of one of our richest opportunities for experience itself, in a sense our only opportunity, and hence the neglect of the chief source of all actual knowledge.

Discriminating senses select specific features of the world which thus become distinctly characterized objects in perception. Such selection and the further discrimination of details in these chosen formal objects, are the sole avenues to æsthetic pleasure. And this means that without discriminating senses, and without the cultivation of these senses, one remains in elementary and primitive ignorance of the world as it is actually presented to us to dwell in and to dwell upon. This has been the burden of so many wise admonitions that men might well pay more attention to it. Plato was as clear on the subject as Aristotle's practice was clear in exemplifying it. In later times Emerson's famous address on the American scholar is an almost dithyrambic prophecy on the text, and the same principle constitutes the central significance of Bergson's insistence on the incomparable value of what he calls absolute metaphysical knowledge. In æsthetics itself, the lack of discrimination in appearances is the cardinal sin, a sin apparently white and harmless in other realms, but, as we shall see, leading almost inevitably to a general blindness as to all values, even that of human character. For human beings, like other objects, come to us first of all through the senses. Those of us who neglect the discriminating of appearances, not the cut of clothes and color of skin, but the thousand and one marks left by life upon the surface of men's bodies, their motions, their features, their manner of speech, their whole bearing —those of us who neglect such appearances come gradually to judge men by no clear marks. We cannot judge by something in them which does not appear and is mystically divined, for what does not appear at all is in all probability a fiction of our own; and we cannot in any case avoid judging, perhaps only half consciously and far from frankly, on the basis of more obvious features. But we are likely to judge vaguely and loosely as to general type, or stupidly and blindly altogether. Such neglect of detailed discrimination leaves us a world where, for example, the distinction between foreigner and compatriot is more attended to than differences between human beings in actual human traits. In important decisions on such a basis we choose men for friends or for positions either without any sound criterion, or on the strength of the judgments of others, whom for some accidental secondary or indirect reason we trust. But to turn back to more specifically æsthetic judgments, recording the results of discriminating as against indiscriminate observation, let us take examples where the matter will be, if not, conventionally speaking, more strictly in the æsthetic realm, at least in the realm of distinctly sensuous experience.

If we leave the office and go to lunch at a restaurant in the neighborhood, we come to a place where choices are clearly a matter of taste, properly so called. And what is the meaning of such judgments as we make here? The coffee is good. The tables look fresh and pleasant. The meats are well seasoned. In such judgments there is finality. We do not choose good coffee for nourishment or any other practical purpose; the vilest would serve the purpose of stimulant, like the boiled tea of old England. That the coffee is good simply means that it tastes good, and perhaps also that it looks the right color and clearness. The judgment that it is good refers to an experience satisfactory in itself, and if we do not contemplate our cup of coffee for hours in complete absorption, we do really dwell on it a little in an act of attention directed to its qualitative nature alone, not as means but as end. Here is a directly satisfactory sensuous content, simply good to have in itself, a moment of directly felt pleasure, taken in isolation from the hurried business of a long day, and dwelt on fondly. If it is not the highest sort of æsthetic satisfaction, it is at least a simple, clear example of disinterested sense pleasure on the very surface of experience directly had. It is a pleasure, too, to which we return over and over again through the years, not for any extraneous reasons, but just because the hot, clear, brown liquid is, as directly experienced in its perceived na- ture—not accurately or exhaustively describable, of course, but familiar and in no need of description or definition— one of the satisfying features of the surface of the world we live in, a feature we may dwell upon a little in aloof happi- ness, isolated in our contemplation from all the ramifying practical activity of business and all the pursuing zeal of inquiry into the origins and causes of coffee in nature, or its economic significance, or its consequences and cost in our own future.

§ 3

Such isolated sensuous pleasure, distinguishing in perception the special discriminated flavor of its object in more or less lingering and loving contemplation, is the very mark of all æsthetic experience. There are of course benighted persons who, as we say, cannot tell good coffee from bad. And they may be blind to the delights of coffee because of the intensity of the brilliance in which other beauties of the world of nature or of art shine for them. In general, however, it is not fanciful or irrational to distrust the genuineness and sureness of any taste, the discrimination of any man, who in small matters shows himself indiscriminate. Indiscriminateness here is at least just indiscriminateness; and if this is our total evidence so far of the taste of the man in question, it is evidence of lack of taste, the lack in one field at least, of that discrimination without which any developed æsthetic experience, and so any significant reliable æsthetic judgment, is a flat impossibility.

These simple sense pleasures of taste furnish an example of the meaning of æsthetic judgment and of the essential function of discrimination even at this level of natural experience. Clearly enough, however, the world is not a cake to eat or a measure to be danced, and if æsthetic possibilities are to be realized at all fully, we must find most of our æsthetic satisfaction not in truant excursions from business, but in the forms and surroundings of our main activities and tools, graciousness or even physical grace in daily human relations and transactions, and colors and forms and sounds that are not intolerably unpleasant and chaotic in factory-buildings, streets, traffic, and office-furniture, as well as in public monuments and parks and school-houses and gardens, where æsthetic concern is normally, if vaguely and too often unsuccessfully, taken into account. The active city of our practically busy lives is after all more upon us and about us than our suburbs, where we sometimes dream or play a little before we go to sleep.

Nor are such æsthetic matters altogether neglected in modern practice. If the voice of the telephone operator is monotonous and her intonation and enunciation bad, her modes of speech on duty are at least defined and formalized with an eye to a standard ambiguously called service or courtesy. Advertising itself has found that individual taste and smart color and design have an "appeal." Obvious and crude and undistinguished as bill-boards and posters may be, it would seem that a public demand for "artistic" ones is a turn in the direction of attention to the actually appearing surface of the world on which our eyes must dwell if they are not fixed altogether on dreams of future success or a heavenly rest. Once attention is directly focussed on appearances as such, it may not be out of the question to go further than these appearances as they are, to a demand for very different ones—involving even the absence of bill-boards for the sake of a landscape naturally pleasant to look at and infinitely more absorbing in its subtleties of line and form and color. Even the most blatant of our magazines makes a half-hearted separation of what we have bought to read from what advertisers pay to have us look at, with a respect for appearances that somehow refuses to be completely effaced by the most thoroughly commercialized press that the world has ever known.

With useful paraphernalia this negative solution is not possible. Means of transportation and office fixtures are not likely to vanish. No one but an irrational and irresponsibly romantic visionary supposes that we ourselves want or ought to want the classic beauties of the age of Pericles, with the accompanying lack of most of what makes our lives significant in our own modern world. What does move in the direction of improving the surface of this world for our contemplation, is evidenced in the fulfilment of such æsthetic demands as those of neatness, cleanliness, polished surfaces, finished and efficient apparatus of all sorts, such apparatus as happens to be useful or to be thought useful for our practical everyday purposes. Not that usefulness itself is beauty. A telephone would work just as well in a less immaculately smooth black casing; the instruments on an automobile dashboard would be as convenient in less symmetrical arrangement and without ornament; rough edges and red lead would allow a train of Pullman coaches to cover the same long miles in the same short time. But once any useful article reaches a stage of clearly defined and limited purpose, and is an adapted mechanism not immediately in need of improvement, the lavish attention to perfection of functioning naturally plays also on appearances. The machinery of a brewery may be painted ornamentally and even floridly because the gaze resting on it can then more fully enjoy not merely the grandeur of its physical proportions and the economy of its intricate arrangement, but the very externals of painted supports that keep it in place. The whole, being an object of the greatest solicitude and pride, receives the attention to detail of appearance that is always bestowed upon objects of fond contemplation, though usefulness is not one whit increased, and vast care and labor may be expended, not only in the original decoration, but in keeping the paint fresh and the brass polished. We are always told that such expenditure is merely in the interest of "good business"; but if that is even true, it is only because æsthetic appearance is felt to count with the general public and so to be indirectly valuable to hard-headed business-men themselves. But one cannot always credit this explanation. Instead, one places these supposed paragons of efficiency among the gullible and æsthetically demanding general public where like the rest of us they are very much at home.

Such æsthetic efforts may be quite futile, of course, for they may fail to give satisfaction in themselves and so be not only otiose but actually offensive. Moreover, in decorating the useful in the most superficial and obvious sense, attention may be more and more concentrated on the merely useful, or the merely comfortable, in such uses and comforts as are themselves irrelevant to any mature rational living. And to decorate and perfect means—office-files, say —which absorb the whole lives of individuals for no purpose of their own and for no even plausibly just or humane purpose at all, is to add in ornamentation and in perfection of form an external appearance rightly taken as the visible insult added to the fundamental economic and human injury. Such perfection and ingenuity in form, and such decoration, may easily direct attention away from better forms and more felicitous decorative opportunities, and so substitute the lesser for the greater happiness and loveliness possible, or it may fail of its intent altogether and, being either unsatisfactory in itself or inappropriate and hence irrational in its occasions, be in the end actually offensive or even disastrous.

But the natural inclination to dwell in perception on useful equipment, or the means of industrial art in general, is not only unavoidably and always present in men, but the root of all finer art, either in ornamentation merely, or in the positive creation of new forms and objects for sensuous gratification in discriminating perception. A reasonable order of living and of society would bend its energies towards making the surface of its own practical active world satisfactory to the perception that must in any case dwell on it for most of its waking hours. If the forms of human relation and the interactions of individuals also partook of such grace and satisfactoriness to the discriminating view, society would be living a more rational life in a more rationally controlled environment. Such a life would also be more nearly beautiful, and as happy, one may suppose, as the power of man over himself and nature allows. Death and disease and pain and risk would not vanish; but as funerals themselves have long been occasions for solemn and tender memorial rites, or even for social pleasure, pain would be suffered and risks run and exhausting toil endured, only as incidental or as fully integral to satisfactions important to those concerned. The ends in view would color and light these evils with some semblance of human happiness and beauty. Men would still err and follow false gods, but at least they would live liberally so far as their gods were of their own choice, their forms satisfying to men's vision, and thus beautiful in men's eyes. Such forms would beautify men's whole world, not by suggesting to them what it might be were it another world, but by offering them beauty as its actually present and apparent surface.

CHAPTER IV

THE ÆSTHETIC SURFACE OF PRIMITIVE LIFE

1. Primitive life as illustrating the development of art on the basis of surface discrimination. 2. Refinement and ornamentation of the useful; pattern supervening upon spontaneous activities. 3. Significance of primitive art in the vitality of its expressiveness and in its natural sources.

§ 1

WHEN the tools of living—our machines and office supplies and mechanical "parts"—are not merely useful but actually necessary to men if they are to live at all, the case we have been making out is still clearer. And in primitive life under simpler conditions, where the needs of men are food and shelter and protection from enemies, and their aims are thus easily defined for them and unanimously agreed upon and accepted by the community, the natural growth in the direction of expert technique, and the refinement of this into the regions called fine art, are most easily seen and most convincingly exemplified. Hence it is worth while to consider such development, not with any historical or scientific interest, but simply to be clear as to the nature of art itself as growing directly out of what we have seen to be typical æsthetic experience, as expressed in the most elementary sorts of æsthetic judgment.

It seems to be agreed among anthropologists that the so-called æsthetic motive is one of the outstanding springs of action among primitive men. While there are interesting and important relations between religious ceremonies and more purely social dances and celebrations, our only concern here is with the fact that spontaneous activities, naturally enjoyed, develop even in primitive life into clear forms, adhered to of course traditionally, once they are established, but not to be accounted for unless we notice that primitive people take direct pleasure in them both as performers and as onlookers. And it is not only music and dancing and pageantry that we find, but baskets and rugs and robes that are ornamented, and cave dwellings with drawings of animals on the walls. It has also been shown, fortunately for our purpose, that while the objects and symbols of religion and magic play a great part in primitive life, it is in purely secular works that primitive men produce their most technically developed and happiest works of ornament and decoration.

From what we have already noticed as familiar æsthetic aspects of our own busy industrial civilization the sanity and acceptableness of such an account of primitive æsthetic activities is clear enough. We are interested in the facts of the æsthetic aspects of primitive culture only as illustrating the meaning of æsthetic judgment as we have already defined it. What primitive life has to show us in particular is the naturalness or even the inevitableness of artistic activities and æsthetic enjoyment in a state of civilization a little simpler than our own, and at a sufficient distance from us to define itself in outline and in some of its main features.

§ 2

First there are the dwellings, the clothing, the utensils and the weapons, needed for survival in primitive society, and the ornamentation of these or their modification under atten-

46

tion into forms satisfactory to contemplate. Here in general, utility, whether strictly practical or religious or magical, comes first, and upon it supervenes, on account of attention and the satisfaction that perception craves, ornament, or at least a finished and perfected form not required in such finish and perfection of appearance for the ends in view. A bow or an arrow may be polished and tapered not merely to shoot straight and far but to gleam brightly for the eyes, to feel smooth to the touch, to look satisfactory as well as to serve its practical purpose of bringing down game or enemies. A thatched dwelling may be constructed not only so as to keep out water, but so also as to have finished edges and symmetrical form. And beyond the actual finish and perfection of form and surface, there may be added decoration, painted designs or carved shapes of animals. That this does so regularly happen is a simple illustration of the fact that men devote their energies even in the most natural social conditions, in robust and undecayed civilizations, in the wild open places of the earth, to making serviceable objects satisfactory to perception, to beautifying the useful. That their patterns become stereotyped, that religious symbols and magical objects have the greatest importance for them, that specific forms and shapes come to be socially and traditionally demanded instead of freshly and freely invented— none of this need obscure the fact that both active creative effort, and the pleasure derived from sensuous appearances and social conventions, are characteristic of primitive life as clearly as of the most developed or even decadent cultures. Not that the same forms of objects or types of ornamentation satisfy all peoples, or the same social arts, the same dances and ceremonies; but even in form and character primitive works of art find ready acceptance and recognition among civilized men as art, and while we may not like Navajo rugs as well as Persian, or Indian chants as well as the songs of Brahms or of Strauss, we can all see the effectiveness, the specific, distinguishing, æsthetic quality, of Indian baskets or archaic Greek sculpture or Koryak carvings.

If the cave dwellers of France and Spain, the jungle tribes of Africa, the natives of Java, and the Indians of America give us undoubted evidence of the time and energy that primitive men expended on such works of supererogation as drawing and music, carving and ornamentation, dances and dramatic spectacles, we may at least admit that the fine arts themselves seem to be an appropriate and genuine part of any human living; and in connection with primitive art we may discern the elementary aspects of the meaning of æsthetic judgments in general. Moreover, since primitive societies are in a sense completed and defined, their whole reaction to a given environment worked out fully, and repeated for generations with perhaps very little change, their artistic activity is seen in its completed natural functioning in their life, and its central characteristics are clearly exhibited.

These characteristics may be indicated, perhaps as spontaneity of expression on the one hand, and on the other, rationalizing and formalizing of such expression. And to this, we must add a sort of reversal of this development. As mere spontaneous expression may take on gradually the most rigid formality through being repeated and imitated for generations, and given social and even religious sanction, so many useful or necessary activities and artifacts, their forms determined by the ends they serve, may in the light of spontaneous feeling, be decorated or modified in the direction of sensuous satisfactoriness. As merely spontaneous expression may be beautified through taking on definite recognizable form, so the useful or practical forms of objects or activities may be spontaneously adapted to suit the organs and modes of perception. The natural cry of grief may become the traditional and highly conventionalized formal funeral dirge by taking on definite structure and form and cadence; and the necessary arrow or hut or boat, or the necessary coöperative labors of war, or hunting, or fishing, may be made to yield pleasure by a more sensuously acceptable exterior appearance, or by chants or dances or other accompanying rhythmical forms, that modify the presence of the useful or lighten labor in the direction of beauty, and so modified are still expressive and vital with the significance of their original function.

The natural occasions for artistic expression and for the development of beautiful forms and appearances in general, are thus seen to be the useful or otherwise desired objects and activities of ordinary life. We come to see at once in primitive man how normal, healthy activities and useful objects or objects serving any genuine specific purpose of the individual or of society, because the occupation with such objects and activities calls for attention to them, lead to the additions in finish of form and decoration, and rhythmical elaboration of activity, which will make the objects and activities in themselves, and quite aside from original practical or religious purposes, acceptable to perception and expressive of conscious feelings and meanings.

Some of our so-called fine arts—carving and painting and architecture and ornament—would thus appear to supervene naturally upon the making of practically useful objects, and to derive their meaning and acceptableness from making what is already necessary to us a pleasure to handle and look upon and to be concerned with in perception; so that this sort of vital and genuinely functional artistic expression, having its occasions and its foundation in these necessary things, will keep its strength and health and its vital emotional significance only so long as the underlying need for the objects is at least indicated in their forms, or emphasized and accented, not blurred or concealed, by refinement and ornamentation. Whether this is the historical origin of some of the fine arts is not at all our question. In any case the obviously natural course of events suggested is illustrated by the way in which the beautiful does supervene upon the useful in a life sufficiently free to allow perceptive activities to be indulged in for their own satisfaction.

§ 3

Another phase of primitive art illustrates this equally well. As in a city office the images in a man's memory sometimes blot out his immediate surroundings, and he sees the distant river swirling under the bridge he crossed in the morning, so primitive men, in their cave-dwellings, had time to live in the images of the beasts they had slain or escaped from; and these familiar objects of their outdoor experience they reproduced not only in memory but externally on the rocks that sheltered them. While their inspiration was nature, whence alone, of course, they could derive the forms they carved, their graphic art succeeded in being more than realistic imitation; it expressed in form and line the sense of power and swiftness that they themselves had felt, and that they felt again in recollection. Not mere factual reproduction of detail, but the choice of those details which meant to them that in the objects that was important and interesting, the size and strength and power and fleetness of bison or buffalo or horse, the exciting qualities of these animals. These qualities were what called for expression in graphic art, because it was these qualities that were called up in memory images upon which one would dwell long and attentively to catch just that which in the actual appearances of the animals was felt and then remembered as stirring and significant.

While such graphic art was thus not the ornamentation or refinement of form of the useful, it was the free expression of the interest in the nature of stirring objects of experience, whether rare and especially exciting, or familiar in everyday activities as stimulating occasions for action and the accompanying feelings and emotions. Primitive art thus gives us examples of the free expression in graphic forms of those inner images and feelings and emotions that could be externalized in the exciting and significant details of the represented objects themselves.

And primitive life offers us a still purer form of art, where the very ground of it ceases to be either useful objects or acts or the familiar objects of experience lending themselves as subjects of representation to express in peace and at home the dangers and thrills of fighting and hunting. For there appear to be spontaneous activities not explicitly useful or even consciously directed, such as the production of sounds by the human throat and movements of the human body in general, which are still natural, and which in themselves give relief or pleasure and express emotions for their own sake. Savages perhaps took no thought to indulge such instinctive tendencies, but it seems at least not fanciful to suppose that there were long hours in which merely accidentally experienced motions and vocal sounds could be reproduced, simply to be felt or heard. And whether this happened or not, to bring music and dancing into the world, at least these arts are most easily recognized as spontaneous acts, gradually taking on distinctly pleasant form, and being elaborated into forms both recognizable and capable of being reproduced from memory for still greater pleasure. Natural physical processes producing rhythmic sound and motion, cultivated primarily because they incited men to more effective performance in war and work, but felt as pleasurable in themselves, were capable of an intrinsically felicitous structure which could be learned. Then without the war or the labor to call for the beating of drums or the cries of encouraging ferocity or the exciting dances stimulating the emotions into bravery of action, the rhythmical movements and sounds in the recognized structures of music or dances could be produced simply for their own sake, their effective magic transformed into natural enjoyment.

The simple fact of the existence of the various primitive arts themselves, whether primarily useful or primarily free and spontaneous, whether purely free expression of emotion or attempts through representation to appease or cajole gods or beasts or nature, but always formally defined in recognizable and rememberable structures, give us in clear examples the cardinal points for æsthetic theory. For æsthetic judgment is always the record of æsthetic experience, and in æsthetic experience primitive life is rich by virtue of its naturalness and its freedom from historical theory, and from the sort of linguistic prejudice that finds knowledge in mere verbal records instead of immediately grasped sensuous content, or the forms of expert activity. In primitive art we find that active æsthetic experience in its genuine and simple actuality is first of all expressive, and that whether it be representative or merely spontaneous, it is formal, not in the sense of being prescribed in traditional forms, although these of course occur characteristically too, but in the sense of creating and elaborating forms, whether in the representation of objects to express the feelings and emotions that those objects in certain of their aspects can stir and satisfy by indulging, or in the sense of defining and specifying and arranging in a recognizable structure—largely rhythmical—elements of sense experience reproducible by human organs, or by crude instruments. Once put into such forms, these elements make up dances or ceremonies or music, works of art in the full sense.

If primitive art offers us æsthetic data somewhat simplified and accented, colors vivid and in sharp contrasts, drawing that is sometimes too crude to be interesting, and sometimes flatly photographic in its accuracy of representation of particular details, sounds that are limited to the possibilities of the roughest instruments, and dances which, for all their elaboration, are made up of comparatively simple bodily movements, more successful in expressing particular aspects of tribal life than in making their rhythmic patterns felicitous, this is only saying that primitive art is after all primitive. It is not ours, but that of primitive men in a world less shielded from external natural exigencies, and with a social tradition more fixed, perhaps, but less evolved and artificial, nearer to the natural inner interests of men whose physical life was as vigorous as that of other animals, and whose instinctive desires were to be fulfilled more or less as they occurred, and at least without quite our modern civilized and sophisticated indirection. Thus if on the formal side primitive art has to teach us only the elementary lessons of the general requirement of form as such and the values of simplicity and directness, on the expressive side it is perhaps quite beyond our capacities; for, inadequate as the primitive instruments of technique were, and limited as was primitive knowledge of the media in which primitive men created their æsthetic forms, what these forms expressed was not concealed from them under quite such a maze of material surface complications, and they had less than we any dread of being crude and natural and animal. Their interests and their emotions could be expressed more directly, even in the media at their disposal, and in the comparatively simple forms and structures they could create. Since the vitality of æsthetic experience depends upon or consists in the meeting of perceptive demands and the coloring of perception and activity with felt satisfaction, the direct expressiveness of their art is the very acme of æsthetic success.

Moreover, in many ways we can never quite lose just those æsthetic qualities in sound and rhythm and color and form that are their pure expressiveness rather than their formal satisfactoriness. Here sound is perhaps the easiest example. If certain qualities of sound are, so far as psychology knows, among the very few genuinely natural sources of fear, this may remind us that those sounds simply carry fearfulness as their felt nature to any ears and minds that belong to bodies developed through long ages to be human beings, whether primitive islanders or dwellers in the steel structures of New York. Apartment buildings are immune from the attacks of ravaging tigers or stampeding buffaloes or trampling elephants; but the apartment dweller still vibrates within to low rolling sounds or shrill high ones, and much of what we mean by the significance of even symphonic music is neither pitch relations nor distinguishable timbre nor loudness nor swiftness, but specific, so to say absolute, quality, qualities drawing from us inherited semiconscious but deep-seated and stirring emotional response. As an aboriginal South Sea cannibal did not really fear the music made by tribal musicians before his very eyes; so we do not shudder at the sounds from tympani and oboe and bassoon. But for us as well as for primitive men there is a resonance set up within, coloring our feeling with an emotional tinge no less absolutely and directly affecting and expressive because that which it expresses is an age-old inheritance of fear or hope or native human vitality itself. If we stop a moment to think of earlier, simpler men in nature, the inevitable expressiveness for us as for them of sensuous elements of sound, and, one may surely suppose, though to a lesser degree, of color and line and form and texture in general, is clear enough. And it is in expressiveness that the vitality of art lies.

One other fact is worth taking note of before we leave the data of primitive æsthetic experience as illustrating essentials in all æsthetic experience, and in art itself and its creation and enjoyment. Primitive men had no more truly than we have, but only in a more obvious sense, but one source for feelings, æsthetic or other, and but one source for the material elements of art—nature, that is. And it is a little strange that so palpable a fact should sometimes be forgotten. As primitive men discriminated sensuous elements spontaneously generated by their own vocal organs, or by birds or beasts or winds or waves or thunder; as they saw in a horse those outlines which were to them its swiftness or its strength, and in rocks those colors or shadows that meant lurking danger or healing herbs; as drum-beats took on the rhythms of fear or hate or ecstasy; so nature's elements were all they had to put together and stir again within themselves that discriminating perception with which comes æsthetic experience. While we have poured the rocks into steel frames to live in, and turned the flowers into poisons or sleep-inducing drugs in a physician's phial, all our materials, and all their forms and patterns, are given to us as natural animals looking within or without. Strength in art and in æsthetic life is the fruit of discriminating in nature, external and internal, rock forms, flower forms, throat sounds, body rhythms, animal colorings, ocean shadings and gleamings, river sinuosities, the lines of bird-flights, the swirling of dust clouds, the grooves in parched naked soil, the texture of bark or of steel girders or varnish or dyed fabrics—discriminating those infinitely varied, and always absolutely specific, forms and shapes and colors and lights and sounds out of which all art is always created, and which in all art constitute the elements and even the structures we can appreciate.

In the false notion that art is photographic representation, sound minds saw the destruction of art itself and the fertile soil for misleading theories. But this should not blind us to the simple and obvious fact that all the possibilities of artistic creation and enjoyment depend upon the discriminating of sensuous elements offered to us in nature, and that rich and fruitful art, like all our world, lives fully only as it keeps its life fresh by its intimate hold upon these elements in all their absoluteness of specific and infinitely various qualities.

From this slight and only illustrative glance at primitive art, we turn now directly to an attempt to distinguish and group the sensuous elements of experience in general. For these are the very materials of beauty. Although our knowledge of them is after all very inadequate, they are our first concern, the primary subject matter of æsthetic theory.

CHAPTER V

THE ELEMENTS OF ÆSTHETIC SURFACE IN GENERAL

1. Æsthetic elements that lack intrinsic order, and composition in nature. 2. Elements defined in an intrinsic order as the condition of human composition. 3. The orders intrinsic to elements of sound, color, and spatial form.

§ 1

DISCRIMINATING perception focussed upon an object as it appears directly to sense, without ulterior interest to direct that perception inward to an understanding of the actual forces or underlying structure giving rise to this appearance, or forward to the purposes to which the object may be turned or the events its presence and movement may presage, or outward to its relations in the general structure and the moving flux—such free attentive activity may fairly be said to mark the situation in which beauty is felt. It is the occurrence of such activity that makes possible the records put down in what we have called æsthetic judgments. Only the red that has really caught our attention fully, and upon which that attention has actually rested, is more than merely red—bright or glaring or hard or stirring, or lovely and rich and glowing, or fresh and clear and happy, or harsh or muddy or dull or distressing, ugly or beautiful in any one of a thousand determinate and specific meanings of those words.

But though these variations are indefinitely great in number, they are after all limited, as appearing upon the æsthetic surface of our world, by the limitations of the variations in that surface itself. There is a limited range of hues to see, a limited range of sounds to hear, and even a limit to the dimensions of shapes perceived or imagined. Not that the number of possible variations in color, for example, is the number of the possible beauties of color, for the beauty of color is not simply its specific hue or shade or tint or intensity or saturation, but that specific color as upon an object, and not merely as distinguished there by vision, or noted in passing or for further reference as the color it appears to be, but also as appreciated, as felt to be delightful or the reverse to the perceiving subject. And this is plainly indicated, this relational character of the situation in which the beauty of sense elements is present, a relation involving feeling, in the long list of typical words used in describing such elements.

As we pass from the perceptually discriminated quality, taken as sensed, to the intuited beauty immediately felt, we pass from terms like bright and clear and red, to warmly red, pleasantly bright, charmingly clear, or to attractive or lovely or fascinating. As the æsthetic nature of the judgment is more and more unambiguously expressive of beauty as against ugliness, the terms used to describe it more and more definitely assert the relation to the perceiving subject which is attracted or interested or fascinated by it, or who finds it lovely as he loves it. Not that all qualities are not found in a relation to a subject who finds them, but that strictly æsthetic qualities involve not merely this finding, but such quality as is found, such quality as is perhaps only constituted at all, when the feelings of the subject are involved in its relation to the object. But the range of possibilities for delightful or ugly color, for example, bears some relation to the range of possible variations intrinsic to color as perceived; and if we are to know what we mean when we assert that colors are beautiful or ugly, we should know first a little about color itself.

So of the other elements of sensuous content; so of all the materials of æsthetic experience, sounds and shapes, textures and lines, and as it would also seem, so of tastes and smells and various recognizable kinds of bodily feelings which have distinctive character of their own. But if æsthetic character is properly limited to the object of attention, which takes on as directly apparent to sense its own specific beauty, felt in intuition but felt as a quality of itself, it is clear enough that fully appreciable beauty must be that of objects upon which this beauty actually shines as their own nature when we perceive them. Now we do perceive fruits, for example, as clearly upon the palate as upon the retina, although as the rationalists would say, not so distinctly; clearly, in that the taste is present as what it seems to be, indistinctly, in that what it seems to be, what it appears as, is not in its own essential nature rationally transparent, self-explanatory, native to mind as understandable by intellect. We are using the distinction within a field where historical rationalism did not make it, but the distinction itself, as we do make it, is exactly parallel, and worth putting into these old terms to show how troublesome, though in the end fruitless, this kind of distinction has been for all thinking. In our example, the exquisite aroma and taste of rich, ripe strawberries, marked by the palate and the organs of smell, are qualities exactly parallel in perception to their visual qualities, their specific form and color and texture as discriminated by the eye. And there is no doubt either that strawberries or foaming milk, or cabbages, for that matter, have clearly characteristic savour. But these sense qualities, subtle and specific and characteristic and objective as they are, seem to lack just the possibility of giving such fully satisfying æsthetic experience as is given by colors and shapes and sounds.

It is not that they are unworthy because they are so close to our bodies. The palate is no more internal than the ear, and the taste of strawberries is no more a function of the human body than their color or their shape. It would be a very determined esoteric theorist indeed who should deny that the fragrance of roses or gardens or orchards or perfumes was not merely not part of their visual beauty but not part of their beauty at all, even as its richness. And it is not their intimate connection with our vital bodily processes and motions that makes tastes less characteristically æsthetic than sounds or colors or shapes. Part of the appreciation of form itself, as in jars or vases, is without question incipient motions or motor tendencies in our own bodies, and the beauty of the morning is in part the freshness of our vital functioning as well as of our perceptive faculties. We cannot rule out the specific character of tastes and of bodily feelings and of smells from the materials of genuine æsthetic experience on any clear ground. Certainly the fact that we usually consume what we taste but not what we see or hear does not furnish such a ground; for we do not need to consume and absorb it in order to taste it, though, as with tobacco or incense, we sometimes appreciate its savour best by passing the smoke of its destruction intimately over the organs by which we apprehend it. Such distillations of beauty are common enough even with roses or lavender, with the resin of pines or the oil of bays. It is only accident, then, that bodily consumption is the means to the full æsthetic flavor of objects, and this without any relation, either, to biological needs or interests. Appetite is not hunger, of course, and even appetite need not precede enjoyment except as a tendency or possibility or natural disposition of the human body and its organs, scarcely different on principle from the disposition of the eyes to see or the ears to hear. Moreover, we could be nourished by our food perfectly well, though our senses were anæsthetized. And in any case the perception of tastes or odors is never as such the devouring of them. We devour the substance not the quality. And the smell of boiled cabbage, as of blooming roses, is a distinctly discriminated and easily remembered quality, eternally a quality to delight in or be offended by, were all the cabbages in the world consumed, and all the roses dead forever.

Nor does the transitoriness of smells and tastes in their occurrence rule them out as materials of æsthetic pleasure. Nothing is more transitory than sound. And what is more transitory than beautiful expressions upon human faces, or than beautiful young human bodies themselves?

But the fact remains that we do not say of the taste of even the most subtly blended salad or the most delicately flavored ice that it is beautiful. Hence it is clear that smells and tastes and vital feelings are not the materials of beauty in the sense that colors are, or sounds or forms, or even textures, for they are obviously not the contents of typical æsthetic judgments. If they are not to be ruled out on grounds of their nearness to the body, or their destruction by consumption, which is contemporaneous with and sometimes necessary to the very act of perception, or because of their transitoriness of occurrence, or because they are associated in our minds with fulfilling biological needs, or because of any lack of objectivity or specificity of quality, we must find some other ground for the obvious fact that though they occur in delighted perception, though attention may be focussed on them, as specific qualities directly apprehended in sense experience, they are not usually pronounced beautiful, do not become the content of æsthetic judgments, and thus apparently are not the characteristic materials of the æsthetic experience that such judgments record.

Now this ground is not far to seek, and when we stop to notice just what it is, it will offer us three points of clarification for general æsthetic theory. In the first place, smells and odors are unquestionably and emphatically sensuously delightful, and so far are elements of æsthetic experience, however elementary. In the second place much of the beauty of nature is made up of just such elementary sensuous materials, which also enter into complex natural beauties just as truly as other elementary materials, more commonly called beautiful. But in the third place, smells and odors do not in themselves fall into any known or felt natural order or arrangement, nor are their variations defined in and by such an intrinsic natural structure, as the variations in color and sound and shape give rise to in our minds. Hence our grasp of them, while it is æsthetic very clearly, since they may be felt as delightful, is the grasp in each case upon just the specific presented non-structural quality, which is as absolutely different, unique, simple, and unrelatable to further elements intrinsically through its own being, as anything could be. One smell does not suggest another related smell close to it in some objective and necessary order of quality or occurrence or procedure, nor does one taste so follow another. There are apparently more or less compatible and incompatible smells and tastes, but there is no clearly defined order of smells and tastes, or any structure of smells and tastes in which each has its place fixed by its own qualitative being. Our experience of these elements is always of elements properly so-called, but also æsthetically elementary, of course.

Tastes may be subtly blended, and so may odors. Cooks and perfumers are in their way refined and sensitive artists, as tea-tasters and wine-tasters are expert critical judges. But such art and such criticism have no intelligible, or at least so far discovered, structural or critical principles, simply because the elements they work with have neither intelligible structure nor apparently any discoverable order in variation. It is this lack that rules them out of the characteristically æsthetic realm, not any lack of spatial distance from the body, nor of objectivity in themselves as specific characterized elements; nor is it their admitted occurrence in the consumption of the objects of which they are qualities. Their extremely transitory occurrence only marks them as not suitable elements for æsthetic structures that are to remain long before us. They do have a degree of distance after all, as great, if measured from our minds, as the distance of any sense quality; and it is the mind or the mind-body, not the body as such to which they are present at all. They have complete and well-defined objective native character, clearly discriminable specific natures, often even very subtle and refined and exciting. If they are more fleeting in their occurrence than some other beauties, they are no more fleeting than the colors of sunset, nor than many beautiful forms, and they are just as readily reproducible or more so. No beauty is more than a little lasting, for whatever occurs at all, to present us with any quality, also by its very nature passes away.

But relations objectively clear in given orders and a defining structure of variation, tastes and odors and bodily feelings do not have, and it is for this reason that we call them not merely the bare materials of beauty—colors and sounds and shapes are also only materials of beauty—but elementary æsthetic materials. For they remain merely elements, refusing to become for us, in any kind of intelligible human arts, within relational structures or movements or processes, that is, such composed and complex and elaborated beauties as we build up out of shapes and colors and lines and sounds.

Before we turn to these latter it is important to repeat with emphasis the fact that, while taste and smell are not the æsthetic senses *par excellence*, they are capable of æsthetic experience merely by virtue of being senses at all. For like all sense presentations, smells and tastes can be pleasant to perception, can be dwelt on in contemplation, have specific and interesting character, recognizable and rememberable and objective. They offer an object, that is, for sustained discriminating attention, and in general they fulfill the conditions necessary for æsthetic experience recorded in æsthetic judgments. While they remain only elements in such experience, like bodily feelings, and offer no intrinsic structure or formal relations in variation or combination by which they might become the materials of conscious arts of smell and taste, they are still beauties, the elementary materials of certain limited æsthetic experiences.

They do also enter into higher, that is, less elementary, æsthetic experiences, if not of all the arts at least of some representative art, and without forcing themselves upon attention they help compose beauties definitely expressive, the recognized elements of which are forms and colors and sounds. Organ tones depend without question, for even their strictly æsthetic effect, at least in part on the feelings not due to hearing and ears, but stirred by quite other bodily processes. The beauty of flowers is enriched by fragrance, the beauty of Catholic ceremonials by the odor of incense. Thus while they are only elementary æsthetic qualities, they are in exactly the same sense as sounds and shapes the materials of beauty and even of complex structural beauty. While they themselves are but elements, they are materials of more than elementary beauties. So far science and art have discovered in them no order or structural principles by which to compose with them, so that they remain either separately appreciated bare elements, or, if they go to make up beauties apprehended in the main by other senses, they enter as hidden or unconsciously employed constituents, with no apparently necessary relations to or in the structures of such non-elementary, that is composed or complex beauty.

Since tastes and smells and vital feelings reveal no principles of ordered variation, it is obvious that the compositions into which they do as a matter of fact enter are cases of natural or representative beauty; for the beauties of art as such, being forms created by man on some principle or other, however vaguely known or crudely followed, require such objectively established relations. Human composing is doing something with elementary materials that are capable of being composed, and elements cannot be put together at all unless in themselves and by their very nature they are capable of sustaining structural relations to one another, relations of contrast, balance, rhythmic sequence, form in general. These relations must be at least dimly discerned by any artist if he is to use the materials of beauty at all. But there is no such system of smells and tastes, and what relations and contrasts we do notice in such matters seem fairly arbitrary and accidental: apples with pork, perhaps, and perhaps not sour wine with sweets; certain blendings of tea and of spices, certain combinations toned into each other with sugar, or toned in general with garlic; but no structure, or any very clear general principles, though the whole matter is in all probability not so formless and accidental as it may seem, as current psychology is beginning to discover. One is indeed tempted to look for articulate principles here as elsewhere, if only to dignify to obstinately verbal minds whole realms of expert activity which seem to them too natural and domestic to be important and interesting, and too illiterate, it may be thought, to have any full moral status in the society of the arts.

What we are to point out here is that natural beauty in general is so largely of just this unprincipled sort, whether in its rank, unchaste profusion, or in its natural but unintelligible selection and composition. Nature at some places, at least, and at various times, without men's efforts, assumes lovely aspects, unintelligibly composed and unreasonably fine. In fact much of what men, artists particularly, know of color combination has been learned not out of any knowledge or perception of the orders and structures that color and line and shapes inherently possess by being color and line and shape, but from the purely accidental and familiar success of such combinations as nature has exhibited to them, in rocks under sunlight, birds and flowers against trees and sky, hills beyond running streams, metals or jewels against human flesh, and the thousand other happy accidents of natural beauty. If we do not know enough of perfumes or colors or sounds to compose with all of them at once, this is not to say that all these may not in nature go to make up rare beauty, nor that nature may not with impunity paint the lily with its own fragrance and add as integral elements in natural beauties the æsthetic materials of the despised senses of smell and taste.

If there is a beauty of August nights, or beauty in the rareness of a June day, or the fresh loveliness after rain, if there is ripe and languorous beauty in the mist and mellow fruitfulness of autumn, or a hard, cold beauty of glittering winter frosts, such beauty is not all for the eye and ear, and if we do not ourselves know how to blend smells and tastes with sound and form and color to compose such beauties, we need not foist our limitations upon nature. The saltiness of the breeze is as integral to the beauty of the sea as the flashing of the fish or the sweep of the gulls or the thunder of the surf or the boiling of the foam. If we know no modes of arranging smells or tastes or vital feelings or even noises in works of art, nature does not hesitate to combine the soughing of pines, the fragrance of mountain air, and the taste of mountain water or its coolness on the skin, with dazzling mountain sunlight and the forms and colors of rocks and forests, to make a beauty intense and thrilling in an unexpected purity and elevation, almost ascetic in its very complexity and richness. The greatest beauties of nature are concrete and full. Nature appears to have no æsthetic prejudices against any sort of elementary æsthetic materials, nor to lack insight into the principles of their combination in the greatest variety. Only human limitations may miss some of these elements and human insight fail to recognize any principles of structure or form to hold them so firmly together and make them often so transcendently beautiful.

But what happens in nature is not, of course, art, and an

artist must work with materials that have relations, degrees of qualitative difference, established orders of variation, structural principles of combination. While we must be careful to include in the materials of beauty sense elements of all sorts, since all the senses, by virtue of being senses, may take such pleasure in their specific objects as is in all rigor to be called æsthetic pleasure, we must admit that these elements of smell and taste remain mere elements, except where natural occurrences happen to combine them, and through familiarity sometimes to sanctify the combination to men and to art, on no principles intelligible or available to human beings, but as some of the richest of natural or of representative beauties. As æsthetic materials they remain for us elementary in the simple sense of being elements, specifically æsthetic in quality, but still merely elements, not amenable to composition through intrinsically established orders.

§ 2

For less elementary æsthetic experience the materials are sound and shapes and color and line. The simple distinction that marks these materials is that they present objective structural orders intrinsic to their qualitative variation, through which we have control over them to build them into the complex formal beauties characteristic of the human arts and no longer the beauties of elements alone or of merely accidental natural combinations. If nature loves tastes and smells and vital feelings as well as she does colors and sounds and shapes, we may be ready enough to appreciate the beauty both of her materials and of her compositions; but in our own human compositions we are limited to such materials as order and arrange themselves by their own intrinsic nature. And to know even a little of humanly made beauties or even of natural ones involving these intrinsically ordered elements, we must know their order and their formal variation, and learn from this the possibilities they furnish, not for mere fortuitous, if often felicitous, combinations, but for composition in which the principles of such order and form have been consciously employed or at least intuitively discerned.

The essential nature of these orders or structural principles, which are intrinsic to the materials as such, which lie embedded in the very nature of color or sound or shape and line, vary of course with the varying materials, since it is just the defining nature of the material that is its falling into that sort of order that it has, that unique kind of relation that establishes the place of any one given determinate color or sound or shape in the range of colors or sounds, or the structural possibilities of lines and shapes and masses. It is clear that what is peculiar to color, for example, is not any quality that sounds can have; what is peculiar to sound is impossible to color; and spatial form as such is simply spatial, not colored or resonant. Thus no intrinsic order or structure of colors can be the order intrinsic to sounds or shapes, much less to smells or tastes or muscular imagery.

There are also, of course, orders common to several materials. Clearly enough, sounds occur and in occurring involve temporal sequence; and if they occur in throats, they involve the feelings of muscular coördinations and activities besides. Clearly enough, also, colors are found in shapes, along lines, and in general in spatial order. What we must look for here is that peculiar order in color which is not temporal, and for that order in shapes that is uniquely spatial. Time orders we shall find common to the occurrence of any color, any sound, any shape, and so, available for composing with them and making structures out of them, but not intrinsic to them and their nature in the sense in which the order of hue is intrinsic to color, the order of pitch intrinsic to sound, and geometrical structure intrinsic to line and shape.

While all this directs us to these intrinsic orders as fundamental, it indicates clearly enough that still more fundamental factor in all æsthetic experience, a factor in all occurrence and therefore in all experience of form or color or sound, in all the experience to be had in an existing—that is, temporally occurring—world. This most fundamental fact of order and arrangement is of course rhythm, and rhythm, as we shall see, is applicable to composition with *any* materials whatever. But that which rhythmically occurs is in itself æsthetic material, and, though sound embodies it more obviously than line or shape—for even space is temporal in all motion—shapes, too, may be rhythmical, though not unless their spatial nature defines them as what moves rhythmically or progresses in a pattern. Rhythm is all-pervasive in its application, since all there is in the world moves to its own peculiar measure, rocks and trees as well as waves of sand or of ocean, or drum-beats or dances or songs, or laboring bodies or machines themselves. But only perceptible rhythm is æsthetic, and for perception motion on too great or too small a scale is rest.

To complicate matters even here, however, perception and feeling, occurring as they do in time, have their own rates, and these may introduce rhythm into movements or spatial structure where it would not otherwise be felt. But it will be easier to grasp both the nature and the significance of this possibly all-pervasive and absolutely—even metaphysically, perhaps—fundamental character of æsthetic experience and of all objects of such experience, all manifestations in beauty, after we have surveyed those intrinsically present orders of the very materials of beauty that manifest rhythms so variously, faintly or clearly, directly or indirectly, making rhythm sometimes a primary, and sometimes scarcely even a secondary, consideration.

§ 3

Before we pass to a detailed account of these intrinsic and unique orders in the very materials of beauty, we may here mention them briefly and then leave this general account to turn to more specific description of the separate kinds of æsthetic material in their peculiarities, their possibilities of variation on the one hand and of combination and composition on the other. It is clear at once that in color the intrinsic variation, peculiar and unique, is what we call difference in hue, so that absence of color in the rich, lively meaning of the word means absence of hue. We contrast colored surface, colored walls, colored toys, colored glasses, colored light, with white or black or gray primarily, not with absence of all visual sensation. The colors of the rainbow are what we mean by colors, the breaking of the white radiance into the discriminably different hues from red to violet. Colors vary in other ways, of course, but it is variation in hue, and combinations and contrasts of hue, that are intrinsic to color and nowhere else to be found.

This is what is sometimes called the specificity of sensation. It is the fact that color, being color, being the specific hue that it is in any case, is just uniquely its own quality for vision; and if we apply loosely the term color to musical sounds, or mental states of depression or the reverse, or if we speak of the colors of tones or the toning of color, we go beyond what we mean by color itself, to apply terms not in their specific literal senses, but either by analogy, and often vaguely and with resulting confusion as well as the suggestiveness intended, or else by letting these terms color and tone carry as their meaning the principles of order and variation common to both but not uniquely present in either. For color or sound may vary also not in specific hue or pitch but in intensity, for example, although even here the specific intensity is in the one case brightness or darkness, in the other, loudness or softness, and these are not directly but only indirectly or even only analogously comparable.

In sound it is clear enough that pitch, differences in pitch or combinations of pitch, is the uniquely ordering quality. Sounds may vary in intensity too, as we just noted, as colors also may; but as color has no pitch, so sound has no hue, and nowhere but in the æsthetic materials called sounds do we find an intrinsic order of pitch established. We may use abstract terms such as value in its technical meaning for painters, and say that as color-value is higher or lower, so pitches are higher and lower; but here the confusion of the parallel is obvious and the work mostly of words. What we mean by high in pitch depends entirely on the meaning of pitch itself, which simply is this specific way in which sounds differ from each other more or less, and in which colors do not, the way in which a high note is above a lower note, not the way in which a high color value is above a lower one of the same or another hue. For this last is a difference in what is usually, but after all ambiguously, called saturation, a way of differing peculiar to color not to pitch; so that while there is an analogy between higher and lower color value and louder and softer sounds, there is an equally good analogy, perhaps a better one, between higher and lower color-value and differences in timbre, the difference, for example, between brass and strings, and only a rather faint analogy between pitch differences and differences in color-values. Even these analogies find little but abstract words to base themselves upon, words which refer to abstracted aspects of what in reality are full concrete qualities, the abstraction being sometimes useful enough to make a comparison, and forceful and enlightening enough as indicating in both fields genuine structural possibilities, but as applied to the materials themselves and their specific intrinsic orders established by their unique qualitative specificity with which we are all so familiar, only analogies, which, since there is no common principle involved, no identity of these two structural modes of variation, but only the fact that in both cases the variations are ordered, lead almost inevitably to confusion and often to actual error.

When we come to lines and space-forms, the intrinsically ordering feature is harder to name, but is after all clear enough except that it is two-fold. We have two principles, which we may call that of simple extension or extendedness itself—shape perhaps is the best term—and that of geometrical order, which permits what we call different perspectives of the same spatial configuration, such different perspectives being often not merely geometrically correlated but apparent to vision as the same. While the geometrical identity may remain, however, a change in perspective may result in such great changes in the spatial appearance that for vision there is no identity recognizable, but only a difference. It will be necessary to explain the two principles and differentiate them not only from each other but from other meanings suggested by the terms we seem forced to employ. But mathematics is, in its strictly geometrical, non-analytical methods, at least in part visually intuitive, and we have therefore to seek the intrinsic orders of the æsthetic materials of spatial form not only in obvious appearances but in the mathematical nature of spatial order. So far as we can give any clear account of all this, it is to be deferred to a later chapter. For the present we may be content with illustrations that suggest the difficulties.

A shift in perspective makes the circular elliptical, the vertical horizontal, and so on. But also the eye sometimes sees the elliptical as circular, sometimes not. Thus the character of shapes and lines may or may not vary while the strictly geometrical order remains the same, as a mathematically defined conic section may in limiting cases be a line or a point, and still possess all its geometrical order and the corresponding properties. So too lines or surfaces or solids lose none of their mathematically ordered properties by being revolved through angles or referred to a new system of coördinates or moved to greater distances or projected upon planes or solids at various angles. But for æsthetic perception such shifts are often all-important. A circle is one shape, an ellipse another. A group of horizontal parallels is one appearance, a group of vertical parallels another. Shapes and directions and sizes are absolute for our sight and not to be confounded with one another simply because geometrically they may be mere transformations in reference not affecting intrinsic mathematical order or structure.

In fact spatial form itself is one of the striking illustrations that any beauty is absolutely its unique self only in relation to the perceiving subject, his spatial orientation and habits in general, and his space location in particular. But for such a subject, so constituted and placed, the spatial characters of objects and their visible beauty are what they are uniquely and absolutely. Objects are of one specific size and shape and proportion, they lie in one direction, and the lines themselves have the direction they have and no other. Obviously the unique and intrinsic ordering quality and structural principles of spatial form are a complex and difficult matter, but we have at least seen that they are present, and their uniqueness is plain. Colors have as hues neither shape nor direction but only hue, sounds may move in space and time, but only sounds have pitch, and pitch itself has neither dimensions nor shape nor direction, nor is even duration of sound its actual intrinsic quality. Thus we have marked and distinguished from one another these three orders of variation, each intrinsic to its own realm. We may now go on to treat these three different kinds of differently ordered æsthetic materials separately and in greater detail.

CHAPTER VI

THE ÆSTHETIC MATERIALS OF SOUND

1. The vital significance of elements of sound. 2. The orders intrinsic to tones: pitch, timbre, loudness.

§ 1

No doubt the most obvious characteristic of the surface of our world is color, and it is often the arts of color and of spatial forms and masses that we mean when we speak of art as distinguished from poetry and music. But if we use the word more broadly, it includes not only painting and sculpture, but music and poetry as well. Still more broadly, *art* is everything produced artificially, as we say, that is, by the operation of men upon the materials of the world, consciously undertaken for any purpose—not only painting and sculpture and architecture, or even these and music and dancing and poetry, but also the great field of the industrial arts. Here too, as well as in the natural world itself, as contrasted with these arts of men, we find the very nature of all surface experience to be color and shape and spatial relations. But for all this, it still seems simpler and more useful for understanding æsthetic experience to begin with the elements of this surface that come to our ears instead of our eyes; and this for several reasons.

In the first place, sound is for us in many cases the primal mark of life and even of actuality. If motion is still more elementary, motion is not so much the surface of our world as its permeating inner being, and our own inner being, the very heart of human vitality and existence. Motion is rather the substance and soul of nature than its appearance. And when motion is manifest to sense, it is in changes of surface appearances that we are aware of motion as within, as the active principle of natural life. Now since æsthetic experience is, as we have seen, rather the experience of the appearing surface of the world than the perception of its inner structure and relations, the intuition of permanent qualities in forms, retained by mind as they appear, these static forms, being, as it were, taken from their transitory occurrences and made the possession of memory and imagination after they have once struck upon the senses in direct and immediate intuition, it is these appearances and not motion as such that is directly sensed. Motion itself is known rather than sensed, and it is known not as the surface but as the underlying actuality that manifests itself to sense only indirectly in appearances, subject always to change, but capable of being held before the mind in their permanent, that is, eternally identical natures.

Now for human experience, sounds seem to be even closer to motion in their nature than colors. A painted ship upon a painted ocean is the very symbol of the unreal, though it is not lacking in color or shape or space relations. And such a painted scene is dead. It is silent. We speak of the silence of death to mark its most salient and imperious feature, its absolute finality, its inhuman distance and separation—still as death, silent as the grave. If motion of some special sort *is* life, sound is its mark and sign. Vitality always sounds: the babbling brook, the roaring surf, the whispering breeze, the calls and cries and songs of beasts and birds, the speech of men. So that it is at least not merely arbitrary to begin an account of the elements of æsthetic experience not with colors and shapes but with sounds themselves.

And there is another reason for so doing. Sounds are the elements of those arts rising from the purely spontaneous performances of human beings, music and poetry. Whatever the origin of language, sounds from human throats must have expressed from the beginning the same unmistakable emotions that we always recognize in the joyful barking of a dog or the comfortable purring of a cat or the happy squeals of human infants or the equally unmistakable cries of fear or pain from suffering animals or sorrowing human beings. Unlike colors, the very elements of sound are not only the immediately apparent content or object of intuition, but always directly expressive, whether as spontaneous cries or as the elements of music. Color is of course expressive too; but while, for example, red is vaguely warm or rich and green is cool and thin, sharp, high-pitched tones are directly exciting and rolling low ones directly ominous. Sound is, as unequivocally as any æsthetic element could be, expressive of significant feeling even without being composed into structures. And sound, instead of mainly imitating or representing beauties found in nature and expressive of moods and feelings, may almost be said to be these moods and feelings, to be the loves and hates and fears and joys it carries to our ears. For these emotions themselves are in substance complex systems of bodily vibrations in us, and sound somehow carries in itself directly to the ear the very vibrations of living feeling.

There is, of course, one still more fundamentally expressive art, dancing. But, as contemplated, as æsthetically enjoyed from without, dancing has a content not merely of rhythm but of colors and forms in space. It is not in its elementary nature a content *sui generis*. And if dancing embodies rhythm and motion more obviously than any other art, still on the one hand rhythm is of the formal nature of all arts as well as of dancing, and on the other hand, dancing is never the mere rhythmic elements themselves, but the rhythm appearing through other elementary materials of beauty, color and shape and space relations. The rhythm of dancing is after all manifested in moving shapes; it is in an order of time, and such temporal order, as we have already seen, is applicable to, if not necessarily involved in, all of the arts, certainly not least so in the arts of sound.

In another sense too, the arts of sound are closer to us than the arts of color. For the instruments of sound are first of all our own bodies. The human voice is limited in range, but within its range it is a perfect instrument, capable of the infinite variations of pitch involved in passing from one end of its range to the other.

Thus, while there are no absolute grounds for calling sounds more primary or more fundamental elements of æsthetic experience than any other elements, there is some justification for treating sound first among æsthetic materials on the ground of its being the very mark of vital life in a sense in which color and form are not, of its being spontaneously and natively produced in ourselves, and of its being, even as elementary material, always expressive of feeling and emotion. If dancing is a more purely rhythmical art than music, and so closer to expressing that most fundamental characteristic of æsthetic objects and activities in general, rhythm itself, dancing as an art involves more senses than that of the feeling of temporally patterned motion; in its appreciation, it involves the perception of changes in visual appearances, whereas sound is heard without being seen. And while dances are of course structures, sound elements are still more highly æsthetic than dance elements, since they are, through their intrinsic defining order, more capable of differentiation in an ordered range, and so more clearly and fully felt as related to one another in heard agreement and disagreement and sequence. It is on this account that they are capable of being built up into the indefinitely elaborate but always fully defined structures of musical art which employ and even tax the fullest human capacities.

We are interested here, however, not in any possible primacy of sound as elementary æsthetic material, but in the intrinsic order of this æsthetic material, the materials of heard beauty, beauty that comes to the ear. And sound has the advantage for us of requiring no other materials of sense to be itself manifest in beauty. While colors are always upon surfaces and shapes, sounds come directly to our ears as pure sounds, unmixed either with the materials of beauty from the other senses, or with the meanings which, as in colored surfaces, we read into æsthetic appearances, directing us away from these appearances themselves to the natural objects we recognize, and so to that whole world of further interests and relations that is involved in our knowledge of the world. Sounds are, as we actually have them in the arts of sound, pure, unentangled with representing anything beyond themselves, and yet so intrinsically ordered by their own nature as to be capable of an infinite variety in specific detail and an infinite variety of composed structures, all for the ear alone, all made of elements of one sense realm. It was sound that Augustine used to reveal the meaning of creation out of nothing; the word that was with God was a sound, and it was the sounding word that made intelligible the creation of an ordered world out of the chaos of sheer nothingness.

As we go on to an account of this order intrinsic to the very nature of sounds, and these possibilities of structure inherent in the realm of the audible materials of beauty, we must not forget, however, as we have just noted, that even as elementary materials, sounds are always directly expressive. If in music we may become absorbed in tremendous structures, themselves expressive, in their dynamic relations, of both subtlety and volume quite beyond the power of words to express or characterize with any degree of determinateness, so that single elements are no longer felt by themselves but only as transitive connections and relations in a whole that demands all our attention and absorbs all our conscious feeling, it is still true that the very elements themselves never lose their expressive power, stirring ancient fears and hopes that are no longer parts of our habitually recognized or even consciously felt world. If we are to confine ourselves just now to sound as merely one of the kinds of beautiful material, we need not lose sight of the fact that this material itself carries within it an emotional content of unknown depths, and feelings appropriate to the ancient dominion of nature over all her creatures. Our main purpose here, however, is to mark out the elements of sound as intrinsically ordered by their own nature, and this is in itself a sufficiently complex matter.

§ 2

First of all we must notice that in nature as we hear it, few of the experiences of sound we get are unmixed clear tones. Noises rather than tones come to us from waves on the shore, wind in the trees, thunder-storms in the clouds.

Even insects and animals make more noise than music. And in our modern world we are enveloped in a ceaseless and confused din from which it would be very difficult to extract intrinsic principles of order. Tones, then, not noises, are the æsthetic materials of sound that we can best use and know. Nature and industry resound, and our world is surfaced and enveloped with noises that may or may not strike happily upon our ears, that may or may not go to make up natural or accidental concrete beauties. But beauties that are composed of sounds by human beings are made of chosen tones, and it is tones that musical art employs in all its main works and all its formidable and comprehensible structures.

We must not forget that music is only a very small part of audible beauty; but the beauties offered us in nature's noises as well as her tones, combined on no principles intelligible to us, furnish æsthetic experience to be had merely by attention to the finished concrete situation, for which no conscious training fits us to apprehend it quickly and surely; and there are no guides for taste and no principles of structure here for us to notice and make use of in building beauties ourselves and in understanding our appreciation of beauties built by others.

Tones then are our proper subject-matter, and among tones, as we have already seen, the principle of discrimination and so of differences in an order, is the continuous range of pitch. This principle may be very simply stated. Of any tone it may be said that it lies between other tones in an order of pitch running through a one-dimensional series from end to end. Pitch is a continuous qualitative stretch, from that of huge organ pipes to the last distinguishable notes of the piccolo or fife, from the bass notes of Russian choir-singers to the shrill whistle of a school-boy, from the bottom of a fire-siren to the top. The words we use for these extremes are high and low, but we must remember that we use them after all somewhat figuratively, as ultimately we use all words. Height is spatial and so is depth, and it is something of an accident, perhaps, that high and low are our most nearly literal description of variations and extremes of pitch. To children beginning the study of music the terms have often to be explained in this application. High and low are so regularly used in this sense, however, that they cause no misunderstanding, and in any case they are the sole words we have for the purpose. The facts are simply range or sequence of pitch in such order that any one pitch lies between others and is defined as the pitch it is, and in terms of pitch, relatively to these others. Fortunately for definiteness, the mechanical production of tones is a process involving measurable numbers of vibrations, and we can for convenience name any determinate pitch with reference to the number of vibrations per second of the body that emits it. Thus we may make instruments to produce tones within a given range by choosing material bodies whose rates of vibration we know. And men knew comparatively little of the means of the controlled production of sounds in given orders upon instruments until physics had taught us in terms of vibrations per second what sizes and shapes of material bodies to construct.

But it was not the mechanical means of producing sound that gave us music, and much less is it a knowledge of vibration rates that arranges pitches as higher or lower. For that, all we need is ears to listen to tones of voice. That men's voices are lower in pitch than women's is a fact observable by the crudest ear, and music began, we may suppose, as vocal. In vocal tones, too, the terms high and low are especially intelligible. For when we produce them, it is those from lower regions that we call low and those from high in our heads that we call high. And perhaps it is also true that all high sounds seem to come from higher spatial regions than low ones. Thunder itself, though it originates in the clouds, comes to us as from the trembling earth beneath and all about us, and it is not entirely figurative to say that sounds from heights are high and sounds from depths are low.

One more point before we turn to our proper subject here. While we hear sounds with our ears, there is no doubt that our vocal organs themselves play a great part in discriminating them as higher and lower. The coördination of ear and throat through the brain we know very little about, but a very slight psychological investigation, even a purely behavioristic one, is enough to inform most of us positively that vocal organs and their connections play a very large part in æsthetic discrimination in the realm of the audible surface of the experienced world. Even if there is no conscious feeling from the throat, the mere fact that a heard pitch can be reproduced by the voice indicates a coördination of great refinement, and how much this inner or even unconscious relation of throat and ear has to do with distinguishing one pitch from another, no one seems to be in a position to say with any degree of assurance.

As we have already seen, the specific peculiarity of sound as elementary sensuous content, aside from its simply being sound, and not color or shape, is that any pitch, by being the pitch it is, is discriminably different from every other pitch in an absolute order of higher and lower. A given simple pure tone must be a specific pitch, with no movement in it of course, but in an ordered range, through which, as in a siren, we pass from lower to higher or higher to lower with a sense of perfect continuity. There are no leaps in the range, one sound simply appearing to rise or fall into another by an unbroken gradation. If we stop at any given point in the range, we feel the pitch to be either higher or lower than the one we started with. And any pitch passed through in the course of the rising or falling is between the two extremities in the order native to any continuous one-dimensional extensive magnitude. Thus specific pitches, like points on a line, are at various distances from one another; and for the purposes of construction, we may choose a number of these pitches at certain intervals, neglect the intermediate ones, and confine ourselves to arrangements in those we have chosen. Since these remain fixed, we may also name them and so be able to indicate in these names the intervals which we are to employ. But since these pitches themselves have no relations except that of being first, second, third, and so on, among those we have chosen, there are no settled points to begin at or conclude with, and no special relations or tendencies calling for movement from any given one to any other one. Nor is there any fixed point at the bottom or the top except as defined by the lowest or highest note we can discriminate, nor could the number of intermediate notes be decided upon except according to the degree of discrimination of our ears, which varies enormously from one person to another. If my ear is crude either by nature or through lack of training, I shall fail to distinguish a note as higher than another, which to a more delicate ear lies at some distance from it with several notes between. Thus the order of betweenness which gives the possibility for distinguishing elements as higher or lower, neither offers us any one set of discrete pitches at regular intervals from each other, nor any focal points to begin with or pass through or rest upon.   And, as we shall find, it is not pure pitch itself that offers us these further ordering principles.   It is to the mechanical accidents, or rather the natural constitution of the physical instruments of sound production, that we must turn for such principles.

When any pitch is actually sounded, it is by virtue of a vibration, transmitted through air-waves, set up in physical bodies, whether columns of air themselves, or human tissues, or stretched strings, or other resonant material—wood or metal or whatever it may be.   And the sounds we ordinarily hear, produced, as they always are, by physical means, are never one pure pitch, because bodies, unfortunately for the simplicity of theory, vibrate variously themselves and set up various vibrations all at once in contiguous things.

It is about vibration itself, then, that we need more information before we find the principle of order we are now seeking.   Physical bodies simply have their own vibration rates, rates at which they insist upon oscillating, if they oscillate at all.   As a taut gut string always vibrates at the same rate when we pluck it, so huge balanced rocks, weighing many tons, may be set in motion by the pygmy strength of a man, provided the impetus is given in time to the native vibration rate.   The fact is familiar to us all in the pendulum, upon whose regularity we rely more firmly than upon our own words or upon our friends.   A pendulum of given length, if it swings at all, swings at its own rate, so many oscillations per minute or per second, until it ceases to oscillate at all. If the clock runs down, the oscillations become less in spatial magnitude, but their number per minute remains the same. Any one who has "pumped" a rope swing knows this phenomenon too well to need any other example; the swing has its own timing, its own regular rhythm, and one's efforts can be exerted to increase or diminish the height to which it rises at either end of its arc, but they are useless and fruitless unless they fit its own native rate of oscillation, and while we may set a swing in motion or stop it, we can do nothing to change the number of times per minute or per hour that it rises and falls.

Now the sounds our ears can distinguish are produced by vibrations that are fairly rapid, and instruments producing tones must therefore be bodies capable of being set into rapid vibration, at least sixteen or so per second. It is rather small-sized objects that vibrate at such rates, so that fortunately we can handle and control such objects and even arrange several of them close together, and so in quick succession produce a variety of pitches at will. Moreover, the rate of vibration of bodies is inversely proportional to their magnitude; a stretched string twice as long as another of the same character vibrates half as fast. And when we set the longer string to vibrating, it vibrates not only throughout its length and as a whole, at its native rate, but also in its halves. That is, the halves vibrate at the native rate belonging to their size and length and weight, the length of half the whole string which is vibrating also as a whole. Thus when a body vibrates rapidly enough as a whole to give an audible pitch, its halves are also vibrating less strongly to give another audible pitch, which merges in the main pitch heard and helps give it what we shall later come upon as timbre or quality. But for the present we need notice only that when we hear a sound of given pitch produced by any sort of vibrating body, we are also in almost all cases hearing at least one other pitch, which seems to us simply the fullness or richness or characteristic quality of the sound of the former. If we take a separate string, half as long as our first, which vibrates therefore twice as fast as it, instead of its giving us a new note higher than the first, this new note is really part of the original note of the longer string and sounds to us like the same note only a little thinner and higher up. We name this second note the octave of the first. If we pass along a range of sounds from low to high, beginning with the note of our original string, we shall come, then, among these higher notes, to that one produced by the half-length string, and this will sound indeed higher; but since it was all in the sound of the lower note, since it was indeed a part of the sound of that note, it will give us the sense of familiarity. We shall recognize in it the sound we heard before and call it the same note an octave higher. At least in the development of music in western Europe this is what has happened, and the physical conditions of the production of tone seem very simply to make it what we call a natural happening, especially when we consider that even in very early music men's and women's voices, trying to sing the same tune, met with just these conditions.

Here then we have the new principle of order we have been looking for. Once we pick out a note of any particular pitch in the whole one-dimensional range of pitches, the continuous stretch or line of pitch variation from low to high, this note recurs again and again as we go up the stretch. If we name the first note by a letter, A, the second note will be another A, perhaps a little a. And since the same holds as we mount higher, we shall have the whole stretch marked off by our ear as from A to a, to a', to a'', and so on. What was one long uninterrupted single line or stretch of an infinite number of pitches, becomes thus naturally, and simply as striking upon our ears from the physical bodies that produce it, a recurring short stretch, from A to a, from a to a', from a' to a'', until we reach the end of our powers of distinguishing sounds at all, because the vibration rates are of such frequency that our ears do not catch them as tones. And we must notice that although it is the physical production of sound that makes this phenomenon clear to our minds, it is simply our ears, attending closely to the audible surface of our world, that make out for us the recurring short stretch from one A to another, as lying along the one whole stretch of all the pitches, these recurring short stretches occupying it completely and continuously, and dividing it conveniently and naturally. The octave, which names the interval from any given pitch to that pitch which is produced by a vibration rate twice as fast, serves to divide the whole range of pitches as tens divide the number series for us, and with a comparable effect, not giving any new relations in the whole series; for the one intrinsic relation in pitches, as in numbers, is that any one pitch follows its predecessor and is followed by the succeeding pitch. But the range is now punctuated for us into recurring intervals; it is divided into stretches all alike in length and in possibilities for further division. Instead of having a mere unbroken stretch of always higher sounds in one long line from the lowest to the highest tones discernible, we have the periodic recurrence of a short series of pitches, each series a single octave.

It is the further division and order within the octave that gives us the basis of all those structures that are built of tones, a starting point, a resting place, and characteristic transitions through determinate intervals. But we have not given any account of this division, the marking of the intervals between one A and the next, the choosing of a scale of discrete notes; and this process varies with the ears and feelings of peoples and times and places. It is clear enough, however, that whatever intermediate points we may choose to stop at and select and name between *A* and *a*, may be found again and repeated from *a* to *a′*, from *a′* to *a″*, and so all the way up or down. It is also clear that since the variation upward from *A* to *a* seems continuous to our ears, we might choose a very large number of intermediate stopping places, and make a scale of many, many tones. In fact we might arbitrarily divide the so-called octave, the interval or stretch from one *A* to another, into two or three or four or seven or ten or twelve, or twelve hundred equal divisions, and name them all. What has actually been done in western music, however, is to choose seven steps of different lengths by which we move by pronounced intervals from one end to the other. If we call the note we begin with, say *la*, our first step, the next *la* will be our eighth step, to be called first again if we go further up. It is this quite special, but in many ways natural and effective arrangement, that makes octave, eighth, that is, the name for the interval from *A* to *a* in our account, or for the first *a* above any other *a*, of which this higher note itself is called the octave. In the paragraph above, *a* is thus the octave of *A*, *a′* of *a*, *a″* of *a′*. In careful scientific accounts of sound, the twelve hundred divisions are used, one hundred so-called cents to each of twelve equal divisions. But since it is the ratio of vibration rates, not numbers of vibrations arithmetically added, that corresponds to heard distances of pitches from each other, this method of division uses logarithmic calculations, and is too complicated to be made out in a few words. If we have good ears, we distinguish many more than the seven different pitches from *A* to *a*, however. Even for familiar tunes we must distinguish twelve pitches before the fundamental recurs, and musically trained or natively gifted ears distinguish so-called commas, some fifty odd in the octave.

When we actually define the seven steps, and so indicate the relations of pitches to each other in the familiar diatonic scale, we have, of course, gone beyond an account of the intrinsically ordered variations of tone, to that of a specific musical combination, beyond the material elements of auditory beauty to a defined relational structure, dependent for its richness and its stability and power on the native possibilities of tone-relations, but distinctly a work of art. If this structure is so fundamental in music as to be felt as part of its elementary defining form in western countries, it is after all elementary in the art of music, not elementary as being the auditory material of beauty, of which it is constituted, as itself a complex and specific and even idiosyncratic whole of tonal relations, the familiar major scale or, with modifications, the various minor scales.

What we have further to notice here is two other sorts of variation in sound, one of them subtle and characteristic, the other neither subtle nor quite in the same sense characteristic. Sounds vary not only in pitch but also in what is called quality. But this is a confusing term, since pitch itself is obviously one sort of quality. A less ambiguous term is timbre. And sounds also vary, as all sense materials do, in intensity, which, in this realm, is accurately and familiarly designated by the terms loudness and softness.

When we mean by quality of tone neither pitch nor degree of loudness but the distinguishing character of, say, the human voice as contrasted with piano tones, or the characteristic quality of a violin tone as contrasted with that of a flute or a whistle, which is sounding the same pitch with an equal degree of loudness, we need a word other than quality; for loudness and pitch are qualities too. In the realm of tone this special sort of variation is called variation in timbre. Whether timbre has been completely accounted for or not in scientific analysis, it is at least intimately wrapped up in the occurrence of overtones, and these we must stop to notice. Examples of sounds rich in overtones or partials, as they are also called, are in the first place likely to be lower sounds in general, since even the first overtone of any note is an octave above, and hence for very high notes the overtones are not distinguishable or even present in any sense to audition. The higher we go the fewer overtones there are, and timbre in very high notes is difficult to distinguish—harmonics on a violin almost whistle, and very high soprano notes sound hardly more vocal than the notes of a flute or even a triangle. Single notes well above the human vocal range are all very much more alike on different instruments than lower notes on these different instruments, which have clearly distinctive timbre, discernible by the least trained or gifted ears or even unmusical ears. Even such comparatively like sounds as those of tympani and tom-toms, when they are so low that the pitch is not accurately discriminated except by a very good ear, differ very markedly to the most ordinary ear in timbre itself. The denotation of the term is clear enough, then; we can all tell the difference between sounds from a trombone and those from a 'cello, we can all distinguish pianos from violins even on a gramophone, or any of these from a human voice, within a large part of the range where we can distinguish tones at all. But we are interested here not only in qualitative differences, but in the fact that such differences establish for us intrinsic principles of order, of contrast and relation, out of which we may build genuine structures. For genuine structures are such as are held together first of all by an order or form native, and therefore applicable, to the elements that go to make them up.

Now the one intrinsic characteristic order in tones is pitch, and while we may have various timbres at the same pitch, timbre itself is apparently in the main a matter of pitch combinations. If we stop to listen repeatedly to the rich quality of a low note on the piano, we soon notice that within this single note there is not only the fundamental low pitch that marks its place in the whole range, but various qualities like high notes produced by metal on metal, and it seems to be the simple fact that fractional vibration amply explains the effect. If a long string, vibrating as a whole, is also vibrating in its parts, we hear a tone made up not of one pitch but of many, blended no doubt partly physically outside our ears, but also by the elaborate mechanism of the ear itself, which allows us by sufficient attention to distinguish these various higher pitches within the fundamental pitch as actually the specific higher pitches that they are. Less training of the ear, or less sensitiveness, fails to distinguish the pitches as such; but even the ordinary untrained ear never fails to give us in sensation the specific character or timbre, and a very dull ear indeed can tell a violin from a piano on most occasions, even when just a single tone is sounded. Nor does the highly trained musically expert ear miss the timbre in distinguishing the overtones, any more than the epicure misses the exact flavor of his salad by distinguishing clearly in its taste the specific flavors of which the composite flavor is made up. If the garlic is a suspicion only, and the sugar a heightening of other flavors, there is still the recognizable garlic, the recognizable sweetness, as well as the recognizable subtle whole. And so of overtones. They may be heard as distinguishable higher pitches, and rare ears with much training and attention have distinguished them up to the sixteenth or so in the high and brilliant ringing fullness of men's bass voices. But for the expert listener, as for ordinary ears, the specific quality remains as the characteristic timbre of the instrument producing the tone.

Just which overtones are sounded, and with what varying degrees of intensity in various musical instruments, has been pretty fully investigated; but all we need to notice here is that since timbre is at least very largely a matter of overtones, and overtones are specific pitches, there are ordered relations in the realm of timbre itself, making it possible to compose musical structures which have within them obvious or subtle contrasts and combinations of timbre as well as of pitches considered simply.

The third possibility of variation in sound itself is that of intensity—loudness and softness. And since degrees of loudness and softness lie in one single range from silence to deafening intensity, which finally becomes painful instead of merely very loud, here is another principle of structure to serve the purposes of balance, contrast, climax, and form in general.

Every tone we hear is complex; it has pitch and timbre, and a degree of loudness. In all three ways it is intrinsically differentiated from and related to other tones, of other pitch, or another degree of loudness, or of different timbre. And since it is not only kinds of instruments that vary in timbre, but almost any two particular instruments of the same kind or any two voices, neither a chorus nor a group of stringed instruments, much less an orchestra, of course, is simply bigger and louder than a single voice or a single instrument. Not only is the range of pitch increased, as well as the range of intensity, but the variations and combinations of timbre are indefinitely multiplied.

Music proper is not due merely to these intrinsic orders of variation in tonal elements, but it does depend for its peculiar nature, its characteristic appeal through the ear to the appreciating mind, on just these ordered elementary materials. While its own character, in even the simplest melody, includes more than these, without them and their beauty as elements and as sensuous material, it would not be the art of sound at all.

CHAPTER VII

THE ÆSTHETIC MATERIALS OF COLOR

1. The variations of color as intrinsic order: hue, lightness, darkness. 2. Ostwald's color notation and some
traditional color terms. 3. Colors as ultimate ordered
differences. 4. Sound and color as specifically different
orders.

§ 1

WHEN we turn to the surface of our world as colored, to
find the intrinsic order in this second sort of material beauty,
by which it may be satisfactorily arranged in its intrinsic
variety, and the variations systematically noted as elements,
we are met first of all by that in color which corresponds to
pitch in sound, namely hue. Nothing can give the experience of hue, these elementary beauties characteristic of visual
experience, except just hues themselves; and the great variety of them is at first glance overwhelming. They range
from bright yellow through orange, red, and purple, to
violet and blue-green, and through yellowish green back
to yellow, in a continuous circular series in which we can
distinguish some hundreds of variations, the number dependent in part upon the fineness of our visual perception,
but the order being established by the intrinsic color quality
itself in such wise that any given hue lies between two others,
into which in either direction it gradually melts, as we say,
so that yellow lies as clearly between yellow-green and
orange, as orange between yellow and red.

But these clear hues themselves vary. Mixed with increasing proportions of pure white each of them runs into a

scale of lighter clear colors, and, with increasing proportions of black, into a scale of darker clear colors, approaching white itself at one end and black at the other. From white to black there lie all the intermediate grays, which are again distinguishable in a scale where each has its fixed place between two other grays, lighter and darker. A diagram which should keep strictly to these objective facts of order requires thus at least three continuous one-dimensional scales of variation, one line to represent the variations from

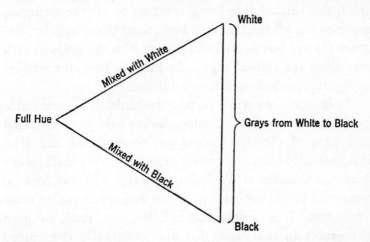

the full clear hue itself through its mixtures with white to clear white, a second to represent the variations from the full hue to black, a third for the grays. Of these three lines the first two have one point in common, namely that representing the full hue undiluted with black or white, and the end points of the third line are the extremities of these two scales, so that a closed triangle gives us a representation along its sides of the three scales at once, as in the above figure.

But as the full clear hue may be mixed with either white or black, so it may also be mixed with white and black at once in varying proportions, each mixture giving a new variation on the hue. These last variations are the so-called neutral colors with which we are familiar; the actual colors of the things we see are always such mixtures, pure white, pure black, and pure full hues being in general difficult to prepare by artificial means with pigments and available rather in laboratories, where they can be produced as colored lights, or in nature in the rainbow. The actual number of variations of one hue is indicated by the points enclosed in the triangle of the figure, including those points along the two oblique sides, the vertical side being common to all the triangles, representing all the different hues, since this triangular diagram fits one hue as well as another, with the grays in each case along the vertical edge. And clearly then, the number of the represented variations is infinite.

As in music we name certain mechanically determinable pitches, so, in the field of color, devices have been perfected and physical theories worked out to mark off and then systematically name the variations in color. We shall follow here the theories of Wilhelm Ostwald, who has been so successful in solving color problems and systematizing color variations. It is obvious that in color, as in pitch, we have differences to deal with that are intrinsically determined and intrinsically ordered; that is, determined and ordered by the actual nature of the colors themselves as they appear to human eyes. What must be done further, as in the case of sound, if we are to compose structures with these elements, is to choose starting points, determine appropriate intervals or steps in the gradation of hues, name them systematically, and note the principles of harmony, contrast, and balance that the material offers. A scheme of notation has even been worked out by Ostwald which, if adopted, would give us not only color norms and color scales, but also some general principles of harmony and progression in precise terms. The single achievement of a scheme for unambiguous color-names, or rather color-notation, covering a range of some 2500 odd variations, and the theoretical and practical procedures for establishing such norms and making them available, is an enormous advance for industrial and artistic color technique. But, as we all know, there is no historical art of color in any such developed and elaborate form as music, even though there is a modern color-organ, Mr. Wilfred's Clavilux, which is of genuinely artistic significance. Artists have of course used colors, balanced and harmonized them, designed with them, composed with them, but never merely as colors; for lines and shapes are involved in the very presentation of the color-elements, and there is besides in painting, and even in much of pure design, an expressive or even strictly representative factor that gives to works of art in color a great deal of their traditional character and their æsthetic value. Nor have artists always had at their disposal the means to produce the specific colors of their actual intentions, so that such an art of color as would be at all strictly analogous to music remains among the possible achievements of the future. What we have in the history of painting and decoration so far is a very mixed art, none the less important or satisfactory for that reason, but not solely dependent upon the visual materials of beauty and the principles of intrinsic order in these materials, in the sense in which music is constituted in ordered structures of pure sound.

It is important to notice, however, that not all of the variations of color lie along the same one-dimensional scale, like pitches. The pure hues themselves run along such a one-dimensional range, as we noticed, which returns in a circle upon itself; but the surfaces of visual experience are made up almost entirely of other than pure hues, and such color-elements require more than the designation of the hue itself if they are to be correctly indicated. In the first place, our triangle is only one of many; in even the most elementary and conventional experience of colors we distinguish red, orange, yellow, green, blue, violet, and purple. And since there are complementary colors, colors that is, which added together in equal amounts neutralize each other in an unhued variation along the white-black line, any circular diagram of hues, to be accurately representative of color-order, must find a place opposite any given hue on the circle for its complementary hue. Thus, if we attempt to arrange the hues in this circle, and if we draw a diameter from, say, clear yellow to the blue that is its complement, the hues marked off from yellow, through orange, red, and purple to this blue, must have their complementary hues at points on the other half of the circle from blue back to yellow. Such an arrangement using laboratory technique to establish norms and to make clear what we are to mean by equal amounts of color gives us eight main colors, which may be variously named. Roughly we may call them yellow, orange, red, purple, blue, green-blue, blue-green, and yellow-green, and for convenience in Ostwald's scheme these are divided each into three: first, second, third yellow, first, second, third orange, and so for the rest, twenty-four altogether.

Thus we should have at least twenty-four triangles fitted together by using the vertical line of the grays for an axis. If we make the circle of hues continuous the result is a double cone, representing every possible color variation, the clear, full colors on the circle around the middle, the clear light colors on the surface of the upper cone, the clear dark colors on the surface of the lower cone, white at the upper apex, black at the lower, the grays from white to black on the axis, and the rest of the colors in the interior. A vertical cut through the cone in the plane of the axis would be a diamond-shaped plane. It would represent all the variations of two complementary colors from a full, clear red,

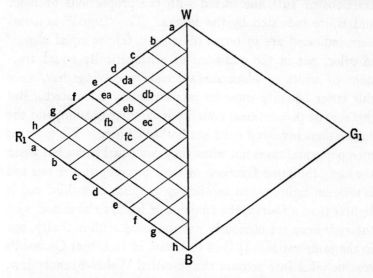

say, at the point of one triangular half of the diamond to its complementary green at the opposite point, with all the grays along the vertical division down the middle. The surfaces of the two triangles vary upward to lighter red and lighter green, downward to darker red and darker green, and inward towards the central vertical line to grayer red and grayer green in proportion to the black and white content indicated by lines in each triangle parallel to its sides, as in the diagram, one half of which, representing the variations of one hue, is filled in.

§ 2

Here if the letters along the upper edges represent degrees of white, with *a* the maximum of white, and those along the lower edges degrees of black, with *a* the *minimum* of black, each of the small diamonds in the figure indicates a variation of the hue that is actually measurable in terms of fractions of full hue mixed with the proportions of black and white indicated by the letters. The "equal" amounts here indicated are in terms of what is felt as equal change in color, not in the additions of arithmetically equal fractions of white or black surface on a revolving disk, since this latter equality must be proportionally calculated. But this sort of proportional equality is familiar enough, and the correlations involved need not bother us here. We say that men pay equal taxes not when they pay equal sums, but when they pay the same fractions of their income; and if one red is to seem lighter than another by as much as a third red is lighter than a fourth, the amounts of white to be mixed with the reds here are obviously not the same arithmetically, but in the same ratios. It is in this way, in fact, that Ostwald's scheme takes into account the so-called Weber-Fechner law, with which we need be no further concerned. For we are dealing with æsthetic judgments, with judgments recording beauties of qualitative variation, not with the physical conditions of the production of such qualitative differences. The whole point of the scheme for our purposes is its success in arranging all the variations of color in such a way that the intrinsic order of their qualitative variation is unambiguously before us. Not only does red lie between purple and orange, but red *e b* lies between red *e a* and red *e c*, also between red *f b* and red *d b*, also between red *d a* and red *f c*, and red no. 2 *e b* between reds no. 1 *e b* and no. 3 *e b*. All these orders are given in the nature of red itself as a series of qualitative differences under the general name of color, which is nothing but the abstract term designating the whole completely and intrinsically ordered range itself.

In the present chaotic state both of the popular knowledge of color variation and of the terms employed to indicate specific variations, and orders of variation, it has seemed best to indicate these variations as above, though the scheme differs noticeably from those familiar in text-books in psychology or in color manuals. But of course the actual differences in colors have long been felt and employed by artists and others, and some of the principles of color harmony and contrast are very well known. In the light of Ostwald's scheme many of the current terms can be unambiguously referred to their intended meanings, certain familiar phenomena of color vision can be objectively described, and some corrections in terminology can be made for the sake of clarity.

In the first place neutral colors, constituted of certain considerable proportions of black and white mixed with the full hues, appear as single unitary colors, though the trained eye or the natively sensitive eye recognizes the black and white constituents in the single complexly constituted color, much as the trained or naturally musical ear hears the pitches that are the partials or overtones in characteristic timbres. But painters' colors are physical stuff and not simply the colors themselves, and the mixing of pigments is not in general the mixing of their respective colors. Thus, while the addition of yellow color and its complementary blue color give by such addition white color, the mixing of yellow and blue pigments gives green pigment. In the first case we are dealing with æsthetic materials themselves—the colors; in the second with the technical media upon which the æsthetic material proper, the color as seen, supervenes after the technical operations have been completed. Our concern here is only with the properly æsthetic materials themselves, the colors that may or may not be beautiful, not with the pigments used in their preparation. Æsthetically, then, the complementary colors are those naturally seen as such, those which mixed in equal proportions for vision give us no hue at all. This may be done by revolving a disk, half of one color, half of the other, thus for purposes of vision adding the colors together, spreading the two—not the pigments of course—equally over the one circular surface. The two colors are said to complement each other if the result of revolving the disk is its appearing as of no hue, colorless light being as we know the total of the spectrum colors in combination. It is thus appropriate to call two colors which, mixed in equal proportions, give this total, the complements of each other. Another familiar phenomenon further justifies this name complementary for any such pair of colors. If we look attentively at a spot of one of them on a white ground and then look away to the white ground itself, we see a spot of the complementary. Since the circle of our hues was so constructed that the two extremities of any diameter indicate such complementary colors, it is clear that our division into eight or twenty-four hues, as indicated above, was properly made. And we may remark here that the older division into six hues failed to indicate complementaries in the important and unambiguous sense defined above.

§3

What we have done so far is simply to indicate an order given by the nature of the seen colors themselves, as æsthetic materials, in which they all fit, the arrangement exhausting the possibilities of color variation. If it is still asked what æsthetic interest this order has, the answer is simply that any appearing color is defined to vision itself as a given point in the scheme, the shade it is being exactly that shade that lies between two other shades, whether these are in the sequence from light to lighter, or from dark to darker, or from what is lighter as having more white to what is lighter as having less black with the same amount of white, but more of the full hue. Whether we are conscious or not of the scheme and the total range, the color appears necessarily as of the special character it is, and this character in turn is exactly the variation defined in an order of surrounding variations which it is felt and seen to approach in definite ways, its place among them being its actual definitive nature. It is worth noticing, then, that colors are a series of differences in the clear sense that one is nearer to or farther from another by virtue of its own intrinsic appearance, that colors in their actually appearing qualitative nature have nothing qualitative in common, but are a set of such intrinsically ordered differences. If we try instead to make out a common nature, color itself, say, or hue, we can do so only by naming the differences in terms, not of any common qualitative character, but of the order itself, which is not color at all and not colored, in which they come.

Hues fall into an order clearly enough, and this order is given through their own nature, but just what no two colors in the circle of the hues have in common is their specific hue, since each occupies its own unique location in the ordered range in which they all fall. If they did have a hue in common—and here we are speaking only of the clear full hues themselves, though for any other variation the principle is the same—they would be absolutely identical instead of being two different hues. And the order, while it is given by the whole range of differences, is not given in any one of them separately, nor is it anything in any one of them over and above the specific hue itself. Thus it is brute, natural, physical fact, including of course the physical and nervous constitution of eyes, that presents us with the differences, and these differences, these specific irrational, inexplicable, ultimate qualitative natures or essences, are the materials of visual beauty, of which the complex beautiful structures of the visual arts are composed.

But as we saw, the historical visual arts, even decoration and color design, are not pure color arts; for elements of color are in these arts built into structures not by the use merely of colors in their intrinsically ordered variations, but on the one hand by the use of geometrical patterns where a spatial order not intrinsic to colors as such is employed, and on the other hand in representation, where the subtle and unexplored principles or absence of principles in nature's compositions come into play. Here men, even artists, use forms and colors given in nature and weave these into wholes which are only to a slight degree patterned on consciously recognized principles. And if for the artist there are half-intuited, vaguely felt principles of structure in all his work, and even in what he finds in nature to adopt, or to adapt to his uses, these remain mostly beyond clear knowledge, and hence can only be admitted as undefined possibilities, not as philosophical principles or æsthetic knowledge. Men are without question sensitive to structural or composed beauties far exceeding their theoretical grasp, at least at present, and no present æsthetic theory is in a position to give anything like a full analysis of even the most obviously satisfying painting. When we see how varied the one elementary material color is, how elaborate an order its variations fall into, we are forced to realize that in the simplest works of painters on canvas the color structure itself in all its detail of elaborate variety is far beyond our theoretical grasp. And when we notice that this color structure is only a very small fraction of the composition, which includes familiar natural shapes or geometrically patterned designs, which uses perspective, and which often represents objects immediately calling up feelings quite irrelevant to the mere color structure and the design, feelings at least as important in the direct perception of the whole as those stirred by the beauty of the colors or lines as such—when we notice all this, we shall be sufficiently warned against thinking that æsthetic theory has as yet more than the most general, indirect, and unscientific statements to make about the beauty of developed works of pictorial art. It is in fact this realization of the complexity involved, and the absence of even any very general knowledge of the fully analyzed actual nature of works of art, that any rigorous æsthetic theory has to teach us at present. Positively, however, about the elementary materials of such beauty, even color alone offers us an enormously full and elaborate field for that discriminating of differences and that attention to characteristic specific objects of color vision which is our only path, in this general realm, to full perception of them, and hence also to discerning and appreciating their beauties.

If, however, the arts have gone far beyond theories of

beauty, so that we appreciate infinitely more than we understand through analysis, both of elementary content and of composed structures, artificial or natural, the theory of color elements once fully made out offers us, on the analogy of music and its use of sound, the suggestion of an art of color not in static balance and space relations, but in temporal sequences and pure color harmonies and contrasts; and the modern color organ may very well be the forerunner of instruments arranged so to project changing colors in moving forms as to give us a whole new art. But even here, since color must appear in shapes or upon surfaces, the purity of the elements and their intrinsic order will be modified. The colors will necessarily be mixed in spatial proportions as well as in temporal orders. Sound offers us after all a clearer view of the way in which the natural materials of beauty may be built into beautiful structures, the internal qualitative relations of whose elements are intrinsic to the very nature of those elements themselves, though time sequence is also employed to make these structural relations explicit, as well as to insert extrinsic temporal relations, as it were, into the intrinsically non-temporal quality of sound as such, to give music a structure in time as well as in tone.

§ 4

Before we turn to beauties which are thus structural or composed, what we may in general call formal as distinguished from material beauty, we may stop here to consider the similarities and dissimilarities in the two materials we have already discussed. Since this involves also the different orders intrinsic to these two kinds of æsthetic material, in doing so we may throw some light on the arts which are founded on these materials chiefly. Then we shall be ready to discuss form itself and the kinds of order and structural principles upon which form depends for its possibilities of variety and of coherence in unity. We shall find at least two different sorts of order applicable in different ways to different elementary materials, temporal order which gives rhythm, and spatial order which gives us spatial balance and contrast, symmetry, and spatial completeness and unity.

As we saw in sound, however, there is besides the intrinsic order of pitch an order of intensity or loudness. And even timbre, being largely a matter of pitches in combination, makes the requirement, for tonal structures, that intrinsic relations of one timbre to another be taken into account, if a composer is to be fully conscious of the inner structure he is building. In color too, besides the order given by nearness or distance of hues from each other in the serial ranges already noticed, there is an order of brightness intrinsic to the hues themselves which is to be distinguished from variations of lightness or darkness within each hue. This latter variation, as indicated by quantities of white and black in varying proportions mixed with the pure hues, is one of the general principles of order in the whole field. But the clear, full hues themselves vary in brightness from yellow through orange, red, and purple to the blues and greens, the so-called warm colors running in this order from yellow to a reddish purple, the colder colors from a very blue purple to green. Warm and cool colors have long been so called, and our present knowledge of color variation makes it plain on the one hand that of the variations as given in our circle of hues it is the bright colors that are warm, the less bright colors that are cool, and, on the other hand, that the stretches of borderline hues, purples and yellow-greens, are either warm or cool as they approach the characteristically and emphatically warm and cool colors. Warm and cool as a distinction serves to name only what we have already indicated in saying that the pure hues themselves are of varying degrees of brightness. This variation too is measurable in a scale just as the lightness or darkness of gray is measurable.

In the painter's use of the term value as applied to color we have another term definable and measurable on our scheme. Higher value means simply a greater proportion of full hue, and colors are of the same value when they have the same amount of dilution with black or white, or with both in the same proportions. Here the scientific account in terms of measures lagged far behind the recognized fact, and the obvious conclusion for æsthetics is that direct artistic perception recognizes much that æsthetic theory has been very slow to give an adequate account of. Usually color variations are given under three headings, hue, saturation, and intensity; but the account we have followed, while it includes hue in the same sense, has indicated more precisely in terms of quantitative additions of white or black alone, or of both white and black in varying measured proportions, a much more accurate and unambiguous order, which allows of a strict color notation, in which the exact discriminable tint or shade is unmistakably indicated and capable of being checked by scientifically determined laboratory norms. And the scheme is based on physics, chemistry, psychology, and laboratory technique, to make it sound and adequate.

The comparison of colors and sounds is useful mainly for emphasizing their ultimate difference, and avoiding the confusion due to the application of the same terms to both sorts of elements. As tones vary in pitch, intensity, and timbre, so colors vary in hue, intensity, and saturation. But as hues are not pitches, so intensity in sound means a quite different sort of variation from that of the intensity of color; louder does not mean brighter nor does softer mean darker; much less does louder mean lighter. And in colors brightness and lightness are to be distinguished as well as their opposites, for which the same word darkness is used indiscriminately. The sense in which full clear blue is a darker color than full clear yellow is not the sense in which the same full clear blue is darker than a lighter blue, for this latter difference occurs correspondingly between two yellows indicated by the same notation. While intensity of sound may vary without varying pitch, the same pitch being capable of all degrees of loudness and softness, any one of which matches the other exactly for the ear as to pitch, a variation in the brightness of illumination actually changes the appearance of a color so that it is no longer felt to match the hue it was under another degree of illumination. Thus while sounds, differing either in timbre or in loudness, may be heard to match exactly as the same note, different shades or tints of the same hue are never felt as matching in color.

In other words, modifying a color of a given hue to make it lighter or darker or brighter results in what is felt to be a different color, not the same color at a different intensity, though this last description of it is abstractly accurate enough and even useful, and hence justifiable. In words we may make the two cases, color and sound, parallel; in experience recorded in æsthetic judgment they are primarily specifically different. Pitch predominates so in sound, no doubt because it is pitch that fundamentally and most characteristically orders all sounds in a serial range, that we feel two sounds of the same pitch to be the same note, however they differ in the two other dimensions of variation. If the hue of a color, however, is modified to lighter or darker, we feel it to be another and a different color. Brown, for example, is a distinctive color with a special name, though it is only an orange with a good deal of black and some white, or by special courtesy a kind of green or a kind of yellow. That is, the variations in black and white content, not the variation in hue strictly taken, often seem more characteristic than the hue itself.

All such discussions are of course fruitless as demonstration, since logic can be used to make the parallel between different material elements in their modes of variation abstractly satisfactory. But what we have been saying may serve to indicate the vital importance, for any account of beauty discerned that is to be adequate to the facts of perception and feeling, of the specific kinds of differences to be discriminated in different kinds of sensuous materials. While it is perfectly intelligible to say that all such material elements are subject to increase or decrease of intensity, these changes in intensity mean variations within specific intrinsically ordered sensuous materials, where not only the material elements themselves, particular sounds and colors, are absolutely other than each other in quality and in no clear sense comparable, since they exhibit no degree of similarity or difference, but also the ordering principles native to and definitive of these materials are in each case exhibited in incomparable orders of variation. It is therefore a mere abstraction leading away from our subject instead of more deeply into its nature, to insist that varying color intensities are in any full, clear sense parallel to varying sound intensities.

Further illustrations of the confusing dangers of such attempted unification under common principles come naturally to mind as we try to apply these orders themselves to different realms of sensuous content in the same sense, and not merely as parallels. But here we come at once upon the beauties of form, not of material elements, to which we are mainly confining our present discussion. And of course there are orders not intrinsic to the qualitative elements which may be applicable to elements of any sort. We might spray perfumes in regular time intervals, and colors may be rhythmically projected on a screen. Dance movements and sounds may be so correlated in time as to become one unified event, a colored and sounding motion fused in a temporal rhythm. But what can be so fused in rhythm possesses anteriorly, as elementary material, its own specific sensuous character actually defined to sense in its intrinsic order of variation. This intrinsic qualitative order, whether consciously taken into account or not, insists upon being present and entering into the account—of itself so to speak—when any further structural order, not intrinsic to the qualitative elements themselves, is to be impressed upon those æsthetic materials to make out of them works of art. If the differences between mixing tones and mixing colors are obvious to any one with hearing and sight, and hence require no further emphasis, it seems clear that we should admit the fundamental differences not only in the specific elements themselves, but also in the intrinsic qualitative orders in which we can exhibit all their variations.

One parallel in particular may be summarily disposed of on these grounds. It is sometimes urged that pitches actually have hue, that on hearing a certain high pitch, for example, we experience pale green, or that the blare of trumpets is red or orange. Now no one need deny that red is at least possibly more appropriate to a trumpet blast than pale blue is, or that in some minds colors and sounds are so associated as to be called up the one by the other. This latter association is honestly asserted as recording individual experience, and the appropriateness of red to trumpets may be felt not on the basis of any qualitative likeness between the hue and the sound themselves, but on the basis of the volume of response or the kinds of feeling or emotion stirred. We are not arguing that the beauties are not comparable, but that the qualitative natures of sound and color are intrinsically specific and distinct, and ultimately other than each other.

And there are two obvious facts to interfere with holding that such associated colors are intrinsic to the pitch or the timbre with which in some minds they are actually associated. First it is to be noticed that pitch always lies in a series which runs out at both ends, and that these ends are the farthest apart from each other that pitches can be. Hues on the other hand lie in an order in which, as we pass from one to another, we finally return to our starting point, so that the colors farthest apart are those opposite each other on a circle, and the two members of *any* pair of complementary colors are at this distance from each other; whereas in pitch, as we run up the range, the distance constantly increases, and no two intermediate pitches can be so far apart as the lowest and highest discernible notes are from each other in pitch itself. If somewhere in the high part of this range of pitch some one of the colors is to be found, which, in the native range of hues, moves as it varies in hue, by even gradations around the completed circle of the hues, we are faced, if we are to make out any strict parallel between hue and pitch, with the odd task of determining the end points of a never-ending circle, so as to find a hue nearer to one end than the other.

And if we break the circle and straighten it out into a line with extremities far from each other, it turns out that the line no longer represents properly the variations of hue, since the two extremities, considered as hues, melt into each other.

A second fact is still more disconcerting. It is obvious that the character of different colors is so distinct as to be fairly absolute both for perception and for memory, whereas absolute pitch, as it is called, is a comparatively rare gift among human beings, and very difficult to acquire by training. Hence, also, while the same tune, an arrangement of pitches in time, may be produced anywhere along the range of pitches, it is hard to feel any clear likeness between a color combination of two tones of yellow with an orange and two tones of blue with a violet, though the word tone itself is of course drawn from the realm of sound. While parallels could be made out without much ingenuity and even justified on various grounds, the obvious and even absolute distinction both between the specific elements in the two sense realms, as well as between their intrinsic sorts of order, would seem to be an essential point for æsthetic judgment, which here as elsewhere is always primarily concerned with recording that specific discriminated qualitative content present to it in attentive perception, intuited as uniquely beautiful, if beautiful at all, with the beauty that lies upon this sensuous content, characterized primarily and also ultimately as just the specific presented qualitative character that it is, and no other.

CHAPTER VIII

THE ÆSTHETIC MATERIALS OF SPACE

1. Practical prejudices and spatial wisdom. 2. Platonic fallacies, moral and intellectual. 3. The fallacy of independent objectivity illustrated in Hogarth. 4. Mathematical character and intuited shape. 5. Dimensionality as the type of order intrinsic to elements of spatial form: length, area, volume. 6. Spatial character as order in general.

§ 1

WE have already noticed that the materials of beauty include more than color and sound, that especially in what we may call natural compositions, those occurring in the world accidentally, as we say, tastes and smells and vital feelings, as well as the imagery of all the senses, constitute materials of beauty both as separate elementary sense beauties and as component parts of beautiful structures, occurring naturally and directly or arranged artificially, and presented to sense. But of all of these æsthetic materials, besides sound and color, only spatial shape and relation offers, in our present state of acquaintance with the surface of our world, the intrinsically ordered character that allows us to distinguish its specific sorts of variation and the principles on which spatial elements may be conjoined to form genuine structures, which are at the same time at least in part comprehensibly made up of elements in an order.

But we can hardly approach this subject quite directly and

without prejudice; for our earliest formal training directs our attention to the rigid requirements of spatial forms in our practical world of activity. A square room has only four corners. A quart measure will hold only two pints of milk. The maximum area that can be enclosed by a string or a fence of given length is the circular space of which that length is the circumference. What lies to the north cannot be seen by looking south. Right-angled triangles are so absolutely dependable, as to the ratios of the lengths of their sides to each other, that they help measure not only fields and city lots and the heights of mountains, but the sizes and distances of the sun, moon, and stars. With much of this geometrical rigor and finality attached to our conceptions of lines and shapes and angles in our constant dealings with them, it is a little hard to turn to the appearances of these as actually presented to the unprejudiced eye, and to see what is more or less immediately there for æsthetic contemplation.

In the first place, we do not so much see as judge of these shapes and distances and spatial relations and directions. We see spots or areas of color beside other colored patches, and our mind rather than our eye draws a boundary-line between them or a boundary line around one of them. What is clearly enough given to immediate vision, though we sometimes do and sometimes do not drop our practical habits to look and see—and the one fact is as important to æsthetics as the other, of course—is simply the contrasting colored surfaces. Modern painters have realized this, as ancient painters no doubt also discerned it without erecting it into a first principle of their art, and have been able to produce by color masses alone beautifully vivid effects, in which the shapes are read in by us as we read shapes and lines and sizes into the natural objects about us. Nor is shape given by color alone or always by actually drawn lines in pictures or in the mind seeing them. Shape is appreciated as well by touch and by muscular activity. And shape and distance and even direction are as clearly matters of muscular sensation as they are also matters of vision and sometimes even of hearing.

§ 2

Besides these prejudices of our early and practical learning, which is itself so important for all of our working activities and which therefore cannot be neglected in our considerations, since perhaps it is never discarded even in æsthetic contemplation; besides the complication introduced into our appreciation of line and shape and space relations in general, as directly present to intuition, by the use of so many senses at once instead of the use of one sense only— touch and sight and muscular imagery and the immediate impression of distance due to subtleties of color and outline as well as to familiar experiences of locomotion—there have been introduced into our general notions of spatial shapes and relations ideas based upon theory itself, sometimes elaborate and confusing, sometimes clearly mistaken, and even tinged sometimes with ethical and political conceptions and ideals.

Plato, in his moral and intellectual enthusiasm, definitely felt that geometrical shapes and relations and abstract mathematical forms were purer and more beautiful than mere sense objects, full of color and sensuous richness but subject constantly to change. And this was partly because to Plato true beauty, being of the mind, not of the senses, was necessarily to be appreciated intellectually. In his view of the scale of value, we rise from the many beautiful sensuously rich objects to their sheer forms, then on to pure mathematical form itself, which only the reason can grasp, and then to that pure Platonic and altogether mythical abstraction, still held to by some philosophers as the sole concrete æsthetic object, the Idea of Beauty. If the lover and the artist had most hope of heaven in Plato's opinion, it was not because of their love of actual beauty and their devotion to it, but because this love and devotion in them was an intimation of immortality. That is, to speak more flatly and simply, because the eye that dwells lovingly on a concrete particular beautiful object is in Plato's theory the eye of the unconscious lover of the Idea of the Beautiful and through the Beautiful of the Good, which really attracts this discerning eye by its beneficent divinity, a divine reality somehow hidden behind or within the false sensuous appearance. Devotion to the appearance itself, what we should call actual æsthetic appreciation, seemed to Plato good only so far as it annulled itself and thus led the soul on to cast out all love of mere transitory objects and their appearance to fleshly senses, and to rise to the mystical discernment of true Beauty itself, which means not our æsthetic surface beauty but Plato's rationally comprehended Forms, not even geometrical shapes, but pure dialectical form itself. Taken at his word, Plato thus despised actual familiar æsthetic experience as a professional swimmer might despise water-wings, a help perhaps to a weak beginner, their use at best the sign of an inner desire to swim, but the very negation of swimming itself, and, if adhered to for long, its effective prevention. At any rate, in Plato's mythical ladder of values it is easy to see that purely formal geometrical beauties are at least a step above the mixed concreteness of sensuously satisfying colored objects, and Plato leaves no doubt in our minds that he did rank abstract geometrical shapes higher than the full-textured actual surfaces of beautiful objects of sense perception.

There are two resultant and connected mistakes here, both of which have passed into common human prejudice on the subject. And these survive quite cut off from, or at least in addition to, Plato's own primary, if mistaken, doctrine of Ideas, which after all, though it is still held in many minds as deeply but somewhat vaguely significant in various ways, is no longer an æsthetic doctrine seriously accepted. The two prejudices, as still current, are mere floating notions with no anchor in even this consistently elaborated and honestly believed, if quite false, groundwork of Platonic metaphysics.

The two mistakes are closely connected, but perhaps fairly distinguishable from each other, and often separately adhered to. One is simply the notion that the degree of beauty in spatial shape and arrangement is measured by the absence of any filling, of color chiefly, although texture is almost as important perhaps, though less emphasized because it is less fully within our clear knowledge. That is, spatial beauty, to be pure, must be purely formal in the sense that this form is to be the abstracted shape itself instead of this shape as of and upon the colored and perhaps richly and subtly textured concrete surface area or felt volume. So we may be told that the highest æsthetic appreciation is the mathematician's, an error easy to make plausible by using the term purity instead of emptiness or thinness, in the same way in which ignorance is so often called innocence, and so lauded as virtue when it should be merely tolerated, or actually condemned, or as quickly as may be removed. Or a special æsthetic response, whether empathy or not, may be supposed to be called up in great intensity, even when the volume of sense stimulation is lessened, as if the senses were not the very names for our avenues of communication with the surface of our world, so that all the presumption is in favor of a volume and intensity of reaction in direct proportion to the fullness and variety of the sensory responses, up to the point where the mind is oppressed or distracted, as in mere barbaric din and display. This insistence on the purity instead of the amount and richness of quality lies very close to the old self-contradicting thesis of asceticism, that the highest and noblest pleasure is after all excruciating pain, or the greatest good the suffering of the greatest evil. This mistake is not so popular in the morals of our day; but, through a judicious use of terms, abetted by a traditional and far from ignoble idealism, it is still easily thrust upon us in the field of æsthetic judgment. For in æsthetics, we have not so fully taken our bearings with modern and efficient instruments, and it is only through science, based on a more adequate acquaintance with the natural world, that we come to view our own life as a mere incident in the larger world about us, however specially significant an incident it is bound to seem to our human selves.

The second mistake is still more commonly made, although perhaps only in part, and at least not so uncomprisingly, as Plato made it. Following his general thesis as to grades of beauty as grades of reality and also of value in general measured in terms of pure rational comprehensibleness, Plato found the familiar geometrical figures, the circle particularly, to be eminently beautiful. We are no longer taught that geometrical regularity and harmony, or simple symmetry, is the most beautiful spatial arrangement; but, as Plato did, we are very likely to think that a circle is a more rational figure than a complicated curve or a zig-zag line. In other words, we forget what Plato perhaps never realized, that any one spatial form is as rigorously mathematical and geometrical as any other. The only variation in this respect is in our degrees of knowledge and ignorance. If geometry deals with space, an ideal and fully adequate geometry must have within its range all possible spatial forms and relations. Hence triangles and circles are, so to speak, not more but less rational than irregular figures, with their high degree of intellectual content. And even on his own ground of rationality as beauty, Plato must be reversed. The more irregular the figure and the more difficult it is to follow, the higher its pure logical and mathematical content must stand in his scale of intellectuality and value. If the subtlety and irregularity go beyond our ordinary grasp, the figure is no less determinate for that, and no less an object for intellectual appreciation of a high order. If its æsthetic charm is lost in a maze of lines and spacings utterly bewildering to even the trained eye, it is clear that the criterion we must and always do naturally apply to space as æsthetic, is the criterion not of intellectual fullness or complexity, but of the senses. Here, as elsewhere, moderate simplicity is necessary if we are to intuit relations and shapes at all, instead of a great blur of confused masses and lines, and moderate complexity, if the object in its spatial character is to interest us. Some degree of immediately felt order is necessary, not because we like formal order as such so much as because without some degree of such order we have no sufficiently defined object to look at, much less to appreciate in its specific character and its internal detail. We literally cannot see a sufficiently complex space configuration even of a sort that we could, with enough mathematics, rationally comprehend.

But we certainly intuit spatial arrangements as *somehow* ordered and arranged, when we do not at all fully or consciously comprehend their order and arrangement with our intellect. As artists have used marvellously successful color combinations through instinctive gift and without offering us any theory of the intrinsic order of their colors, so the compositions of draughtsmen and painters have far outrun our comprehension, much further our formal theories, of the intrinsic order in shape and distance relations, and depth and balance of masses, and contrast and connection through lines. So we come back to the necessity we found in the material elements of color and sound, of distinguishing what little we can as to the intrinsic ordering principles native to shape and space relations in general, the principles by virtue of which in combinations we have not mere blurred inextricabilities of lines and shapes, but, however loosely and however vaguely grasped, genuinely composed and coherent structures.

§ 3

But we must first notice one other point. While divinity as somehow intimated through lower beauties to sense was a favorite idea from Plato's time to the nineteenth century, with Plotinus and St. Thomas and Hegel all espousing and expounding it in various systematic metaphysical contexts, the eighteenth century set up another prejudice with regard to the nature and beauty of spatial forms, which is met with in most men even now as the outstanding opposed and perhaps contradictory doctrine. It is not the beauty of spirit somehow intimated in sense materials that the eighteenth century saw, but characteristically, in its hard and common sense enlightenment, an objective choice of this or that line or curve or proportion, natural or even accidental forms, though also mathematically definite, lying ready at hand to be adopted for the artist's use and arranged in drawings or buildings to please good taste, much as the various patterns in a foundry offer us varying moulds for more or less ornamental brass door-knobs, or key-escutcheons, or hinges, or electric-light fixtures, to fit the current fashions in such accessories. And here again the error is fairly striking, though it is not quite so easy to make it out convincingly in its downright erroneousness, because it is of course not all error. One typical example will perhaps suffice, and if before citing it we remind ourselves that the error in question is simply the notion that beauty is entirely independent of a mind that intuits it, instead of being constituted in an occurrence as a quality of an object only—so far as we know, at least—when that object is being perceived and felt as beautiful by a human being or at least a conscious organic creature, we may find the example to be given more enlightening for our general grasp of æsthetic theory.

Hogarth, like Leonardo da Vinci before him, was wont to classify and enumerate and note for future use the varieties of shape and line that he came across. As Leonardo listed ten types of nose, or, as seen from the front, twelve, so Hogarth, not content merely with the varieties of lines, decided upon the most beautiful one, as if neither spectator nor context were fundamentally determinant of all beauties as definitely as the physical object presented, and as if the materials of beauty were a sort of stock in trade.

Thus objectively Hogarth could divide all lines into the straight and the curved, and then by combining the convex and the concave in various degrees decide upon a compound curved line of the greatest beauty. Aside from the fact that his line is only the line most acceptable to his own eye, his further error in æsthetic principle is clear enough. For it is plain that for our actual visual experience there is a difference between one straight line and another at least as important as the difference between curved and straight lines. A vertical line has one visual character, a horizontal line quite another, as the words vertical and horizontal indicate in the first place, and as the enormous difference between Gothic architecture with its preponderance of verticals, and Roman architecture with its preponderance of horizontal spread, fully enough emphasize. Now this difference between vertical and horizontal, while it is clearly enough made out, is a difference in the relation of the bodily position and conformation of the observer to what he is seeing, not a difference, in Hogarth's eighteenth century sense, between the objective spatial forms in question. The point is simply that we cannot afford to neglect, in our account of the intrinsic æsthetic nature of spatial forms and relations, the matter of the human point of view, a point of view determined by the size and structure of human bodies and the specific nature of their modes of sensation, especially, of course, the physical, spatial peculiarities of human vision, bi-focal, chromatic vision, that is, from a point five feet and a half from the ground. Thus the size of objects as compared to the size of the human body is fundamentally important to their specific æsthetic character. And so, also, all the space-relations and spatial characteristics of objects, for æsthetics, must be considered with this human point of view in mind, if we are to understand at all the variations and combinations that affect us as felicitous in spatial structures.

Thus, not only must we free our minds of our purely practical prejudices about spatial objects, or at least take these prejudices into proper account, if we are to see things clearly as presented to sense; not only must we avoid false notions of purity or spirituality of form as the greatest formal beauty, and the equally false notion that perfectly and easily understood, namely geometrically simple and even elementary configurations, are the only rationally ordered ones and so the only ones that minds can fully appreciate; but we must also keep in mind the fact that the æsthetic character of spatial shapes and relations and harmonies is in an order involving the physical and spatial peculiarities of men, so that no purely objective mathematically defining order more than partly determines the intrinsic æsthetic structure in space that we have to consider in works of art or nature presented to vision and intuited as beautiful.

§ 4

But if the logical or mathematical natures of spatial objects are not their full spatial natures as seen and enjoyed through the human eyes of human bodies, neither are these mathematical properties of spatial forms and relations to be neglected in æsthetic theory. They are not only grasped intellectually; they are also in part directly discerned in vision, and they are clearly the beginning of any understanding knowledge of the æsthetic character of these objects of our visual and spatial appreciation in general. Modern psychological investigation in two general directions, has thrown some light upon our appreciation of the beauty of shape and spatial character in the theory of *Einfuehlung*, or in the more developed current theory where what was called *Einfuehlung* comes to be a much more general so-called empathic response. But in this general form, such response is what we have already made out as the human side of the feeling of delight in specified and discriminated objective character, and important and fundamental as this is, it is rather what conditions beauty in its occurrence than what we feel as objective beauty. In a second direction psychology has made much of the attempt to discern, by long series of experiments, a normal preference for the division of a line in one ratio rather than another, or for rectangles whose sides bear one proportional relation to each other over rectangles of other relative proportions. But here again we discover no principle of order intrinsic to shape or space-relations, since one kind of rectangle is as geometrically and visually ordered as another and, as present in complex structures, no doubt also as beautiful as another in varying contexts.

And we can not turn directly to mathematics to discover the intrinsic principles of order in shape and spatial arrangement, for, as we have already noticed, we do not usually see mathematical structure, which in its full and precise character as such is of course logically known rather than sensibly intuited. In any case what is given us as one mathematical structure in equations, in the strictly intelligible logical nature of curves and shapes, may be present visually in forms as clearly distinct from each other for æsthetic contemplation as circles and ellipses, or straight lines and curves, or points and spheres. Size, too, which is not logically or mathematically absolute, but relative to measuring standards more or less arbitrarily adopted as units, is æsthetically absolute as being relative to what for each of us is fixed, namely the size of our own body, and the scope and power of our own movements. However useful to us the strictly mathematical analysis of spatial forms and relations may be for a basis in æsthetic theory, we must take as our fully applicable principles the standards of sense perception itself, through which we may, with proper respect to logical and mathematical guidance so far as that is available, discern the intrinsic order within purely spatial sensuous æsthetic materials of beauty.

Even here we must abstract to some degree; for it is clear that spatial materials, as we have been calling these elements of beauty, are not so plausibly material elements as sound and color are; they are often seen and felt as structure or form itself. There is no absolutely clear line to mark off material elements from formal ones, for of course no elements are purely material and quite formless. And now that we have come to shapes and space relations, it becomes obvious that these elements themselves cannot appear to us except as structural. Spatial forms cannot be intuited directly upon visual appearances except as the forms of colored surfaces and objects, never the bare forms themselves. But obviously enough these bare forms are distinguishable and important, as is illustrated in every black and white reproduction of colored originals, as well as in any design in lines and shapes which remains the same in proportion, size, and spatial characteristics in general, regardless of its possible or actual application to materials of varied color and texture, in which it may appear as one contributory element of structure in single concrete visual characters vastly differing in æsthetic effect. And it is equally clear that particular lines and shapes and patterns may approximate the status of material elements in composite wholes almost as obviously and theoretically as plausibly as color or sound elements do. No concrete case of actual beauty is merely elements or merely structure, and we shall see later that even structures concretely holding æsthetic elements together do not constitute fully beautiful objects, since there is always a still further aspect involved.

For analytical purposes, then, we seem to be well within

our rights in treating spatial forms as material elements of beautiful structures, since we have also emphasized their formal structural nature itself, and since without analysis any understanding whatever, as distinguished from just æsthetic appreciation, as had and felt, and so in this more elementary sense realized and known, is out of the question. Æsthetic theory is a matter, that is, of analytical understanding as against familiar acquaintance with what is to be analyzed. Any objection to a treatment of spatial character as material would be unreasonable, so long as this treatment is conscious of the abstraction involved, and finds such abstraction necessary to an understanding of the mode in which, in the concrete objects of æsthetic appreciation, the elements treated separately cohere, as aspects of the beauty we are trying, so far as may be, to understand. Our whole view may be quite erroneous, of course; but only some better analysis, some other chain of abstractions in discourse, can improve upon it.

§ 5

This more or less abstract æsthetic material of shapes and lines of given character is clearly seen to have some kind and degree of intrinsic order, even if we can not be content with mathematics as the complete elucidation of that order in the strictly æsthetic aspect of its nature. For vision and imagination there are lines and areas and volumes, which are on the one hand three distinctive concrete kinds of magnitude differing from each other in their primary character as directly intuited, and on the other hand related to one another by the fact of dimensionality and the order intrinsic to extension as such. Thus lines and areas may be considered distinct elementary materials for spatial composition, to be related in structures in unique ways, suitable to their peculiar characters; and within each kind only certain types of relation are possible. Lines used as lines and seen as lines give direction only, never flat or curved surface or expanse, as areas do, nor depth and fullness, as volumes do. And plane shapes fit each other or not, and vary in the degree of difference from and congruity with each other, in strictly specific ways not possible to lines or volumes.

There are numbers of empirical technical theories of design, based on various special notions of balance, symmetry, and proportion, and these notions are all derived from intrinsic and specifically spatial character. As matters of artistic technique no such theories are to be too lightly considered. Their value, in fact, is very great in application, and particularly in early practical training in the arts. But they are usually theories, not of the ordering principles to be found in spatial form and arrangement as such, but as to what is the most acceptable order in special cases of combining spatial materials. Thus they are theories of design, not accounts of the elementary spatial materials and the intrinsic possibilities of order within the primary nature of these materials.

Our question here is rather directed to asking what in visual experience of extension itself corresponds to pitch in auditory experience, and the answer has been given roughly above in the word dimension. Indeed, if we notice the kinds of order intrinsic to sounds and colors, we find that we are likely to use spatial terms to make these orders clear. In spatial form itself the same terms are applicable more literally. Lines have a structure in which points are fixed as lying between other points, and every point of a line has its own necessary place, which defines it. This seems too obvious to mention, but it is worth noticing that this determinate order of points in a direction is what allows intersection of one line by another at a given angle, or tangency of a line to a curve, or the specific spatial relation of one curve to another. And in areas, where we have two dimensions and the fact of areal spread, the possibilities, while no less definite, are infinitely great in a new order, where we see not mere lines and directions, but shapes of extended and bounded areas. In volume we have depth added to flat or curved extended area, as well as the specific feeling of volume or bulk or solidity itself; and the complications of the possible ordered configurations, all purely spatial, are so great as to baffle us when they go beyond the simplest geometrical figures and their modes of intersection in points and lines and planes and curved surfaces.

While natural objects, especially human bodies, hands, feet, throats, noses, ears, exhibit subtleties of relation and juxtaposition among lines and surfaces and solids, the actually established orders here are obviously far beyond mathematically accurate exposition for most of us, and it would be absurd to suppose that these elaborate, intricate beauties, definitely felt of course and very highly prized in the greatest detail by eyes that have dwelt long and familiarly on their infinite subtleties—it would be absurd to say that we know on what principles of order, and in exactly what mode of application of these principles, such natural or copied spatially composed beauties have been constructed. No doubt too, if we were animals of another shape, other solid forms and surfaces and lines would be those called supremely beautiful; and it is significant in another direction that among human features eyes are so universally and traditionally appreciated, eyes of which the shape is comparatively easy to see fairly completely and in fairly complete detail. The old difference of opinion as to the superiority of the female form over the male, indicates again that æsthetic appreciation, even in sculpture, is only to a very slight degree a matter of purely spatial elements and their composition in spatial structures.

What is peculiar to spatial shapes as elements for structural compositions is clearly enough the order involved in dimensionality, a simple order of betweenness in a constant or constantly varying direction in straight and curved lines, a two dimensional order in plane or curved areas as æsthetically viewed, and a tri-dimensional order in solid volumes. The possibilities here are obviously very great, especially when we remember that spatial elements of all three orders may be combined with one another in a single structure. It is natural that analytical accounts of works of art have picked out elementary geometrical forms as constituting the order or form of a given picture or statue; but the rash absurdity here involved is palpable, and we hardly need to be warned against it, once we have noticed the subtle possibilities of variation involved, and the infinite detail in any adequate analysis of the complete spatial forms in all their specific character and fullness, which is so clearly what is characteristic and differentiating about them. A triangular composition may be entirely unsuccessful, and it should be clear that the approximation to triangularity in the main color masses of many famous pictures has as little to do with their concrete artistic structural value as the narrow rectangular shape of a coffin or even a wrapped mummy has to do with the structural beauty of the human body whose outlines it so neatly encloses. Some general form any specific form must of course approximate, but to confuse the complex specific form which is perhaps beautiful, with the simple approximations given by triangles, or suggested by theories of dynamic symmetry in terms of simple geometrical proportions, is the adoption of such a royal road to beauty as no intelligent mind could very well travel on the way to an adequate theory of the æsthetics of space. Beauties are always specific, and their analysis in terms of general concepts is fruitless, if those general terms are taken to name the specific features given to discriminating perception as the genuine elements in a genuine and always, if beautiful at all, uniquely beautiful structure.

But this is not to say that simple geometrical shapes have no beauty, nor that Hogarth's line is not graceful. As in all sensuous fields, the elaborate composed beauties of form depend very largely for their own beauty on beautiful sensuous elements. The materials of beauty are no less truly beautiful for being mere materials or elements, but only less complexly beautiful. And too great complexity simply falls apart for actual vision, and so offers no one single beautiful object of attention. Nowhere is this more apparent than in spatial compositions, and this accounts perhaps for the tendency to analyze such compositions in terms of the simple forms which are the merest approximations to the actual form presented, and which would fail completely to distinguish the specific character of any one composition by virtue of which alone it is of precisely the form it is, and so either beautiful or not. The rejection of this obvious fact is akin to the sort of plot analysis that thinks to describe a plot adequately as triangular, as if triangularity here were not a commonplace of subject matter to be used in any one of a thousand different and even unique plots, ranging from the cheaply obvious to the most subtly convincing and expressive.

§ 6

Our results after all this discussion must seem very meagre. What we have found as the intrinsic ordering property of spatial forms is simply spatiality—continuous one-dimensional order in lines, a two-dimensional order in areas, a three-dimensional order in volumes or solids. But if this seems a small result in words, it is perhaps because the very meaning of order itself is so largely thought of in spatial terms. To get things into shape, as we say, just is getting them into intelligible or practically useful order. Once we reduce any subject matter to a linear scale, we seem to have an ordered account of it, and spatial forms themselves are the very diagrams which reduce all knowledge to comprehensibility; even time, if we are in any way to retain unambiguously our grasp on its nature or our controlled knowledge of its passage, must be spatially indicated on dials and other instruments, and its variation recorded in pictures. Thus mere dimensions, by virtue of being spatially extended, would almost seem to give us all the possibilities of all the kinds of order there are.

If it has been thought by many philosophers that space itself is nothing but established order and ordered relations, nothing but the manner or way in which co-existent objects are related to each other, such a view could seem plausible only because being spatial, having shape at all, means being spatially ordered. Thus the intrinsic kind of order to be found in shapes is just the archetype of all order that is visualized in lines and planes and solids, an order as native to a point, which has definite location only by co-ordination in a system, as to a line, where the betweenness of the points establishes relations of greater and less distance and length, or to the most intricate arrangement of the surfaces of solids, where intersections, relative magnitudes, distances, and directions are all determined uniquely in any given case by the very nature of the spatial elements involved. If the order of shapes and space relations is so obvious as to seem nothing but their being spatial elements, that is simply the reverse of the significant fact for æsthetics that all spatial compositions are highly complex ordered wholes by virtue of the intrinsically and uniquely ordered nature of the spatial elements themselves.

Nothing has length after all but lines, and mere linear dimensionality constitutes a sort of order, not only specific and unique, but at the same time literally infinite in the possibilities it offers for variety and complexity of spatial structures. Those who suggest to us so often that space is abstract and limited, and a mere mechanical conception, seem to have forgotten the specific and unique concreteness of length and area and volume as such, the absolute mystery of that concrete multiplication that turns two lengths into an area or two intersecting lines into an angle, and the literally infinite fullness of variety in ordered concrete spatial structures, made solely of spatial elements, and coherently held together in accordance with those principles so apparently simple at bottom, but adequate to such tremendously complex and exciting wholes, which we find intrinsic to the nature of the very elements themselves. If these possibilities or mysteries are better called the natural face of our spatial world, that is only saying that they are the familiar mysteries, as Santayana has called them, of nature as æsthetically viewed, elements and aspects of the character of the spatially beautiful.

Our account has been prosaic, and it may seem very far

from even suggesting the visual beauties we all know, even with the non-spatial elements omitted. The flight of quail on a hillside with the bark of the dog who has startled them, the fresh smell of fog over the green brush, the whirr of wings, the light and color, the vital tone of the body, is a richly concrete beauty only in small part a matter of visual perception at all. But if an account in terms of geometrical lines, curves with defined direction, seems a poor abstraction, of little avail even to name the beauty of such an event, we have only to turn to Leonardo's note-book to see how a gifted perception marks the specific quality of this line of flight, and in recording its character for vision, as knowledge to be treasured, appropriates for his mind and memory one more of those infinitely precious and infinitely varied elements of beauty in which for him the whole world of nature abounded, and which in the structures of his art would build beauties still undreamed, such beauties as the world has marvelled at from his day to ours.

Leonardo's observations and sketches, with what they reveal to us of his scientific interests, are indications of many things about himself as well as about science and art. In the æsthetics of space they may here emphasize two facts, first of all the infinite importance for such a creative mind of the exact spatial configurations of natural objects and motions of particular sorts; but they remind us still more forcibly that the strict definition of shapes and space-relations in lines and forms, the discriminating and rigorous perception of detail and variety of the æsthetic surface of the world, which is the condition of any actual enjoyment of the full objective beauty of that surface as it lies before us in absorbed attention, is also the condition of any adequate knowledge of the world, which after all must appear, in order to be known, and must be known through its appearance; so that science, as well as art and the appreciation of beauty, demands just this full acquaintance, through intuition, with æsthetic surface, if science itself is to be adequate, or even alive and significant.

CHAPTER IX

RHYTHM AS TEMPORAL STRUCTURE

1. Beauty of elements and beauty of structure. 2. Rhythm as imposed temporal order, felt, but not seen or heard. 3. Spatial rhythm as involving real or imagined motion in time. 4. Rhythm a regular recurrence variously indicated to sense and involving rate and patterned division; compound and complex rhythms. 5. The dancer's appreciation of rhythm and the philosopher's. 6. Rhythm in verse less explicit than rhythm in music. 7. Variation, specification, and determinate character of all rhythms; rhythms as elements.

§ 1

IN most cases of æsthetic judgment it is not mere separate sense elements, single notes, specific shades of color, individual lines, or flat or solid shapes, that we call beautiful; but in many cases of course it is just these elements, and it is somewhat doubtful whether any composition could be altogether beautiful as a structural whole were it not composed of elements beautiful in themselves. In any case the beauty of such a structural whole is largely the beauty of its æsthetic material. If a tune sung by the high, cracked voice of an old man may give us quite accurately its melody, its full beauty as sung by a rich young voice is quite definitely more than this, and the difference is clearly enough that of the quality of the single sense elements, the tone quality, which, being the quality of these material constituents, is

138

also the tonal quality of the whole. So of color compositions. While structure gives us the harmonies and contrasts, these vary in beauty with the beauty of their æsthetic materials, the specific qualities of the colors as such, the intrinsic variations of hue and brightness and clearness, by virtue of which the particular contrasts and harmonies are present or even possible.

If this is not so clearly the case with spatial elements, it is partly because of the difficulty of distinguishing these as elements from the structure of which they are constitutive parts. But certainly the particular lines and shapes involved may be interesting in themselves and so heighten the interest and beauty of the composition in which they occur. And negatively it is clear, for example, that the badly drawn hand of some one minor figure in a composition may detract from the satisfactoriness of the whole, even though the larger structural relations of the design are not at all obviously affected by this particular element of shape. In a seventeenth century baroque saint of small proportions, carved in wood, we may notice only after some time that one of the hands has been broken off and replaced with a crudely fashioned substitute. Our pleasure in the whole will be distinctly less, for this unfortunate hand is still integral to the whole as one of its real parts; but we shall feel it as only a single unsuccessful element, and the formal structure of the carved saint will remain pretty much intact, instead of being completely ruined as it would be by a distortion of the main outlines or balance of masses. Since all shapes, however, solid or flat, are marked out for vision by boundary lines, and since all lines have direction and order, there is a sense in which spatial elements are all structural or formal, as well as being particular elements. While they are distinct æsthetic materials of composition, they are always at the same time in part the structural form of the whole.

Only a little less clearly is this true of color and sound elements, however, and of course no one pretends to hold that in an actual composition the structural relations are merely added to the æsthetic materials. As actual bricks of clay built into anything, or thrown into a pile by the road, for that matter, necessarily define some shape with specific surface texture, so any æsthetic materials merely accumulated, define an æsthetic form; but as bricks may make Assyrian façades or garden walls, so æsthetic materials may be composed into enormously varying formal beauties. In noticing that these æsthetic materials themselves are defined in and by an order intrinsic to their own qualitative nature, we have already indicated clearly enough that structure begins in such material elements. But instead of putting all our emphasis on the characteristically structural wholeness of beautiful surfaces or beautiful objects, it was important to notice also the beauty of elements as elements, and the share that this sensuous beauty has in the beauty of the structures. Abstracted from it these structures might be formally conceived as satisfactory in presentation to sense, but through loss of beauty in the æsthetic materials they would themselves suffer loss, and in actuality, without these sensuous elements they would of course be nothing at all.

If written music, for example, offers to the technically trained musician the very structure of the beauties he silently hears, so that he is presented with the form and quality of a composition on paper, even this silent music is composed of sensuous elements, sounds which memory and imagination summon at the sight of the appropriate notation. The most gifted composer has a new experience in the actual perform-

ance of his music, in which it takes on its proper sensuous
proportions and achieves its full volume and richness and
the precise and specific quality that is given to the outer ear,
and never in its absolutely full, intricate, subtle tonal quality
to the inner ear, the "ear of the mind." To say that one
enjoys music just as fully by reading a score as by a performance of it upon instruments is either a mere affectation
or else a very doubtful assertion. From it would seem to
follow *a fortiori* that remembering music once heard is as
full and satisfying an æsthetic experience as the actual hearing. And neither of these claims, implied or asserted, can
be made in candor, unless one is so intellectually predisposed
as to like the mere abstracted or even logical pattern of a
thing better than the thing itself. One may of course grasp
the abstract form and enjoy doing so more than one enjoys
the music, as for that matter a child at the piano may enjoy
the workings of his own fingers and muscles under the direction of a notation he is proud to have deciphered, and be
exercising no musical feeling, much less appreciating the
given piece of music. As such pleasure in muscular skill and
mental co-ordination is not to be denied, and not even ruled
out of æsthetic pleasure, though it is a far commoner enjoyment than that of music, so it is also true enough that abstract patterns are more easily followed and held by some
intellects than apprehended directly within a full sensuous
tonal content. But to prefer the pattern to the concrete object of intuition is either lack of musical appreciation or else
asceticism again. This is the old mistake, not of abstraction
for the special subsidiary purposes of knowledge, or of
retention through memory, or of practical operation in
general, or performance in particular—all of which are
obviously rational and justified cases—but of identifying

the abstraction with the concrete whole from which it is drawn. One is then able to fill it indifferently with either the good or the bad, but preferably with the bad, since, if filled with the good, it is the very sensuous content that was to be avoided by the purifying abstraction in the first place. This rigorously formal view ends in mere general terms with the thinnest possible meanings, however broad, or else in a supposedly elevating and edifying mysticism that abandons reality and life for Platonic ideas, or even for Nirvana.

Such a view is more or less plausible in its half-way stages, as when Greek sculpture and architecture are seen uncolored and are then thought to lose their pure nobility by being restored in imagination to their originally colored appearance. A photograph often indicates to certain minds, or perhaps to all of us, by its very abstraction from confusing sensuous elements, beauties which in the concrete we either miss altogether or fail to appreciate fully. But since the Greeks themselves, who created the beauties we recognize, used strong colors extensively, an unprejudiced mind must be willing to admit at least the possibility that richness of sensuous content in general simply adds richness to the most formal structural beauty, instead of contaminating it. And while this is not to say that the mere piling up of sensuous materials, with no dominating coherence of structure, is the greatest beauty, it does remind us that beauty is sensuous in its necessary elementary content, and that any judgment condemning sensuous materials as æsthetically base runs the risk of denying to beauty any actual content at all.

We have so far been dealing with these material beauties, and we have noted their variety as distinguished in orders intrinsic to their qualitative nature; but these are not the sole orders available as principles of structure. For as perception itself occurs in time and is thus subject to temporal order, so the content of imagination or of sense comes to consciousness in time sequences. Hence temporal order may be imposed on any sense material whatever, though such order is not intrinsic to the qualitative nature of this material in the sense in which the order of pitch is native to sound or the order of hue to color. Moreover, upon color elements both spatial and temporal orders may be imposed. In the order of hues as such orange lies between red and yellow. But on a surface, while orange may be placed beside red or yellow, it may also be placed beside purple or green, so that spatial ordering of color areas is quite another matter than the intrinsic order of colors as differing in a serially ordered qualitative stretch of hues. To spatial elements as such, that is to lines and areas and volumes, of which we have already given some brief account, spatial order is of course native. But the modern color organ, Mr. Wilfrid's Clavilux, reminds us that colors may also be projected upon our vision in a temporal sequence, where again blue may lie between red and yellow as well as between green and purple.

Such temporal order, not native to the intrinsic quality of any sort of sensuous elements, but necessary to the very occurrence of any such elements at all, we have so far only mentioned in passing. When we stop to consider it, we come at once upon rhythm, which is sometimes taken to be the very nature of the beautiful in all its aspects, the secret of all æsthetics. Whether or not this is so, it is clear enough that rhythm is fundamentally significant in æsthetic experience, and therefore in the intuited character of the æsthetic surface of our world. Moreover, as we have already indicated in earlier chapters, it is not difficult to see why this is so, nor to say exactly what rhythm is in æsthetic experience.

But there are misunderstandings here both as to terms and as to genuine meanings, as well as difficulties in knowing the facts. Hence the subject demands more than summary statements.

§ 2

In the first place rhythm is felt rather than seen or heard. A blind man may keep time silently with slight motions of his hands or feet or head; or feel his own pulses within in the measured pattern of their beat. And if we often connect the notion of rhythm with seen movements and heard sounds, we cannot afford to forget that what is seen is not the rhythm itself, but the content that is occurring rhythmically, or in rhythm, and felt to be thus rhythmically occurring. Its actual pattern is present to mind through the body that takes it up, however inwardly and blindly, and makes it apparent through feeling. So of sounds. Their rhythm is felt through listening, or even given to them by the bodily mechanisms that perform the act of hearing at their own given rate, being often free, as they are, to group unaccented regular pulses in their own way at their own natural convenience. And where the rhythm is introduced by some means into the sounds as produced, this rhythm is what the mind contemplating the sense content becomes aware of in feeling the pattern of these sounds in time. The rhythm has to do with the order and rate and manner of their occurrence to perception, not primarily, or perhaps at all, with the quality of the tones themselves, which is definitely tonal and timeless. A deaf man watching the conductor's baton, may be made to feel the identical rhythm that is felt and distinguished as formal pattern by a blind man listening to the sounds from the instruments of the orchestra. Obviously, then, rhythm is neither sound quality nor color quality, but an order established and marked in the occurrence of these. And it must be equally clear that rhythm is not felt as intrinsic spatial quality or shape any more than it is as color or sound.

The feeling of a distinguishable patterned rhythm may be introduced or called forth, however, by any sense material that occurs in time. And since nothing whatever occurs except in time, rhythmic possibilities prevail over the whole æsthetic surface of the world. Rhythm is always perceived through feeling and distinguished by feeling, by the bodily acceptance or introduction of it to the mind. It can not be distinguished merely by the regularly named senses of sight or hearing or taste or smell or even touch, so far as touch means what receives texture or shape or temperature. It is got by a more generally pervasive sense of touch, which takes up the moving order of what comes to it, though in itself it is blind and deaf, and somehow presents that patterned order to the mind, which recognizes it as the moving structure of occurring sensuous content. But rhythm itself is no more mere feeling than color is merely our sensation of color instead of what is actually apprehended as having its own specific nature, or than sound is merely the activity of the ears or of the mind through the ears, instead of the sounding content heard and recognized and distinguishable as specific qualitative character. What is felt as rhythm is not the activity of feeling, though this is no doubt rhythmical, but the rhythmic character of the occurrence of the sensuous content, the specific moving pattern distinguished *through* feeling.

§ 3

Rhythms may be objectively as determinate and compulsory as any other qualitative characteristics. Since they are all temporal, however, rhythmic order is, like time, one-dimensional, so far as it is æsthetically and directly felt. It is true that modern thought forces us to admit the interrelation of time and space in a more concrete space-time reality or pervasive character of our comprehended universe. But we intuit spatial relations and shapes æsthetically as themselves absolute and static, even though in spatial compositions movement may be represented and the rhythm of that movement therefore felt in seeing the representation. But this is not the embodiment of rhythm upon a surface in the sense in which music or marching embodies rhythm directly in its own moving structure. Spatial patterns, too, being after all perceived in time, may be rhythmically perceived, and even consciously so composed as to induce a rhythm into the perception of them; and the rhythm of this perceiving may be—though always, I think, a very subsidiary aspect of the enjoyment of them—still part of what is enjoyed in the spatial form perceived, as in rugs and textiles and mural decoration. Especially in the spacing of the details of façades or great colonnades, and in architectural design in general, where the spatial proportions are large and involve actual physical movements to follow them out with the eye, does it seem necessary to admit that the order involved is in some sense rhythmical. But it is only very slightly so; for the rate of such perception is never clearly or exactly dictated by the spatial form itself, and the rhythm of the perception is not intrinsic to the form perceived in anything like the intimate immediacy in which the strictly static pattern of the seen shapes and relations is intrinsic. Photographs of such architectural wholes reproduce them in their spatial proportions in a way impossible to the reproduction of musical compositions, where a corresponding condensation of the temporal proportions by more rapid tempo would destroy completely the distinctive rhythmical effect and all its expressive beauty. If this does not prove that rhythm is literally lacking to spatial composition, it at least reminds us that the sense of the term rhythm as thus applied is quite distinct from its ordinary sense. It seems likely that rhythm is at least not an enlightening term here, since the regularity of strictly spatial relations is in first instance the chief structural æsthetic order of composition involved, and since also rhythm characteristically has to do with literal movement, not with static objects, even though such objects may help define a rhythm in visual experience in which they are presented and may therefore not altogether unreasonably be called rhythmical in this weakened and somewhat vague sense.

We may however admit as a needed further use of the term its application to spatial form when it is not the rate or timing of perception that is in question, but the regular recurrence in space of the same or of similar spatially defined units, as in a northern tower that rises in three bell-shaped sections. But the very use of the term recurrence here indicates that it is not strictly spatial character that we are considering, but the repeated occurrence, in a spatial whole, of a particular spatially defined part, and this at regular intervals. In other words we are thinking of the specific spatial part or unit as repeatedly occurring. Whole lines or shapes are called rhythmical so far as they are felt thus to be alive and moving through their parts. The same or a like space-form here below comes again above and then still again. This reappearance or recurrence is felt as motion through the form of the whole, and gives the tower what is called its rhythm, just so far as the similarity of spatial parts is felt to punctuate the movement in time. The tower is thus rhythmically composed, though its whole strictly spatial character is a static shape. In fact it is only as indicating the non-temporal aspect of occurrence that the term spatial has any genuine meaning peculiar to itself. If this meaning is abstract and omits the aspect of occurrence called temporal, it is no less definitely just this abstract static meaning. And for any unambiguous analysis we need to keep it clear. If shape is to have rhythm literally then it must move actually. Thus the term rhythm applied to our tower is rather the felt suggestion of a rising motion marked as rhythmical by the repetition of the same or similar masses than the accurate description of its strictly spatial character. For this latter must be before us all at one time if we are to see it balanced and patterned *in space*. Its form as spatial is a static shape, a primarily non-rhythmical and properly geometrical configuration.

Jacques Dalcroze, the outstanding apostle of rhythm, as material and form and expression in art, is quoted as calling it the symmetry not the measure of motion. And this clearly indicates, since symmetry is a spatial term, the attempt to include in some sense spatial rhythm, or rather to insist that rhythm in its own nature is spatial as well as temporal. But since motion is what rhythm characterizes in this description, the temporal element is left as fundamental or at least necessary. Moreover, the force of the remark seems to be the contrast of symmetry with measure; and if this is to mean anything at all, since measure cannot be completely denied to rhythm or even to symmetry itself, the insistence is upon the possible subtleties and complexities and variations as being what is important to rhythm, instead of its mere measure or regularity. Since spatial human bodies are what present this movement as seen, symmetry is naturally thought of as characteristic. It is patterns in space, literally embodying various subtleties and kinds of symmetry, through which the rhythm is expressed and discerned. But all of this our account of rhythm as strictly temporal allows for, while none of it makes rhythm in its essential nature spatial.

Among art critics rhythm is so fashionable a word as to be employed on all occasions and in an enormous variety of conflicting meanings. But its wide use and the actual insistence on the term itself by genuinely appreciative critics as well as artists must at least be reckoned with, especially when they take pains to insist that rhythm is the proper word and introduces the needed meaning in descriptions of plastic art. This is hardly the place for controversial discussion, and we may be content to cite one very distinguished critic, Roger Fry,* and then merely say that even in his strictly theoretical æsthetic discussion of the meaning of the term as spatial, he includes such diverse content for it that one cannot very well admit its usefulness for theory, unless inconsistency and even contradiction are worth adopting. And in his actual application of the term in even the most convincing critical appreciation, the meaning varies from sentence to sentence, and one can at best say that it describes what some theorists call empathic response and what we have called the pleasurable response marking beauty in objects for us, a response that is not mere perception, but full of feeling, appropriate and authentic just so far as it follows upon and gives color and resonance and volume to full discriminating apprehension of specific presented qualitative character.

* I have cited Mr. Fry not because his inconsistencies seem to me especially bad, but because even in such brilliant and authentic criticism as his the inconsistencies are still present. See, for example, *Vision and Design*, pp. 33-36, and *Transformations*, pp. 71, 72.

In more philosophical attempts to make rhythm out as essentially no less spatial than temporal, success has been verbally achieved, but only, I think, at the expense of clarity. If we define rhythm abstractly and generally as any repetitive division, in the same or a similar manner, of any sort of processes or events, objective or subjective, in time or in space, it looks as if space composition were as integrally rhythmic as temporal composition may be. But in such a definition what makes plausible the co-ordination of spatial and temporal at the end is the inclusion of temporal order as fundamental in the beginning. For any division of processes or events, marked as it may be in spatial or colored or sounding qualitative elements, is, as felt to divide these events, felt as temporal, since events or processes necessarily occur as actually moving through time. The application to concrete cases of any such abstract definition of rhythm becomes useful and enlightening with reference to spatial composition only as it uses terms indicating static spatial relations and shapes. Moreover, it is clear that so far as space comes in at all it is as a content in which a rhythm is embodied by virtue of actual motion involving temporal duration. We are justified, I think, in treating rhythm as fundamentally and literally temporal, rhythmic pattern as temporal order, and rhythmic structure as durational, spread along the single dimension of time. So far as rhythm is æsthetically experienced it is not in the same sense spread over the spatial surfaces of the three dimensions of intuited static spatial objects.

§ 4

Regularity in time order, which of course involves for perception recurrence, is evidently much of what we mean by rhythm. That it is not the whole of it will be plain enough. But first of all the way in which regularity of occurrence in time involves regular recurrence needs to be perfectly clear. If time is, as experienced, one-dimensional, every moment being always and only before or after, never *beside*, another, and if time is not directly experienced as turning backward in its flight but only as moving forward at its own inevitable rate, or perhaps as being the inevitable way in which all life and all existence moves on or disappears from the actual world altogether, recurrence of time itself has no meaning. But what occurs in time occurs at its own rate, as we noticed earlier of the oscillations of physical bodies. Now there is no strictly temporal form or pattern for each oscillation, but only the spatial form of its path. Hence *such* patterns, marking off time into intervals, cannot themselves be purely temporal. Without experienced variation or change of sense content, time appears not as time at all but either as eternity of form,—Being itself, as philosophers call it,—or as the death and empty oblivion to which a static world would succumb. It is in such considerations that the abstractness of space without time or time without space is so clear. But the simple fact remains that by rhythm we mean the moving temporality, even of spatial forms themselves, when these do actually move before the eyes or in our imaginations, and that we do not mean the spatial patterns as such. These must have their own static and non-rhythmical character, even in order to constitute that which is seen or felt to move, and clearly to constitute visual form and beauty, without such movement and without the rhythm of it. And not only spatial patterns, but sound patterns as well, occur and recur in the one-dimensional, irreversible, temporal flow marked off by pulses or beats, the rate of such beats being part of what we call rhythm.

To keep strictly to the one dimension and the one direction of time itself, we must notice that a rhythmic pattern as rhythmic merely, purely as rhythm, that is, and not as sound pattern or shape, can be a pattern at all only as it measures off the felt flow of time. Since this flow is in general experienced as being uniform, the rhythmic pattern is a pattern first of all simply of its own established rate, the marking off to sense of time intervals along the one dimension of their occurrence. But if the occurrences of the sense data experienced are uniformly timed, any one or any two of them, or any group of them, may be felt as the repetition or recurrence of one before, or two before, or of whatever preceding group has been indicated either by our attention or by some intrinsic stress or other emphasis of its own, to give it a beginning and end.

A regularly ticking clock is a ready example. It ticks *one —one—one—one*, or *one-two, one-two, one-two*, or *one-two-three, one-two-three*, and so on, as we mark off an interval by one beat or by a number of successive beats, through attention to them as a unit or pattern of sounding content. Even in this simplest case the varieties of rhythm are intrinsically infinite possibilities, although rhythmic intervals marked by five or six or seven or eight or more beats are either hard to feel as distinctly characterized rhythms, as with five or seven, or such intervals tend to fall apart into sub-intervals filled by groups of two or three. We can also easily distinguish two different rhythms through one interval. One clock may clearly be heard to tick twice while another is heard to tick once, or we may tap three to six, or four to two with our two hands, and with very little practice two against three, or three against four, although our attention finds difficulty in discriminating even such numerically simple combinations as five against seven or eight against nine. In such combinations as we do easily grasp, we not only distinguish the two or more rhythms, but also hear them or feel them as a single complex rhythm. Three against two in sounded notes is a specific single rhythmical effect, as is the famous six-in-three measure of Spanish songs, which involves this same two-against-three. For the six beats are by attention heard in two groups of three pulses each or in three groups of two pulses each, either alternately in different parts of the tune, or both at once in a characteristic complex rhythm with which most of us are familiar, whether or not we have happened to notice its analytical structure. Thus different rhythms may be simultaneously felt as one complex rhythmic effect, or they may follow each other and be felt as contrasted in a sort of balance against each other.

From these simple examples it is easy to see that in regularity of occurrence recurrence is involved as soon as we punctuate the series of regular impulses and mark them off into groups equal in the time-interval they cover, and so, where we have regularly occurring impulses, into groups of equal numbers of beats at equal time-intervals from one another. But the recurrence of the group of beats in the temporal interval depends upon division of the one-dimensional time sequence, and although we can make such groupings quite arbitrarily with the perfectly even ticking of a clock, for example, as auditors we cannot in most characteristic cases of rhythm arbitrarily fix the number of beats in the periodic interval that recurs. That is done independently of us; it is in the given structure of what we are contemplating. All that is needed to force it upon our attention is some sensuous indication of the point of division of the timestream, which is otherwise an uninterrupted uniform flow, or else is punctuated merely by the natural pulses of our own attentive activity.

This indication of a division may be given in any one, or at once in several, of a great many different ways, all of them being simply modes of emphasis to call attention to the point of division into intervals. It must be clear also that this point is felt both as the end of one interval marked by one group of beats and the beginning of another, and that without the indicating of both its beginning and its end no measure can be marked off. Attention may be summoned for this purpose by any sort of sensuous emphasis, and if the impulses come with perfect regularity, the slightest emphasis on the point of division into intervals is enough to make the grouping clear,—a slightly louder sound, a slightly more extended movement, a definite change in direction of line or motion, a sound of higher or lower pitch, and so on indefinitely to all the possible means, along with regularity of the occurring of the sense elements, for calling attention to a grouping of these. Thus the group recurs. Even with no accent whatever, if the sensuous pattern itself is clearly distinguishable as pattern and is repeated at regular intervals in a continuous temporal movement, attention marks some one point of the repeated pattern as its beginning and comes to feel the rhythm involved as the regular recurrence of this pattern, much as in the parallel case of a Greek key border, though there is no beginning or end of any one part, we see the continuous line as the regular repetition of a unitary spatial pattern.

Rhythm is thus seen to consist in its essence in regular recurrence in time. What recurs may also itself be a rhythmic form, as in spatial structures the spatial elements may themselves be spatial structures. On the other hand, the strictly one-dimensional temporal pattern may be filled with any sort of sensuous content in a rhythmical pattern appropriate to this particular sort of content. The motions of a conductor follow, even if with elaborate subtleties of variation and often of condensation, stereotyped conventional patterns familiar to the eye of the performer, who can thus produce the same rhythmic pattern in sounds from his instrument. In dancing to music the rhythmic pattern is given through sounds. But the dancer not only feels it in and through the sounds he hears; he also gives it another filling, reproduces it in inner preparatory muscular and nervous co-ordinations and adjustments and reveals it outwardly in visual patterns, the sequence of shapes and lines defined by the continuous movement of his own body under the control of the felt rhythm in the music. What is added by the music for appreciation in the onlooker is the tonal filling and the richness of sound as well as a definition of the rhythm itself through audible means of emphasis—whether this emphasis be achieved by pitch changes or by accent, that is, stress in increased loudness of sound, at the critical defining points of time-intervals, or by other devices.

While rhythm is characterized in general as regular recurrence in time, the beauty of an experienced rhythmical pattern depends not only upon the way in which the pattern dominates or vitalizes its sensuous material, which is its actually occurring content, but also upon the beauty of this sensuous material itself, whether sounds or colors or shapes. With this clear, it seems less strange to come to the flat statement, that rhythm, the formal beauty of vitality itself, and the elementary nature of all actually moving beauty, is a purely temporal measure or mode of structure determined by the length of time-interval marked off as recurrent. For it is this length that determines the slowness or swiftness of the recurrence fundamental to the character of the rhythm. If the recurrent time-interval is short, since rhythm is continuous, the rhythm is correspondingly swift; and a rhythm is completely constituted for apprehension with the distinct indication of the beginning and end of this time interval. The absolutely simple *one-one-one* is as truly a rhythm, with as clearly defined an æsthetic effect, as any rhythm, however complex. The beating of tom-toms may be of exactly this sort, monotonous indeed but extraordinarily effective and even expressive, despite the simplicity of its rhythmic form. And in all very simple cases counting or "beating time" indicates rhythm unambiguously. Even *one* pronounced at regular intervals defines a rhythm, the recurrence being indicated by the same syllable, itself a defined sensuous sound-pattern, over and over. This same rhythm might be marked by tapping out the same sound regularly and slowly. And if we are to indicate so elementary a rhythm by a spatial pattern, a motion in the same direction and of the same visual form at the same location will accomplish our purpose.

Rhythm becomes less simple in constitution by marking off further divisions or periods within the fundamental recurring interval. For most of the rhythms we familiarly enjoy, at least one such further division is usual. But the principle remains as simple as before. As time-flow itself can be marked off or divided into more or less quickly recurring intervals, so any of these intervals may be divided again into sub-intervals. Familiar music always has at least this degree of rhythmic elaborateness. The conventional time-signatures of musical notation in the form of numerical fractions indicate by the upper figure the number of subsidiary intervals into which the fundamental interval is divided; and this fundamental interval, appropriately called the measure, is full when that number of equal sub-intervals has been counted off, though often these sub-intervals are grouped together, so that the subdivision is primarily into fewer sub-intervals than the figure indicates. In six-eight time, for example, the fundamental subdivision is into two groups of three which fill the measure in a count of six. But the measure is divided into six not primarily but only secondarily, each of the two main subdivisions being itself divided into three. The lower number of the fraction indicates, but only relatively, of course, the duration of each sub-interval in terms of simple fractions of unity, the so-called whole note, so that besides the time-signature we need always a further indication of rate or tempo which is given in a technical term, *presto, largo,* etc. But the time-signature gives unequivocally the subsidiary rhythmic pattern as being constituted of just so many sub-intervals of time within the fundamental time-interval. Naturally for swift movement we are likely sometimes to use a division into many short sub-intervals as well as to shorten the time of the fundamental interval or measure; but it is only this last that really gives rapidity to the main rhythmical structure of the composition as a whole, since the pulse of very slow tempo may easily be emphasized by a contrast between measures filled with long sustained single notes and equally slow measures divided into a very large number of short notes. If we keep in mind the fact that what we call measure here is as such slow or fast, that it is long or short not in space at all but only in time, we shall be less likely to feel that measure involves mechanizing a rhythm or applying to it static units of spatial extension.

The time-signature is in part, as we have just seen, only an indication of convenient units for counting, with reference to the exigencies of musical notation, though of course through convention and association certain time-signatures are fairly required to indicate certain typical rhythms. Waltzes are written in three-four time, though three-one or three-two or three-eight could of course be used. The reverse does not hold, however, for three-four time may be that of a hundred different sorts of composition at almost any tempo. The point of this illustration from musical notation is simply that the rhythm of music is fundamentally a mathematically indicated subdivision of a primary, regularly recurring time-interval, and nothing else, except what is required to indicate to sense-apprehension the division into this specific interval which recurs, and the subdivision of it, either or both of which indications may be given with all possible degrees of intensity. There is the consequent possibility of variation, perhaps not properly called variation in the essential character of the rhythm, but certainly variation in the full concrete manifestation and embodiment of it, so that it may be characterized as what we call very marked and insistent, or at the other extreme, where however the recurrence must be somehow marked if we are to have rhythm at at all, what we call smoothly flowing or continuous rhythm. But continuous here is a misleading term. For in one sense all rhythm is strictly continuous, the end of one interval being the beginning necessarily of another if we are to have any completed temporal structure instead of mere fragments. But no rhythm has the continuity of the unbroken time-flow itself, for this must be marked off, and in that sense broken, if there is to be the recurrence necessary to any rhythm at all.

Rhythms are thus seen to be sensibly indicated and sensibly filled temporal orders which besides having their definite swiftness or slowness, namely, their rate, are subject to variation of as great range as the possible modes of division into sub-intervals of their regularly recurring primary time-intervals. And rhythms may also be combined in all these modes. In other words rhythms, as they can be accurately indicated by numbers, so they offer for æsthetic effect all the possibilities of number so far as number of divisions, combinations of different numbers of divisions of the same interval, or alternating modes of division are available to direct feeling.

We can have in the first place a quickly or slowly recurring primary interval, the length of which, being a measure of time, is just this quickness or slowness; and rhythm thus is always relatively fast or relatively slow, has always its specific rate. If the fundamental intervals or measures are themselves grouped into larger temporal units, obviously the whole group may now be taken as the primary division or time-interval, and there is no further principle involved, but only a more slowly moving and more inclusive temporal pattern, not a different sort of pattern. Musical compositions, for example, in grouping measures in larger wholes, make the measures themselves sub-divisions of the regularly recurring group of measures, and if this longer group does not recur, it is not itself a rhythm but only a pattern of sound within which rhythm is one of the ordering principles or forms. In the same way long narrative poems have often the dignity of the slower rhythm of their stanza length, within which the division into lines and feet is felt as a subsidiary rhythm. And stanza form requires very definite emphasis, such as the added rhyming line of Spenserian verse, or very clear-cut sensuous stress of some other sort, to call attention to the divisions into stanzas, if this division is to be marked for the ear, and so give a rhythmic effect at all different from that of an unbroken sequence of lines. Still larger divisions into books or cantos is hardly rhythmical in any sense, since attention can not in sense-apprehension grasp such long units as units, to feel their recurrence.

At this point we are ready to consider, as easily intelligible specific modes of rhythmical structure in general, so-called compound and complex rhythms and that special sort of complexity called syncopation. The six-eight measure that we noticed above is typical of compound rhythm, as it is usually called in music, a rhythm very different from that which might be felt in a simple division of the primary interval into six beats not grouped into either two's or three's. But further than this, the fundamental interval or sub-intervals may at the same time or in sequence be divided in two or more different numerical ways, the one not subordinate to the other. Rhythms so constituted are properly called complex as distinguished from compound. Often in music they are called cross rhythms, one of them being apparently felt as conflicting with or crossing the other, because the grouping of the pulses in one is not the further division of the other grouping, but a different subdivision of the primary interval, as in two against three or three against four. Here again the numerical possibilities are literally infinite; but only a very small range of them seems to be accessible to æsthetic appreciation and so available for composition, though there is no reason why this range may not be increased in the further development of music and dancing.

Syncopation is that particular sort of crossing or conflict in rhythm that is produced by a shift of the accent to what was previously unaccented in the rhythmic pattern. After a main recurrent time-interval has been established, the accented beat being clearly felt as marking this division, the accent is suddenly shifted to a point between beats. The established rhythm is thus interrupted, and its accent becomes only co-ordinate or even subordinate to the new accent, or it may be actually suppressed. If the new accent suppresses it completely, however, we shall only have introduced a new point of division, not a new rhythm but the old one over again, beginning at a different point in time. For the rate and the pattern of sub-division remain the same. In order to have the effect of syncopation, therefore, we must either keep up both accents concurrently or else shift the accent back to its old place before we have lost the feeling for that place as establishing the previous rhythm.

As in structures in other sensuous fields, when two different rhythmic patterns each fill the same time-interval, not only may they sometimes be distinguished as crossing or conflicting, but together they have the specific and individual characteristic quality of the particular combination, felt in its complex wholeness as one rhythmic character. Untrained perception feels not the two or more distinct rhythms, but only the one complex effect, as an unanalyzed but more or less definite and special character or quality. But all human beings, practised or unpractised, are susceptible to the effects of specific complex rhythms, the constituent rhythms of which they can not or do not at all clearly distinguish, feeling instead the peculiar excitement appropriate to the complex rhythm taken up by their bodies, but not consciously distinguishing the constituents or recognizing the precise rhythmical structure of the composition, though they definitely feel it as characteristic.

If, however, a rhythm is to be felt at all, it must, at least in part, and so far as it is distinctly recognized as rhythmic character, be enacted however minutely in the body feeling it; and for full appreciation of its specific nature, the feeling must be of this character presented to apprehension. There must be not merely the sense content of sound or color or spatial form, but also the marking off by attention of the rhythmical pattern itself. This is more emphatically, perhaps exclusively, accomplished through incipient or overt movement of nerve-controlled muscles. Thus for even the perception of rhythm, and much more for its full appreciation, bodily flexibility and nervous control of muscular movement are necessary, whether of sense organs usually so called or of other parts of the body whose motion is brought by nervous activity to apprehension. When rhythm is fully felt and clearly distinguished, such co-ordinated control is not merely experienced within, but tends, with concentration of attention upon the apprehended rhythmic pattern, to issue in larger and more fully defined rhythmic motions embodying the pattern externally to vision. That we apprehend the rhythm of music through our feet as well as our ears is a familiar enough fact, but perhaps we are likely not to be so clear that the apprehension of rhythm, through any part of the body trained to flexibility in patterned motion, brings just as accurate an account of this rhythm to consciousness. All of which emphasizes the fact that rhythm as such is felt, not heard or seen, and that this felt rhythm is necessarily that of nervous muscular activity itself, progressing in the given rhythmical pattern, which can thus conceivably be apprehended by mind.

§ 5

The most natural and most adequate experience of the beauty of rhythmic patterns themselves is that of the dancer, who by virtue of his training is susceptible to complex and clearly defined rhythmic character in a fullness not available to those whose bodies can not take on or take up such a patterned movement, because their bodily organization is less subtle and refined in this respect and also less strong and resilient. To notice that the dancer, like other artists, is satisfied with the concrete manifestation in himself, apprehended clearly through feeling, and usually fails, even if he tries, to describe it in words, is only to take account of the fact that rhythm is one of the unique characters of the experienced world which, like all other characters, refuses to be literally translated. Rhythms in music and in seen dancing are familiar enough lay experiences, but certainly far less rich and voluminous, less clear and strongly defined, and less subtly discriminated in their specific variations, than rhythms apprehended through the bodily experiences of dancers themselves. And it is clear enough that while rhythm, to be contemplated, must be the pattern of a sensuous content for ear or eye, or for the feeling of impact, this content itself may be very indifferent, and the rhythm still remain an exciting objective pattern. The art of dancing goes far beyond the rhythms involved. It perfects the visual spatial forms in which the rhythm is embedded and enhances these by color and illumination, as well as also using beauties of representation and mimicry proper, and expressiveness as such. But there may be a fine and engrossing fascination in bare complex rhythmic patterns themselves, even when the visual or auditory content is almost negligible, as is obviously the case when dancers close their eyes, and, to the merest tapping or beating of an accompaniment or to no accompaniment at all, focus their whole attention upon the rhythm felt in the body as a dominating formal, but of course temporal, pattern, which their movements fit into and continuously define in all its elaboration and all its precision.

If modern social dances are condemned either as dull and unimaginative, or as merely vehement and intense, or as actually corrupting and loosening moral fibre, the answer is not that we should abandon dancing, but that dancing, like other arts, may be low or high, simple or complex, adequate or inadequate to human capacities. It need not be at its best expressive, even if vividly, of only a very narrow emotional range. Instead of presenting extremely simple structural forms that are primitive in their monotony, or forms that are interesting and exciting, but only as expressive of the most elementary animal impulses in their crudest manifestations, dances may have the subtlest variation and nuance of pattern, the most delicate elaboration and refinement, and all this without the least loss of the rigor and the technical finality of the most absolute jazz.

The vast spiritual, or moral, or merely human, possibilities of rhythmical movement for the good life were as clear to the Greeks as they are to Havelock Ellis, who has identified art itself, as well as life, with the dance, though no doubt with some lack of literalness. Plato put down music and gymnastics, both essentially rhythmical, as the fundamentals of education. The significance of bodily motion and hence of rhythm is still more emphatically indicated, for any natural outlook upon the world, by Spinoza. As the body is apt to many motions, so, and only so, is the mind apt to many thoughts, and knowledge adequate to Nature or to God. Man is neither a mere body nor a mere mind; these are only modes of the one Substance, which in its reality is as truly Man as it is Nature or God. The attributes of Substance are extension and thought, and the primary and pervasive mode of Substance under the attribute of extension is motion. To know our own bodies truly and adequately is to know God. To know their rhythms is to feel the pulse of Nature.

But for æsthetics these authoritative speculative insights are not enough. We may grant the pervasiveness of rhythmical form and even insist upon its unique and inward vitality, and so upon the necessity of concrete acquaintance with it for any the least adequate realization of our world, but we must also be explicit and analytical. Familiarity with the phenomenon itself is requisite to knowing it, but familiar acquaintance is far from being adequate analytical knowledge. Here careful discrimination must come into play not only to distinguish rhythm itself from its sensuous filling of sounds, or spatial elements, or colors, and from the activity that apprehends it and takes on its patterns, or the mere feeling of motion itself, so much of which is not rhythmical at all, but also to distinguish specific variations and combinations in rhythm and their particular effects.

As we have seen, the swiftness or slowness of a rhythm is a rate which can be measured in terms of arbitrary time units. So many pulses per minute, we say. But this rate is in a sense absolutely fast or slow. For units of time, minutes or seconds, bear a determinate relation to the time-rates of human processes, breathing, pulse, and other organic functions, which are beyond our conscious control, including interested perception and attention. And these functional

ÆSTHETIC JUDGMENT

rates constitute a fixed natural basis for the shortness or the length of time-intervals as felt by us. Hence, once we have given the rate itself and the further division and subdivision of the primary regularly recurring time-interval into pulses, we have a rhythm not only completely defined and numerically precise, but also for human beings absolutely or intrinsically fast or slow, whatever the mode of indicating the divisions, and whatever the sensuous content filling the rhythmic pattern. If, as we have already noticed, this appears to be a very meagre account of what we all think of as rhythm in the arts, we may now proceed to indicate its adequacy, at least in principle, to those familiar rhythmical arts in which subtleties and irregularities are all-important and numerical measures seem a little impertinent.

§ 6

So far we have thought mostly in terms of music and dancing, the latter so often associated with the former that illustrations from musical notation apply to both. And it is in music, of course, that notation is most nearly adequate and most explicitly given. The absolute rate is given in the conventional terms applicable to tempo, or still more definitely in metronome markings, which indicate the number of notes of a certain relative time-value to the minute. But the mode of division and subdivision is further defined not only by the time-signature and by bars to mark off measures, but by the notes themselves, each with its relative time-value given by its printed form, and even so spaced as to aid the eye with this further representation of relative lengths of time in the one forward direction in which the music flows, by the one horizontal direction in which the notation is read. The duration of the measure being fixed, and the movement being continuous—for of course "rests" fill out intervals just as clearly as notes—a regular recurrence at a definite rate is established, and the rhythm of the music mechanically and unambiguously represented.

It is also true, however, that without bar-lines to mark the measures, or even a time-signature, the indication of the rhythmic pattern and rate are given pretty clearly by the patterned sequence of the printed notes. This is quite unmistakably so in highly coherent, that is genuinely composed, music as distinguished from such composition as is little more than improvisation. Even the tempo is suggested by the character of the sequences of notes, so that these alone in their one-dimensional time order may give to a competent musician a rigorous guide to the whole rhythmical structure of the composition. But "competent" is a dubious and fluctuating designation, and the whole point would be scarcely worth making, if it were not that in another most familiarly rhythmic art, where competence is equally rare, our written symbolism omits any specific indication of rhythm except by spacing off lines and groups of lines, and so makes the comparison of verse rhythm with the rhythm of music itself more obviously significant.

If for beginners music does not also add this device of arranging the composition in separate lines, it is probably rather on traditional grounds than any other, unless it is just the printing expense; and no doubt verse is not explicitly marked as to rate, much less numerically as to measure and subdivision of measures, because in the first place this would offend traditional taste, but also because previously learned rules of word accent and sentence emphasis and the conventions of reading sentences, of which after all verse as discourse is composed, are more or less correctly supposed to be primarily applicable. Besides this, elocution has been an art rather of the inculcation of specific "readings" than of general principles. Furthermore the content of verse is not, even as directly perceived, mainly tonal or even mainly sound. The sounds of poetry are directly taken as having, or even being, meanings, or as the transparent suggestion of imagery in any or all of the sensuous fields, as well as of emotions and feelings which it refers to and summons only symbolically. Hence to mark off poetry in print, as if it were explicitly rhythmical, patterned sounds, would at once too forcibly emphasize its failings as properly musical composition, and rob it of the appearance of the printed discourse of the human mind, which, though it feels and hears, finds its proudest and most dignified satisfaction in functioning as the strictly knowing intellect.

However this may be, if we are to appreciate verse not merely as expressive of the meanings of its words and sentences, but also as an art of sound in which the rhythmic pattern is at least not negligible, it would help the incompetent—and most of us are certainly to be classed here—and above all the beginner, to have it printed with some indication of its tempo or of its measure. Some contemporary poets have gone so far as to use the familiar musical designations of rate: *adagio, andante,* and so on, but usually rather to set a mood for association than explicitly to indicate the actual swiftness or slowness of the rhythm of their verse. In general, too, poetry is predominantly expressive art rather than formal art; and since we have not yet made out even the relation of art to æsthetic surface, it must be clear that we are not in any position at this point to speak on principle of the effects of poetry as such, or even of the purely æsthetic aspects of poetry. Poetry has an audible æsthetic surface, but it is not appreciated as this surface alone, as the very slightly poetic effect of poetry read aloud in an unknown language is enough to convince us. But more than this, even the audible surface of poetry is not pure tone; the intrinsic possibilities of variation established in the nature of pitch play very little part even in the sounding surface of verse, and loudness and softness are much less definitely ordering principles than they are in music. What the two arts have in common for the most part is only rhythmical structure given through auditory content, which content itself involves, and in both cases, feelings from the vocal chords as well as sensations through the ear. It is the difference between the rhythmical structure of music and that of verse that we finally come to as throwing further light upon the nature of rhythm itself. It is this difference that suggests for our account of rhythm here an additional characteristic.

This difference is perhaps most clearly named as a difference in degree of explicitness. Verse is of course rhythmical, however subtly and variously, and rhythm necessarily involves a measured timing in the sounds of verse. But the very fact that we have not found it necessary to employ a time-signature or a tempo index, as in music, indicates that the "numbers" of poetry flow without so explicitly noted a regularity, and that the artistic satisfactoriness of verse rhythm is a matter of subtlety and even of felt irregularity. What is really the case here is certainly not fully agreed upon by critics and theorists; but in the light of the nature of rhythm in general, it must be clear that some fundamental felt regularity in recurrence is an absolute necessity, since it is in the nature of rhythm to involve such recurrence. But the syllables of words in discourse, whether prose or verse, do not lend themselves in English—or in any other language, for that matter, though English is even less amenable in this respect than Spanish or Italian—to shortening in time or to a regularity of recurring accent, so easily as do musical tones. Rhythm could be applied from without, simply imposed upon, a series of nonsense syllables. But syllables in words and sentences depend in part, for carrying their very meanings, upon the same sort of variations in pitch and loudness that must be used to mark the purely rhythmical structure of any sound sequence.

It is clear therefore that on the one hand the subtle and delicate sound variations native to intelligible oral discourse as such, must be so employed in verse, so arranged and modified to give a sound pattern in a more or less definitely marked rhythm, as not to disregard too violently these primary sound variations without which words and sentences lose their intelligibility. On the other hand, rhythm in the elementary sense of time-pattern in measured intervals, if it is to fit intelligible discourse at all, must be variable and subtle enough, along with establishing felt recurrence, not to interfere with such prior demands in the same sensuous realm as give meaning to verse. At least verse rhythms must be free enough of numerically measured regularity not to distort into unrecognizableness the natural linguistic, and hence symbolically significant, time-values and stresses of words and sentences in discourse.

It is often said that the rhythms of English poetry are a matter of accent instead of duration of syllables—literal length of vowels in time—as in Greek and Latin poetry. But this is a badly confused and confusing statement. Apparently what must be meant, is that in the sounding medium of spoken words, the underlying rhythmical pattern, itself purely a matter of division into recurring time-intervals and their subdivisions, is more usually and more characteristically marked in English verse by louder or higher sound, so-called accent that is, at the points of division, than by actually maintaining sounds longer to hold attention and mark structure. Both devices are common in music, and the first of a series of several notes of equal time-value in a figure is often held out quite beyond this value, and the rest of the series then hurried to come within their total allotted time, simply to make clear the beginning of a new or repeated interval in the rhythm. Neither length of particular syllables nor accent, however, constitutes the rhythm itself. They are both only ways in which the sensuous filling is qualitatively varied at critical points to call attention to, or keep attention interested in, a temporal recurrence, which would otherwise be missed or confused or felt as less insistent and dominating. Rhythm as such, being felt recurrence, is always a matter of time-order and time-division, never merely accent or duration of syllables or notes, but their temporally determinate arrangement, marked now in one and now in the other of these ways.

As we have already said, the number of devices for making any content take on or reveal the pattern of a series of more or less regularly recurring impulses or intervals is very large. If accent or ictus is one of the simplest of these devices, though it is probably never used without others, especially in the case of English verse, that neither turns the rhythm into mere accent, which is manifestly impossible, nor does it in the least rule out other devices, such as introducing pauses empty of syllables to fill time-measures and indicate divisions and achieve continuity, or such as sustaining any one syllable, raising or lowering the pitch of a vowel, stressing in various ways the noises in the consonantal parts of syllable

ÆSTHETIC JUDGMENT

sounds, swaying the body as one recites, beating a drum in
the fashion of an Arabian devotee to mark the measured
progress and the accumulation of his numbers, and so on to
all the more subtle and delicate and less easily named means
of marking time, the holding of the breath, the timbre of the
voice, variations of the slightest sort, or variations of many
sorts at once, all to accomplish the same general purpose.

What is plain from the comparison of rhythm in music
and rhythm in verse, recurrent in temporal pattern as both
must be in order to set up any feeling of rhythm at all, is
first that verse rhythm is less explicitly, less regularly, and
less uniformly marked than rhythm in music. Moreover, in
verse the subdivisions of the primary recurrent interval are
felt as less regular and less specifically measured, and they
are more subtly indicated than in music, where the durations
of notes are simple fractions of the measure itself as well as
of a unit time-interval of notation, the length of which can
be definitely given in fractional parts of a second. Whereas
a musical composition, either throughout its whole duration,
or throughout large parts of this duration, keeps strictly to
this established and measurable rate, so that we can calculate
the number of minutes it takes to perform it; a poem varies
in the speed of movement in time from idea to idea or
from image to image, and the rate of a poem on the whole,
while it is obviously an element of its æsthetic character, is
not so explicitly marked that we feel it necessary to agree
upon it. In fact, in literary criticism it is seldom considered.
How fundamentally or even absolutely important this general rate is, however, any dramatic reading illustrates. Secondly, then, it follows out of this comparison of verse
rhythm and rhythm in musical composition that rhythm itself, whatever the sensuous filling of its patterns, is subject

172

to this further sort of variation, and therefore properly characterized as more or less subtle, more or less regular, more or less marked, or, as we have put it here, more or less explicit.

§ 7

Thus our added point on the nature of rhythm is that any given rhythm varies both in swiftness and in numbers, that is in its fundamental rate and in the patterned subdivision of the primary time-interval; that both these variations may and usually do occur constantly in any rhythmical structure in art, and that what we have left as necessary to rhythm itself is the felt recurrence of the primary time-interval, a recurrence sufficiently emphasized to be marked for attention without interrupting the rigorous temporal continuity running through or under the sensuous content of whatever form, but constantly varied both as to its rate and as to its mode of subdivision. The limits of such variation depend, if they are to come within æsthetic appreciation at all, upon the proficiency we have, through training or instinctive gift, both to catch a fundamental rhythm itself and to feel the subtleties of its variation as still only modifications of the fundamentally recurring pattern of a single temporally ordered structure, no matter how various in its parts.

As the material of music consists more exclusively than that of verse in tone itself, which is the body and filling of its rhythmic character, and as it also depends more obviously upon its rhythmic pattern, music is more explicitly rhythmical than verse. But if verse is less explicitly rhythmical than music, it is no less truly and pervasively rhythmical, for it too is presented only in a temporal continuity where regular recurrence must be discriminable and clearly felt. It is in verse, however, that the variations of rhythm become so subtle and so difficult to measure in numbers, and the subtlety and irregularity so characteristic, that it is the consideration of rhythm in verse that establishes our final characterization of rhythm in general. Thus in concrete cases, whether music or dances or poetry, rhythm, like the sensuous material beauties of color and sound and shape, while it is structural order rather than material æsthetic content, is fully characterized only as in its specific particular form, its constantly varying discriminated sublety, which is not merely the addition to or decoration upon an underlying recurrence of pattern, but the intrinsic and precise nature of the determinate concrete rhythmical sequence itself as actually presented. To repeat in summary what has taken so many words to make out, there must be for rhythm anywhere, in verse or even in prose, an established measure, the primarily felt time-interval or division; else no recurrence is possible in the continuous temporal progress through the composition, a continuity absolutely required if the composition is not literally to fall apart. But once this recurrence is clearly established, the variations in rate, in mode of subdivision, and in grouping, though they may be very great, constitute the concrete specific character that defines the particular rhythm itself, gives it its individuality, and makes it the actual formal æsthetic nature or essence that it is, and is presented as and felt to be.

With recurrence once established in verse, for example, we can hold back our progress to take into the recurring pattern almost any sort of irregularity; an added metrical foot need not at all break the rhythmic flow of the lines. Prose too may take on rhythm by arranging words in phrases and sentences to give the effect of recurrence, though usually in fairly long periods marked by rising and falling inflexion, a

more or less gradual movement all upward, or all downward, with internal accents, or a combination of the upward
and downward movement, accomplished by continuous variation of pitch or of loudness in the syllables as they follow,
and the whole pattern repeated in approximately identical
form and at least in approximately equal durations of time,
so as to be discriminated by the ear as a unit. But as any
rhythmic pattern is a fundamentally distinguishable identity,
whether it appears in prose or in verse, or in music or dancing, and as prose is natively burdened with the meaning its
sentences carry, while music at the other extreme carries its
meaning on its own surface and refers no further to anything symbolized by it, but directly specifies its character in
its tonal structure; while speech is fundamentally symbolic,
that is, and music is almost directly present to sense itself
in its whole æsthetic content, so an explicitly felt rhythm in
prose, as in any other sensuously apprehended content, tends
to emphasize æsthetic surface character. Thus the more
fully rhythmical prose is, the more it is felt to approximate
verse, the form of speech that has traditionally been considered more beautiful upon its surface, that is, more obviously æsthetic. No clear line can be drawn on this ground
between verse and prose, except arbitrarily; for rhythm is
common to both, and rhythm in either is so subtly modified
that the absolutely specific characterization of it fails for
either case, much more any definition of the degree of
subtlety and irregularity or even vagueness that should mark
a clear transition from a free sort of verse to a more or less
rhythmical sort of prose. Prose which is actually metrical
is far over the line, of course, and usually felt to be trespass-
ing, and the extremes are clearly enough marked. On the
one hand there is such verse as is highly and explicitly and

hence metrically rhythmical, and even more or less musical in the strict sense in its use of tone qualities. On the other hand there is the sort of prose that approaches purely intellectual or even logical symbolism, the sensuous content of sound and the temporal order of occurrence of this content becoming negligible as the ideal of transparent lucidity is approached.

Rhythm, even in its least explicit forms, thus involves felt recurrence in time of a sensuous pattern at a fundamentally regular rate, no matter what the variations, so long as they do not interfere with essential continuity and with recognition of recurrence. Rhythm may be compound or complex, but it may also be simple, and so perfectly regular as to be mechanically marked and numerically measured. If it is one of the fundamental principles of structure, it is after all only one sort of structure, the order of the moving temporality of things, not the intrinsic qualitative orders native to sensuous content as such, nor spatial order. Finally, while rhythm is primarily an order, and an order of structure in time, it is often, as rhythmical pattern, an elementary component or material out of which more elaborate rhythms are composed and into which they may be analyzed. Thus it is on the border between the sensuous materials of beauty and the beauty of structure, and we may appropriately proceed from our account of rhythm to the meaning of beautiful form in general as distinguished from material sensuous beauty, and so to the relation which æsthetic surface bears to the nature of art. This procedure is not to suggest that beauty itself can be separated into matter and form; for the very materials of sensuous beauty are discriminated and defined in an order intrinsic to their qualitative nature, and the most fundamental non-intrinsic principle of ordered structure itself, namely rhythm, may also, as particular pattern, enter into structural compositions as sensuous material, capable of being felt and enjoyed in manifestations so elementary and so beautiful in separation from their context, as to be comparable to single color variations or single tones, or single elements of shape.

CHAPTER X

ART AND ÆSTHETIC SURFACE

1. Arts as more than their sensuous content and more
than their strictly æsthetic surface. 2. Artistic value not
identical with æsthetic value: the point illustrated in the
failure of classifications of the arts. 3. The varying
degrees in which perfection of æsthetic surface constitutes artistic perfection. 4. The arts necessarily defined
in part by technique as applied to specific media. 5. Expression as primary purpose the differentia of the so-
called fine arts.

§ 1

THE æsthetic judgments of our illustrations so far have
been distinguished from such judgments as give factual information of one kind or another by their immediate sensuous
content. That is to say, when we look for their meaning we
find that they are records of the surface aspects of the world,
as this surface is spread out for attentive discrimination of
its details and its specific character, which we contemplate
with the direct satisfaction derived from such contemplation. This surface, taken easily into view in sense experience, may be very elementary, as when we sniff the air like
a dog and, not unlike a dog perhaps, feel the freshness of it.
Or we may discriminate the saltiness of a sea breeze, the
scent of pines, the perfume of lavender or heliotrope in a
summer garden, enjoyed with no thought of the source of
the odor and no interest, for the moment, in the garden
itself, or in the pine trees, or the sea. And this breath of

fresh-smelling air may be enjoyed without our having had any previous experience of the odor it carries, without any recognition, any sense of familiarity, that is, with the nature —much less the name—of the quality immediately present.

Say that we are suddenly transported on some still, dark night to a strange land and that we get not even a first view of this new country, but only a breath of its dark sweetness to enjoy and to dwell upon, until daylight reveal its character in the recognizable forms of masses and distances and colors. Of course, so elementary a material beauty as this perfume of the air is anything but simple in its origins and causes. It is conditioned by the elaborate chemistry of nature, which has operated through long evolutionary cycles to produce in climate and vegetation just that fragrance of the still darkness that is now our æsthetic object. But the fragrance remains a unitary quality, a single sense element of loveliness, a material beauty appreciated by the untrained and inexpert nostrils of the novice from the distance as clearly and distinctly as by an indigenous expert, who recognizes it by a familiar name. It is appreciated, too, as just the specific odor it is, an odor which may always be revived by memory, so that its vivid definiteness, recurring even years later, will carry one back to that romantic night of which it may remain the single reliable and life-long witness and evidence, as a whiff of ether carries one suddenly to an operating-room, the scene of a long-forgotten childhood agony. Such simple elements of material beauty apparently gain by the extreme definiteness possible to their occurrence as distinct or even separated sensuous elements, a vivid pleasurableness for discriminating attention that would almost seem to outweigh beauties of fully delineated structural adequacy whose hold on the mind itself, as clear-cut forms, is surer, and, except in exigent immediacy and vivacity, infinitely greater.

But it would be an oddly romantic life that would in the fashion suggested by our example of a vividly pleasant odor set about following Pater's famous suggestion that for real living we bend our energies to crowding into the little interval of our mortal years as many passionate pulsations as possible. If only dogs and children find their intensest natural happiness in a minute observation of the elements of the world's sensuous surface, and if none of us may suck the honey of the world in momentary bliss like Ariel, it is perhaps because neither fairies nor dogs nor yet children are the patterns of adult human appreciation of beauty. If the fragrance of a flower is sweet, the complex full beauty of a garden is, if not sweeter, at least a more enduring and voluminous sweetness for a mind that can do more than smell, for eyes that see its lights and shadows, the patterns and proportions of its masses of green, the fitness of its growth to the buildings it encloses or adorns, the structural lines of its borders and paths, the contrasting and blending colors of its beds of blossoms, its slopes and vistas and expanses of level lawn, the line of its wall against the sky, and the moving shadows of its foliage upon the texture of the wall. But a garden may be too richly and complexly composed—nature's intricacies confounding human apprehension with her multiplied profusions—to be appreciated easily as a single beautiful and completely coherent whole, too full of sounds and scents and changing lights and shadows, of intricate, delicate forms and colors, of subtle perspectives and arrangements, for human minds to do more than choose details to contemplate, or love it all in a kind of homely and familiar wonder at its variety and sweetness and at the inexhaustible subtleties of composition it presents even to the eye alone. A building within it, made by human hands and designed by human faculties upon a plan conceived by a human mind, working in comprehensible spatial forms, while it may be less absorbing to the senses, allows a human mind to rest upon it with perhaps a less immediately passionate response, but with a steady comprehending appreciation of a structural fitness that is more easily grasped and more naturally called beautiful than the most vivid and ravishing odor or color or sound that the garden affords, or even than the garden itself, with all its charm.

The poet whose friend was to pray to be all nose to be enraptured by a divine perfume was after all as much of a wit as a poet, and his verses of invitation to this pleasure, in the perfection of their rich and full brevity, their polished elegance, the directness of their expression of warm friendliness and of an ironically pathetic human love of the comforts and delicacies of good living on an empty purse, were far more to his normal and permanent taste than the perfume he was offering. The same mind that could contemplate a human being praying to be all nose for a divine odor, found his own ampler satisfaction in the beauties of the least æsthetic of all the arts, poetry itself, where, though the sounding surface is for the ears, the whole meaning and life of the lines is an ordered structure for the imagination and the intellect.

The arts, especially the fine arts, have sometimes a surface more æsthetically rich and satisfying, even if sometimes less vivid and arresting, than any mere separate sense elements or casually occurring or partly designed natural beauties; but this surface is not the central life and significance of the arts any more than it is the life and meaning of nature.

And no æsthetic theory is even plausible that fails to notice that the arts themselves are directed human activities, operations and processes of creating, not mere æsthetic surfaces, and that like other human activities,—all of which, so far as they are occupied with forming external matter, the arts ultimately comprise,—their origin, their purpose, and their definition are to be sought not in the realm of æsthetics itself, but in the wider, deeper, and more engrossing realm of human wants in general, human purposes, and human satisfactions.

Æsthetic pleasure is always pleasure in an object immediately present to sense, and whether that object is an elementary material beauty, a sensuous content, a single sound, a vivid odor, a bright color, whether it is a combination of all these offered us in nature, or whether it is a highly artificial object produced by an elaborate technical process, makes no difference to its being rigorously æsthetic. But for most of our experience, surface immediacy is not even an accurate designation; through our ranging memories, the processes of our minds discover in the presented surfaces of objects much that is not there for sense-apprehension; and a perfect æsthetic innocence of vision is hard, perhaps impossible of achievement, for an adult mind. We miss even the blue of shadows in our habit of seeing them as dark places in our way. Being intent upon the practical significance of objects, we see not their precise shapes or colors or textures, not their surfaces, that is, but their uses and meanings, or their place in nature under a vague image or a familiar feeling, or even nothing but a class-name. A concept roughly framing them for our knowledge within a scientific scheme of things is perhaps all that their appearance calls forth from us in response to their actually individual and specifically differentiated appearance. And this appearance we are willing to call beautiful often only by virtue of the association of the word beautiful, as applied to a beauty once actually felt upon a surface freshly seen in younger and less sophisticated experience, with the name we then learned for the object, now only verbally acknowledged as beautiful. At least, if it is not merely verbal, the judgment as at present pronounced is not actually æsthetic; for it is simply the recognition of an object as being of a sort which the word beautiful fits. To say that roses are beautiful is often merely parallel to saying that they have thorns, both pronouncements being mere repetitions of learned phrases or remembered verbal records of forgotten sights and feelings, pieces of a dead sort of knowledge or else of a practically useful symbolism, the meaning of which is not only not of the kind that an æsthetic judgment has as content, but either lies totally beyond the purely symbolic content as what this content refers to, or is altogether absent, the mere form of words left being a surviving habitual response in vocal form, but no more a judgment than any other habitual physical response, a point which was suggested at the beginning of our account of æsthetic judgment in general.

What we are to notice now is a further distinction, that which marks the difference between the meaning and content of strictly and genuinely æsthetic judgments in general and the meaning and content of assertions attributing value to the structural human compositions of the arts. And our conclusions may be stated at once in anticipation of the concrete illustrations which are to make the distinction intelligible and acceptable.

First of all, the value we attribute to works of art is often not primarily æsthetic at all, and to admit this point is neither an aspersion cast on æsthetic value, nor does it involve any confusion as to the nature or function of fine art. Secondly, the various arts differ very greatly as to the proportion of their value that is strictly æsthetic, music being almost purely æsthetic in essence, poetry very slightly so. The various conventional classifications of the arts emphasize this point, and for æsthetic theory in general such classifications and their different or even contradictory basic principles are therefore of considerable importance. Again, the fine arts are first of all, for any intelligent grasp of them, arts, and only secondarily fine. That is, they are specific operative processes, directed to intended ends, and conditioned by various special and often highly complex techniques, which in turn determine in part the very nature and definition of the objects of these arts themselves. For æsthetics, then, it is only prudent to notice the primary meaning of art as such, and so to see just how far the fineness of the fine arts depends upon directed technique rather than upon the æsthetic surface of what are regularly called objects of art,—statues, fine furniture, designed buildings, songs and dances and symphonies and operas, poems and plays and pageants, paintings and drawings, tapestries and rugs and fine fabrics. And lastly, as we find that the surface is sensuous and composed of the elementary material beauties we have already considered, in structures themselves apparent to sense in direct perception, but more fully beautiful and more usually and characteristically called beautiful than the bare material elements, so we shall discover that both sensuous elements and structural forms are by their very nature expressive. It is only as works of art give specification—not linguistic names or any other sort of symbols merely, but actual present determination for direct sense perception—to human feelings, emotions, desires, and satisfactions, embodied in the sensuous surface and felt upon it as being its character and quality— only so do they share in the nature of actual concrete works of fine art.

These four points can be made out most clearly by illustrative examples from the various arts, but first of all we must stop to notice what art itself means as the term applies broadly to the useful or industrial arts of civilized or of primitive life, as well as to the fine arts, where æsthetic surface becomes so important.

§ 2

As contrasted with the works of nature, works of art are man-made; instead of just happening to come about in the natural course of events, they are brought about by conscious processes employed to modify and combine materials given in nature, to produce other materials or manufactured articles, which without these processes might never come into existence at all, as savages, instead of always throwing stones at their enemies or their prey, come to use one stone to chip another into a shape more effective for throwing or for striking. Indian arrow-heads are only pieces of flint, but they are human artifacts, objects produced by the art of chipping and shaping stones into pointed tips appropriate to embedding themselves in flesh. And if in modern industrial arts the very preparation of materials and of tools is itself a long process, involving whole industries, the completion of these preparatory processes being a condition of the manufacture of other tools or utensils or objects of use or luxury, all these arts are one in that materials are worked upon by human beings and so modified in form as to result in something intended and desired by men for given purposes. The process is too familiar to need illustration in a world so absorbed and dominated by it in one form or another, and we need only mention it to remind ourselves that the human arts, producing their works from materials and objects given to us by nature, do so by operating upon these materials and objects in such wise as to meet practical exigencies and fulfil more or less clearly defined intentions in objects of specific forms and natures.

The value of the products of the human arts is then to be measured in terms of the fitness of these products for accomplishing all the various specific human purposes they are intended to serve, and the surface of the products as it lies before discriminating perception is largely irrelevant to this primary value. What we have said of primitive art and what we all know of manufacturing operations and their products makes it very clear, however, that the more nearly we perfect such products, the more widely they are employed, the more familiarly they occur in daily life, the more frequently they are to be seen and handled, the more ubiquitous they have come to be in our surroundings, the more surely do we insist that they be smoothed down so as not to offend the senses, varied in the direction of forms satisfactory to contemplate in themselves, or even ornamented with color or design. Hammers and anvils may be merely of neat and fitting shapes, and horse-shoes merely well fashioned and well attached; but saddles and bridles must be of finely finished leather, and they may also be ornamented with carved design or with precious metals. Even in the kitchen the pots and pans and knives and forks must be in traditionally neat shapes and properly scoured; but the ware for the dining table must be more than this, and as it enters into the processes of domestic life more nearly at their culmination, where they are dwelt upon and repeated not as mere means but in a consummation to be realized and enjoyed, it must be not only inoffensive to perception but an element of grace or ornament.

But even the table silver must still serve its proper purposes, the handles not out of proportion to be conveniently used, the spoons for soup not so small as those for coffee, the plates deep enough for vegetables or gravy. So that the transgression of human standards of convenience in size alone would spoil our pleasure in the perception of the objects. For these are recognized as serving purposes, performing functions, and an impossibly large spoon becomes monstrous and ugly on the table as the most perfectly bred silky-coated dog would appear monstrous and ugly to a mother coming upon it in the place of the baby she had left asleep in its cradle. These illustrations can not of course prove the very general principle that the value of objects, even when they are objects of fine art, is not primarily felt to lie in their æsthetic surface; but they will suggest so many other obvious illustrations that there is little need of stressing the point further. A public building is not judged as we judge the model of it on exhibition, though the latter may give us a clear idea of its æsthetic character. The model is not intrinsically important, and even its own intrinsic beauty of aspect is a very slight sort of beauty, no matter how exquisite, as compared with that of the building itself in its full proportions, where the entrances admit human beings and the spaces provide them with convenient room for carrying on human activities.

Nor does our mind always keep these two aspects distinct. Part of the felt æsthetic value of a dwelling is its privacy, and hence the actual presentation to sense of the beauty of privacy, privacy which is not literally sensuous surface seen, not as such the space relations for perception, or the colors or designs before the eyes, but the quality of fitness to satisfy a human want, to give a human satisfaction, revealed upon an æsthetic surface to the eyes belonging to a human mind acquainted with houses and their uses and their characteristic appearance. If we were to limit the word beauty to the literally æsthetic surface of which in preceding chapters we have sketched the elements, much of what we naturally take to be the beauty of works of art would be lost, the privacy of dwellings, the appropriate size of dinner plates, the tapering or flattening of handles to be held in human hands, the spacing of door-ways and windows, the sizes of rugs and their closely woven texture of durable knots, the steep slopes of roofs for snow and rain or the flatness of roofs for the enjoyment of tropical nights. The fitness of all these objects for their purpose is clearly not itself the æsthetic satisfactoriness of their surface for the barest sense appreciation; for usefulness is not surface beauty. But as all art is seen as under the aspect of its function, houses to live in, knives to cut with, chairs to sit on; and as even nature is humanized and made intelligible to minds in animal bodies that are fit to move swiftly and easily, and bodily organs fit to function properly, so the values of all things are felt in terms of the names of the satisfactions or functions or purposes that they are intended to effect, and we cannot easily, and do not naturally, abstract the surface from the object even for contemplative appreciation.

What we ought to do in such matters has of course scarcely even an intelligible meaning, and certainly no relevance to our discussion, since we are interested here in felt value, recognized and recorded in vital, not merely verbal, judgments. Our point is simply that the primary value of works of fine art, as of all the works of all the arts, is felt and hence judged not solely as the satisfactoriness for contemplation of the æsthetic surface itself. And this is not in the least to deny that the surface as such, and quite apart from recognition or knowledge of the object or its function, may be beautiful; it is in just those cases, in fact, where the object itself is highly prized as a work of art, the product, that is, of operations and processes in the service of a recognized end, that an elaborately beautiful æsthetic surface seems most appropriate and calls forth the most deeply felt response, a response distinctly lessened in the fulness of its satisfactoriness, if the surface in ornament or elaboration blurs or conceals the function of the object or its purposeful structure, or if the object by its size becomes monstrous and repulsive, or minute and merely delicate or charming.

Miniatures may of course be exquisite, as well as accurate likenesses, but we all judge them as lesser works of art than portraits to a human scale; and if heroic figures so rarely succeed in being beautiful, it may be because, dominating or adorning great plazas or avenues or approaches as they often do, their majesty and power, even their intended or effective sublimity, is not quite properly that of those human bodies they so often represent in exaggerated anatomies. Bodies must be of mortal proportions to be human at all and to be felt as functioning in human ways, and a man made divine by size alone, is after all likely to be only a monstrous god. On the other hand, such features either of manufactured objects or of natural animals as are æsthetically satisfying in the strict sense, lend themselves to emphasis in increased size or by ornamentation, as large eyes are beauties because eyes themselves are beautiful in color and shape and texture, or a sword-guard, being for practice and performance appropriately of metal, which can be carved or set with precious stones, and also performing as it does a crucially important function in the play and even the wearing of a sword, may well be itself transformed into an æsthetic surface of striking beauty for the eye, only to add this further richness to the beauty of the sword as a whole, without blurring the sword-shape or detracting from its distinctive total character.

The principle we have been illustrating is that the value of works of art is not felt and judged merely as the æsthetic value of their surface, that their very beauty is felt to be greater as they themselves fulfil more perfectly a function or purpose acknowledged in the names we give them. It will be objected at once that our illustrations are of a very narrow range, mostly, in fact, from mere crafts or from minor arts or from architecture, where there may be some doubt as to whether the fine arts have even been considered; so we must go on at once to our second point and consider the varying degrees to which, in different kinds of art, the æsthetic surface proper constitutes the value or at least the beauty of objects. And here the traditional classifications of the arts will throw some light on the subject.

These classifications have been made on various principles, and it will be seen at once that it has not always been the nature of the æsthetic surface in question that has been used as a basis. From our own account of the kinds of sensuous elements entering into this surface, the classification into visual and auditory arts is seen to be an essentially æsthetic one. But on such a basis, which groups music with poetry, and painting and sculpture with architecture, the classification, as indicating the natures of the arts themselves, is very unsatisfactory. If we must include dancing, for example, or the theatre arts, including drama, the division into visual and auditory fails completely. And while poetry comes to our ears in a rhythmical auditory medium, most of its vital content comes in images from the other senses and all of it in language carrying meanings, in a conventional symbolism, that is, instead of appearing as an immediately appreciated specification to the ear of feeling or emotion. The actual sounds are, more often than not, when felt purely as sounds, utterly irrelevant to the meanings they refer to. These meanings they carry by virtue of a linguistic concatenation of syllables, bound down both separately, and in words and phrases and sentences, to current usage, determined primarily by traditional agreement as to symbolic reference, and this for the purpose of communicating and expressing ideas and emotions, and only secondarily subject to standards of euphony or even of rhythm itself. And if architecture, sculpture, and painting, and carving and etching and drawing, are all for vision, all to be discerned as lines and surfaces and solids by the eye, as arts they perform such different functions that an architect may succeed, may even be something of a genius as a designer of buildings and bridges or parks and cities, and yet have little acquaintance with even the media, much less the specific processes and the specialized skill, that are essential to a painter or a sculptor, and little sympathy or feeling for finished works of plastic or graphic art. The æsthetic surface in all these arts is obviously visual; the arts themselves differ, as being modelling or painting or drawing or planning and designing buildings for given uses.

So we have other classifications not based on the nature of the sensuous elements of the surface content, but upon the purposes in view in making the objects or upon the processes used. There are the arts of carving, etching, drawing, painting, the arts of verse and prose, the arts of rug-weaving and basket-making, of singing and dancing, all the thousand ways in which men employ special processes, special tools, and special media for making or doing particular sorts of things. Such a classification is almost useless, however, because instead of classifying it merely lists or names the arts, each separately, by the name of the technical means and the specific medium employed, or of the end in view.

Then there is the division into the representative arts and the directly expressive, a classification that has no place for architecture at all, and one that falsifies the nature of painting and sculpture only a little more obviously than it falsifies the nature of music and poetry. For though most of the point of painting and sculpture is obviously lost if we leave out the strictly æsthetic surface and think only of copying models, it is almost equally obvious that music and poetry may use direct imitative representation in some of their effects. Spatial and temporal arts may be distinguished, but here again we have the same weaknesses and discrepancies of classification as in the case of visual and auditory as a division, with some slight modifications; for what is in space may move also rhythmically in time, and the classification is neither inclusive of all the arts nor does it draw any clear line between one and another except in a few cases. If we turn to graphic and plastic as against linguistic, we have difficulties again, too evident to need illustration, and it would seem that none of the ordinary classifications is especially illuminating, except in drawing attention to the full nature of the various arts by its very inadequacy. If some of them have a genuine basis in the kind of sense elements mainly involved in certain arts and so characterizing these and grouping them together, or in the types of structure available for certain sensuous media as contrasted with the kinds of structural order available for other sensuous media, the list we always come back to is quite clearly not determined on these æsthetic principles and not a classification at all in any rigorous sense. That is, the recognized and familiarly differing arts do not differ solely or even primarily according to the æsthetic character of their elements or even of their structure, but more fundamentally in the purposes for which their objects are created or the modes and tools and media of such creation. Characteristic media and technique help at least as much to define the specific character of any art as does the nature of the sensuous elements or that of the structural principles mainly involved. But in defining particular arts they still fail to classify the arts in general, and as we shall see later, any classification fails in the end for the simple reason that beauties are not things and therefore do not fall into classes of things.

§ 3

It is clear, however, that for some of the arts a classification on strictly æsthetic principles more adequately indicates the character of the art itself than for others. Thus the art of sound, the auditory art, the temporal art *par excellence*, is music; and so far as poetry is classed as an auditory art, an art of sound, an art of temporal structure, we actually speak of its musical qualities. It is obviously in music proper that a completely satisfactory æsthetic auditory surface is perfect art. But this is not at all the case with poetry. Not even the beauty of poetry is mainly auditory; for poetry, being intelligible language after all, intends to function as all language functions, not merely to produce an æsthetically satisfying surface for the ear, subtle and important as that sounding surface is in heightening its value and even in defining it as verse, and absorbing as this surface is to some artists, whose practice tries to make patterned syllables the whole content of poetic art. If it is sweet syllables that poetry discourses, poetry is still symbolic linguistic discourse; its syllables carry meaning and reference.

Between these extremes lie the other arts. It has become fashionable in modern discussion and criticism to discount entirely from the value of drawings and paintings and sculpture their representative intent; but how false this is to the nature of the graphic and plastic arts, both with respect to their origin and with respect to the nature of their æsthetic effect, is too palpable to need more, to reveal its falseness, than a little attention to the meaning of such a subtraction made in the interest of æsthetic purism, and to the concrete works of the recognized masters and models of this esoteric cult.

So far as the cult is merely stressing the fact that the rigorously æsthetic content of such works of art is strictly a matter of spatial shapes and relations and structural form, of color combinations and of texture, it is not to be disregarded, much less condemned, as our previous discussion must have shown. It is only its exclusion of everything but æsthetic surface in terms of structural and sensuous elements and their intrinsic expressiveness that is false. For abstractly and obviously it is clear enough that even when the most enlightened artist, working for purely æsthetic effect in terms of sensuous and formal beauty of surface, uses familiar natural forms, no matter how modified or even distorted, as in the manner of so-called primitivism, these forms are those given in nature and necessarily recognized as such by any innocent eyes that see them on canvas or in marble. And in adhering to even the faintest resemblance to forms familiar in nature, an artist is using not merely the recognizable principles of design and color combination, but also forms or types that occur naturally and inexplicably, and hence in accordance with no known æsthetic principles, no principles that the artist could possibly be acquainted with, since they have not become explicit to men's knowledge.

In other words, whether representation is his aim or not, and no matter how little conscious he may be of it, no matter how fully his æsthetic conscience may have freed him from such childish obligations, he is using in his design itself forms in shape and color that have been given him by nature to appropriate; and no one, if the artist has really appropriated these in his work, can be required not to recognize them as the representations that they are. What, after all, either of sensuous elements or structural forms, is to be found even in the imagination of a genius that has not been given him through nature? Not that he merely copies what faces him —a flat impossibility in any full literal sense—but that all the form and content at his disposal has been offered him in the life, and on nature's surface, whether it now issues directly from his own imagination or not. And if he uses not the barest sensuous elements only, but actually seen forms, human bodies, tree trunks, rocks, leaves, vine-stems, shadows, and textures of walls or floors or fabrics, he is in doing so representing these forms, which other eyes will recognize and take pleasure in as the forms they know and enjoy in nature, or in ordinary practical living. The beauty of his composition will not lie in the exactitude of the representation, and it may lie very little even in the represented elements he employs, but to say that none of the artistic value of his work is representative is thoughtless and exaggerated or else plainly fatuous.

But more than this. For human beings, as Aristotle noted, imitation or representation is itself a delight, infantile perhaps, but no less truly delightful for that. And to attempt to free art of some of its delight, in order to keep it purely æsthetic, is a new kind of fanatical asceticism no more to be respected as reasonable or sane than more ancient and familiar kinds, though we must remember that any such ascetic cult is likely to indicate some genuinely significant motive towards the achievement of value and its proper appreciation, as we have seen that the present striving for purely formal significance certainly does. Both the rigorous use of naturally occurring shapes and even types, and the effect upon appreciating eyes of the recognition of represented forms and colored surfaces, is plain in the works of Cézanne, who is so regularly approved or even worshipped by the votaries of this æsthetically purist cult, a cult by which Cézanne himself was little troubled, being as he was a painter, not an advocate. In his water-colors, for example, he sometimes represents trees and foliage. True, he does not represent details that the eye can not even discern at its normal distance from such objects, in an attempt to copy all the features of a tree. What he does represent, however, not with lines, but with color masses in his own patiently achieved mastery of a rare technique, is three-dimensional solid trunks of trees, with green branches visibly, and either lightly or heavily, hanging upon them. And this is not purely abstract design at all, but the representation of one specific beauty, clearly felt and grasped, a beauty after all of familiar objects and scenes, but made strange and lovely and vivid because here a gifted eye has taken it away from the distracting details of context in which for most eyes it is effectively befogged and lost as beauty.

Moreover, the great distinction of this painter, as is often forgotten even by other painters in their praise of him, is that the gifted hand, practised in an original and effective technique, has been able by an almost direct representation of the artist's equally rare vision, to communicate to even the layman's eye, by the use of color masses alone, the special beauty that was not only discovered by the artist but given by him to the rest of men. It is this new skill of his that is so often the real cause of the reverence he is paid by other artists and by discerning critics, a skill not so interesting to the rest of the world except in its achieved results. Here again technique forces itself upon us as of the very defining nature not only of the arts, but of their æsthetically felt character, and we shall turn in a moment to a fuller account of this. For the present we are noticing only that visual arts, instead of being merely beautiful as seen surfaces of color and form, gain much of their character and their felt value from being partly representative and thus approaching the linguistic, symbolic nature of poetry in one direction as well as the æsthetic purity of music in the other. It is not only that the recognized imitation or representation of natural objects or forms or even types gives immediately felt pleasure which is not the strict æsthetic pleasure of the surface content of color combination and spatial structure alone, but that the details of line and shape, the fine shadings and arrangements of colors are themselves largely derivative from surfaces offered in nature to the artist's eye, their beauty as elements being therefore rather natural than artistic, and lying in their meaning or reference as much as in their intrinsic æsthetic form. If they are felt as beautiful, who is so informed as to know that this beauty is not partly a matter of habit, and that they are not so felt because practice in habits of perception has taught us to grasp such elements easily as wholes or parts, and hence to be able to dwell on them with satisfaction when an artist represents them to us, whether intentionally or unintentionally, whether aware of their natural sources or not, when he employs them as the materials or the structural forms of his compositions?

If one is unconvinced by all this simple direct feeling, or by the works of the most admired masters of the enemies of representation as an integral and important aspect of the beauty of the plastic and the graphic arts, one is faced with other problems to solve. If one is to support the doctrine of pure design as total artistic value, one must give an account of portraiture, for example. Portraiture is representative by definition, but surely it is still an art. Portraits are not mere abstract designs in shape and color, no matter how consciously and intentionally and successfully they may be designed for direct æsthetic effect. It is true that they are not photographs either, and that they usually fail as portraits if they try to be just that, much more if they succeed in it. But if an artist employs a sufficiently subtle camera instead of paint and brushes, there is no possible *a priori* reason why this tool, the function of which as a tool is representation, should not some day be part of the technical paraphernalia of the fine arts. There is nothing intrinsically spiritual in charcoal and paint-brushes, palettes and stretched canvases, red-lead and ochre and oil, to make them superior to lenses and shutters and gelatine-coated films. And there is no reason in the nature of things why subjects before a camera may not have expended upon them the whole power and skill of a great artist, or why, for the preservation of his vision of them, a camera of sufficient delicacy and contrivance might not be the best means. That photographers are commoner than artists is perfectly true; that photographs often neither select nor arrange their subjects so as to reproduce on their flat surfaces the beautiful aspects of nature and life that only a gifted mind either sees or imagines or selects for seeing, is only to say that often photographs are not works of art. But in any eulogistic sense most paintings and drawings also fail to be works of art. And to suppose that the degree of mechanical complication of tools prevents their full domination and control by a great artist is to overestimate tools and to underestimate artists. Paint-brushes and pencils are mechanisms, and canvas and paint are as artificially manufactured as films or other photographic supplies. For art the question is to use them as means to artistic ends, and since representation is one of these, the camera and photography in general can certainly not be ruled out on any known principles of æsthetics, unless, of course, one makes the false assumption that the perfection of photography consists in literal copying regardless of what it copies, which is absurdly to identify that which constitutes the mechanical perfection of a tool with what constitutes the successful use of it for a given purpose.

At least it must be admitted that in sculpture and painting, whether or not one allows the camera as a proper artist's tool, representation of what an artist finds significant or beautiful in a human being, whether general appearance, or grace, or subtle modellings, or indications of character or wisdom or personality, or costume worn with style, or exquisite texture of skin, or distinction of feature, or nobility of bearing, or degeneration, or despair,—adequate representation of such aspects as the artist discerns and finds satisfying to contemplate is a great part of his art as a portrait painter or modeller; and there is not yet a school of critics to refuse acknowledgment of such success in representation as being artistic success. In portraiture both painting and sculpture achieve their ends in representation, and this effectiveness in representation, instead of sensuous and structural beauty solely, counts as artistic value.

One or two other difficulties in the way of denying the artistic value of representation ought to be mentioned here, perhaps, to reassure the doubtful. If design in color and shape were the whole of the beauty of painting, why should the projected moving patterns of the color-organ not give us the same kind of effect that we get from the graphic arts themselves? The movement is a difference, of course; but even arrested, these color projections have a very different sort of effect from that of paintings. And no one is likely to insist that patterned textiles or rugs, with velvet or silken texture, give us the same sort of effect as paintings. It is not a question of which is finer; that depends on the particular objects, and certainly a fine rug may be infinitely more beautiful than many a commonplace painting on canvas. Our point is that the æsthetic surface, including texture, design, and color, is not the whole and often is not even the most essential constituent of the value of paintings, whereas in works of pure design and color it is. And rugs themselves, if they are particularly distinguished, do not succeed in being fine rugs merely through the æsthetic surface of their sensuous and structural beauty. To the eye of the artist weaver, while design and color are of the greatest importance, the whole takes on value also from the fineness and regularity of the warp and woof, the closeness of the texture of knots, and the quality of the dyes. And the designs, while they are not quite linguistic in symbolic reference—though some-times, of course, actual lettered texts form parts of them—are full of religious and mystical indications, and hence al-most like poetry in their imaginative suggestiveness and the significant character of their appearance. For one who finds the only value of the graphic and the plastic arts in their æsthetic surface, or, as is often said, in their pure design, the very great differences, in their characteristic successful effects, among designs projected from a color-organ on a white screen, designs in paint on canvas, designs in rugs and tapestries and textiles, and designs copied from nature by the lens of a camera, must be accounted for in the terms of textures, lines, shapes, space-relations, and colors; and to carry out such a view would give strangely repugnant con-clusions in the face of familiar experiences. No artist draws lines more subtle or more moving or more powerful than those a camera may copy from nature, or from the artist's own work; no design in pigment on canvas is altogether im-possible for tapestry; and for pure design itself, with no representative element at all, the color-organ is far richer than many great paintings, with which no one would even compare its effects as artistic achievement.

These suggestions may be enough to make it clear that æsthetic surface is not the vital whole of the beauty of even objects of fine art, much less their complete nature and sig-nificance, and further that the arts vary greatly in the degree to which their artistic value is constituted by, or related to, the sensuous and formal aspects of their strictly æsthetic character.

If we list the arts roughly as music, poetry, painting, sculpture, and architecture, our second main contention in the present chapter is now fairly clear, viz., that in the appreciation of the fine arts, while objects of some of these arts are valued in direct proportion to the value for immediate intuition of their æsthetic surfaces, objects of most of them are not. The degree to which artistic value gains or loses with gain or loss of beauty of æsthetic surface varies from one art to another. In music perfection of the sounding surface is perfection of the music. In poetry, the sounding surface, important as it is, is only a comparatively slight, though essential, aspect of the beauty of even the verse as such. The other arts lie somewhere between these two extremes. Architecture, considered as æsthetic surface, as seen masses of color and shape, has the perfection only of its visual content and structure; and it will be granted that these do not name or even suggest its full character, much less its specifically architectural beauty and perfection. In the plastic arts, and in painting and drawing, representation, which is not mere sensuous surface or the structural design of this surface, plays so important a rôle that here again the æsthetic surface is only a part of the success or perfection of these arts, though fitness to human uses is not, as it is in architecture, an important or even relevant consideration. And while the art of poetry makes no demands like those of architecture and is only to a very slight degree directly representative even of sounds—onomatopœia is of course the extreme case of this, though certainly not the only case—poetry is engaged in employing a linguistic, referential medium, and its perfection and success lie in such control of this medium as succeeds in making meanings themselves beautiful, so that the æsthetic surface of the verse as audible sensuous content plays a distinctly minor, though no doubt absolutely essential, rôle.

§ 4

And poetry is as good an illustration as we could find of our third main contention here, namely, that both the arts themselves and particular works of art, are defined in terms of their technique, which, sharing in their essential nature, is also in part their very beauty for appreciation and enjoyment, not merely the condition or means of their production, but definitive of their form and structure and nature, and therefore a main term in the situation in which their beauty is manifest to the other main term conditioning the occurrence of beauty, that is, a human mind in contemplation of its æsthetic object.

This has been suggested already, and a few examples will make it clear. But the point can be made out easily enough on general grounds, so far as it is simply the principle that the defining nature of the various arts is in part a matter of technique; for the arts are naturally enough defined, even as a matter of correct usage recorded in dictionaries, altogether in terms of certain sorts of operations upon certain objects or materials directed by certain aims, always conceived as the production of finished objects or materials of certain forms or structures, which not only serve present purposes, but define and preserve for man's knowledge and for his civilized life the technical functions and processes which these objects externalize and embody. And as the industrial arts thus preserve useful techniques, so of the fine arts. Without the actual physical violins and bows of the Cremona masters of the early eighteenth century to serve both as instruments and as models for other instruments, the technique of producing music from stringed contrivances could not

ÆSTHETIC JUDGMENT

have developed as it did, nor could the actual musical literature of the next two centuries have taken the forms we now
have in the great musical classics.

Or consider the art of poetry as a technique. If language
is confined to the medium of words in intelligible discourse,
then so far as poetry is intelligible at all, it is an art depending for its structure and its significance upon the purely
technical control of this linguistic medium: upon breadth
and accuracy of vocabulary, an expert acquaintance with the
subtle possibilities of phrasing and sentence structure, with
the means of achieving lucidity and unity in composition.
And since these basic requirements of all intelligible discourse are not enough to give the special auditory character
of verse, the composer of poetry must also have an ear not
only instinctively fine and even gifted, but acquainted,
through long practice and intense attention to the sound
qualities of language, with the possibilities for such rhythmical arrangements as will not destroy the significance or
offend the fundamental conventions upon which the intelligibility of discourse in words rests. The poet's ears must
be attuned by reading and practice not only to the specific
denotative shades of meaning, the emotional connotations
and associated images of words and phrases, and even whole
contexts, but to all the specifically auditory or even musical
effects possible to syllables as such, rhyme and assonance, and
various other felt agreements and harmonies, contrasts and
stresses through sensuous means, without which verse fails
of its achievement as a content for the ear in a rhythmical
continuity.

Since we all learn the mechanical, technical uniformities
of pronouncing words and phrases, and of spelling and punctuation and sentence structure, by a long process in early life,

and since we are all taught to read and thus given some acquaintance with linguistic technique as practised by our forbears, so that this technique becomes available largely without consciously directed formal technical training or effort in the habitual talking and writing and reading of every day of our lives for years, we are likely to forget that the technique itself is one of the most difficult and elaborate of any of the arts. The same amount of training in music or painting would make us all equally at home in those arts, and we should not need to learn scale-structure and musical phrasing and the ordinary notation and forms of musical composition late in life as a special sort of "art education," and so fail to appropriate it all as habitual, and think for example of singing from printed music as a rather exceptional, special, or even esoteric accomplishment.

On the other hand language, which is so universally practised in forms of a high degree of structural elaboration, with subtleties of inflection and phrasing learned in infancy, enters with all this complexity into the most ordinary conversations of every day. Hence it becomes stereotyped to such an extent that even slight variations in the interest of brevity, emphasis, accuracy, delicacy of meaning, and those further variations and modifications of accent, order, and arrangement that mark verse as beautiful to the ear, are likely to seem false or offensive. The poet must have not only linguistic skill and a fine ear to control his technical medium to his ends, but such genuine and necessary and powerfully felt significant content to convey, that this modifies and supports the medium that carries it to the ear, to a degree that makes the verse sheer creation of new words and phrases and structures in a new beauty. It is only at this point that we come upon great poetry itself. But however striking and significant, however ravishing or rhythmical, however immediate and compulsive, however lucid and stirring poetry may be, its very character as art is felt as the special nature of the medium itself, the poet's technique becoming externalized in the verse he writes as its effective artistic character and point, as well as its specific individual quality and beauty.

No general statement either as to the auditory surface of poetry or as to its significant content can do more than barely suggest the part that technique plays both in the creation and in the finished form and defining nature of poetry as an art. The numberless works on composition and verse forms and literary criticism are taken up very largely with just this matter. But leaving all the detail aside, it must be clear that if we sometimes forget the all-important and portentously elaborate technique of poetry as entering into its felt quality as art, it can only be because so much of technical linguistic equipment is the common and habitually employed possession of all men who can speak or read or write, that poets seem only to be refining a little on natural processes, instead of carrying on into a sort of magic region, and further developing, or newly creating, a highly technical artificial process such as distinguishes any art as art.

Thus we have noticed both the sense in which the art of poetry may be defined in terms of its technique, and also the sense in which this technique constitutes in part the specific value of any poetical composition, in being directly felt as its particular nature. And since this technique itself is not concerned merely with sensuous and formal æsthetic surface, but with symbolic linguistic elements that have their significance in what they refer to, namely images and feelings and emotions and events and objects, denoted or suggested forcefully or delicately, it must be clear that the beauty of great poetry is only to a slight degree the beauty of its sensuous and formal surface for the ear, unless of course we are to confine the word beauty to sensuous and formal æsthetic quality.

Such a narrowing of the meaning of beauty will appear still more unwarranted when we turn to the beauty of expression as such, which is the value neither of sensuous æsthetic surface nor that of technical artistic perfection of achievement. In fact, at the present point in our discussion we are almost in a position to see that, whereas the arts in general are fundamentally types of technical operation, eventuating in objects or works of art so-called, in the fine arts two further elements are involved. For in the fine arts, as distinguished from the industrial arts or arts as any directed process of giving definite form or constitution to materials, physical bodies or merely sensuous elements—in the fine arts æsthetic satisfactoriness of the appearing surface is a necessary condition of artistic success, though not a sufficient one, since, as we have just seen, the rôle it plays varies in importance with the various arts. And besides achieving æsthetic surface, the fine arts are invariably expressive. In just what sense we shall make out at the end of the present chapter. But before doing so we should perhaps illustrate in arts other than poetry our present point as to the defining function of technique in the arts in general.

Nowhere has technical virtuosity been more abused either by brilliant performers who give their whole powers to exhibiting it or by critics who sometimes mistake it for virtue and sometimes condemn it as the worst of all vices, than in music. Violinists, pianists, vocalists are often simply extensions or embodiments of their instrument, adding the needed motive-power for actual performance, and training their bodies into a marvellous integration in the mechanical process which this instrument, natural or artificial, is capable of carrying out. Their total ambition lies in exploiting its possibilities, whether by composing for it, or performing upon it, or both; and they may find it convenient in the interest of a smooth and elaborate perfection of instrumental operation not only to neglect or suppress the expressive significance of a composition, but even to abandon any but the most obvious elements of the æsthetic auditory surface, in a brilliant swiftness and power of execution that is a marvel of highly efficient, if artistically fruitless or empty, operation.

But if the dangers and offensiveness of virtuosity are so thoroughly appreciated by those who love the arts and their beauties, the indispensableness of a mastery of technique is, especially by the more tender lovers of beauty in the arts, whether of sensuous surface or of expressive significance, only too likely to be scorned in an ignorance not always quite ingenuous. For one who really rules out technique as such, rules out all artistic operation, whether creative in the highest sense or merely decorative or even trifling. One can not make or compose anything whatever of any sort without going through the process of doing so. As spirit is revealed only in bodies, so beauty can appear only upon the objects or events of the physical world, and any beauty of art, not merely of nature, must supervene upon actual operations, which being operations at all are therefore, as practised in any given way whatever, particular techniques, crude or refined, swift or slow, efficient or inefficient, good or bad. To say that all technique as such is bad for true art is pure nonsense, since art occurs at all only by virtue of the technique which is its creation. There is no need of stressing further the obvious generalities that technical virtuosity is not the whole of art, and may even destroy the beauty of its æsthetic surface and ruin the specific character of its expression, and that technique is a necessary condition of the existence of all works of art, and therefore of all the objects of all the fine arts. What we need to do here is to give cases in point.

Take singing, an art so close to nature that its technical equipment and its execution as a practised art might almost seem alien to its own native quality, that of the spirit bursting forth in a song which is its own natural gladness or sorrow, uncontaminated by instrumental mechanisms, and immediately expressive without the intervention of the technical traditions of musical training or the forms of musical art. How æsthetically successful such spontaneous art is, may be heard in the raucous screams or brazen shouts of children at play, or infants in distress, in the cries of men and women suddenly overtaken by danger or great good fortune, adults in the grip of a sudden accident or unconsciously venting their feelings of exultation or excitement at a ball-game or a prize-fight. There is expressiveness here no doubt in all its primal force, but not art with its æsthetically satisfying surface for sense. Even the technique of college yells is more truly art than unconscious and spontaneous shouting. If expression takes on a form here that actually falsifies and blurs the emotions in conventionalizing their expression in the simplest sort of form, this is not an argument against technical form itself, which of course to be adequate to any genuine human feeling, must be subtle and rich and varied enough to be in some suggestive relation to the emotions it embodies and formalizes for perception from without. And as to the necessity for physical apparatus in art, it must be clear that vocal organs of some sort are an absolute condition of singing at all, and vocal organs that are powerful and flexible, a condition of singing effectively in large rooms, and with a sufficient range of pitch to embody the patterns in pitch that are music. Accuracy of intonation and flexibility may be in large part acquired, no doubt; but without vocal organs of the proper dimensions to produce sounds of sufficient loudness to be heard with instruments, one can not be a concert singer, no matter how genuinely one's spirit may long to externalize itself in the sound patterns of vocal music. Furthermore, without vocal organs of certain specific shapes, the sounds of one's voice must simply fail to be pleasant to any ear. The most natural of the arts thus requires very definitely conditioned physical paraphernalia to be beautiful in even the simplest beauty. And it must be equally obvious that to one without either extraordinary gifts or extensive training of auditory perception, none of the more complex reaches of musical expression are even possible of apprehension, much less of full appreciation or of creation.

Without full and familiar acquaintance with the technique of an art, it is the merest pretense that pronounces any judgment whatever on the works of that art; for such judgment is meaningless except as a record of genuine experience, and one actually does not experience any work of art unless one is sufficiently practised in its technique to discriminate its structural and sensuous surface as of the specific nature embodied by that technique in a given application of it. One who actually fails to distinguish minor thirds from majors, or the various melodic intervals from each other—not that he must know their names, of course, but that he must recognize their specific sounds—can not possibly discriminate either the melodic or the harmonic patterns of music that he hears. He does not in fact hear the actual music at all, but is perhaps vaguely pleased or bored by a confused sensuous experience, which no doubt sets up much non-auditory feeling and imagery and even ideation. To the ear trained to listen, and to hear the actual technical structure presented, neither the confusion nor the irrelevant feeling and imagery and ideas are present. For this ear takes in an actually and objectively defined structure of sound, and this sensuous structural content itself demands full and active powers of attention which are absorbed in discriminating its details in their coherent connection, and so in receiving from it its own specification of feeling and emotion, which is not merely relevant but specifically and uniquely and unambiguously expressive. There is no "interpretation" of music as such, except just that minutely specified feeling and emotion that is summoned and sustained by sounds in definite succession and combination, striking upon an ear capable of hearing them when it listens. And the complexity of these musical forms and patterns and movements is so great that a thorough grasp of the intellectually comprehensible technique of musical notation and musical form, to be gained only by a training more or less parallel to linguistic training in its own field, is an almost indispensable condition of hearing them as the sound structures that they are. Thus the technical musical forms are themselves what the mind hears through the ear, and they define even the auditory æsthetic surface enjoyed as beautiful.

But music is doubly technical in that the art requires not only sound structures as such but the instruments that produce these sounds. And the specific beauty of piano music, for example, while it is in part the timbre of the instrument itself, also varies and defines itself in the operations of performing it. Thus a smooth, heavy, rapid *legato* passage is not a sensuous content for the ear alone, but for one who has mastered, or tried to master, the technique which produces such a passage, also the revelation through the specific sound qualities, a revelation upon the æsthetic surface itself, of that specific skill in performance. The performer's muscular mastery is thus heard through sounds by the ear of any body or mind whose own arms and fingers possess it and so recognize it in its functioning.

And this is equally true of the plastic arts. Swiftness of stroke, subtlety of line, a very small number of brush movements to give the exact effect of hair on a head or expression on a face, modelling that makes depths and shadows and high-lights and beautiful textures, come to the eye as not only the sensuous elements of color and shape and line, but also as the skill and expertness of the technique of the art that exhibits its specific nature and beauty.

In architecture, where we all respect a particular technique to the point of making architect the name of a respectable professional calling, its practice compensated in substantial and more or less standardized fees, technical expertness, with which most of us who are not architects are not familiarly acquainted, since we are not professionally trained, is so fundamentally important that we are at least somewhat reticent in our judgments of anything but mere surface appearance or actual social convenience and fitness. We feel clearly the presence in buildings of a structural technique of stresses and strains and sub-masses and inner proportions, which leaves us rather wondering and admiring vaguely, and acknowledging our lack of such acquaintance with the art as would allow us to see its true virtues or defects in what is presented to our untutored eyes. There can hardly be any doubt, however, that part of the architectural success of a high tower is felt, on our seeing it, to be the technical achievement of its stability on its foundations, a stability which is also outwardly expressed. And part of the beauty of a bridge is the technical achievement that allows us to walk over the waters in a security realized as the product of the skill that is expressed in its very form. Not that the formal sensuous structure of lines and masses for the eye alone is negligible in the least, but that it is enriched for discriminating perception not only by salient ornament and accent but by the felt skill of the technical architectural construction.

§ 5

If what produces the actuality of works of art, what brings them into being as objective structures, as well as lending them much of their specific differentiating beauties, is technique, what gives vitality and interest to their beauty is still another aspect of them, intimately bound up with their conceived aims and purposes for human minds—their expressiveness. A work of art may have a lovely sensuous æsthetic surface as form and structure for direct intuition, and reveal in this structure the technical nature of the processes that have produced it; but if it is a work of the human spirit, a work of art functions also in expressing that spirit's feelings and emotions of desire and satisfaction. The beauty of poetry is clearly dependent for its depth and power on this function that it performs. But this expressive functioning does not take place through linguistic symbolism alone, which is common to verse and the least artistic prose discourse, but also through its whole artistic character, including its strictly æsthetic surface, which by means of sounds and rhythms is a verbal and auditory specification of the exact emotional effect that it embodies and thus expresses. And the vitality and life of art and of its æsthetic surface depend almost wholly upon this expressiveness.

If the "significant form" of modern critics has any meaning, this is it. That is, the form of the object or the composition carries by its arrangement and order, its subtleties and complexities of balance, rhythm, harmony, contrast, by all the specific variation and combination of the elements of its particular sensuous medium achieved in any given case, the precise specification, for discriminating attention, of human feeling, so far as human feeling is capable of specification in sensuous form at all. For of course language as such is not rich enough in formal possibilities, nor accurate and detailed enough in variations of denotation, to be able always to name human feelings unambiguously, or otherwise to indicate them. Language as such is not adequate to the infinite fluctuations of their volume and intensity and scope or of subtle and delicate nuance, or to their variety, running from high hope to despair, from passionate love to hate, with all the possible combinations and mixtures. Much more nearly accurate in expression is poetry, with its vastly greater range and detail in specific shades of meaning, accomplished by its greater tonal and rhythmical possibilities. And of all the arts, perhaps music is in the matter of emotional expressiveness the deepest and richest, of the widest range and greatest power, as well as the most flexible and most delicately precise.

But supremacies in one direction or another are not our concern, and they vary no doubt enormously from one person to another. What we need to notice, and what requires the greatest emphasis, is the precise sense in which art is expressive at all, and, for a first example, the sense in which music is expressive, not of course through the words of a song or the dramatic action of an opera, nor through representation of bird calls or thunderstorms; for none of these is determined in form and structure by the intrinsic possibilities of patterns made of variations and combinations, varying also in degrees of loudness and quality of timbre, of sounds of distinct pitch, the patterns spread out rhythmically in temporal order. If music is itself expressive, without any symbolic aid from words or any associated natural sounds that it imitates, or any accompanying significant bodily movements or gestures, then it is because through an arrangement of sounds as such express meaning and significance can come to the mind. To any one who has ever listened fully to music and heard it, any passage of any composition furnishes a perfectly adequate illustration. If the general character of what is expressed in light, rapid runs on the piano is at least not a specification through sound of funeral gloom, so any case of any specific figure, as in a definite tempo and rhythm itself, and in a definite musical context, is the much more accurate rendering, as we say badly but suggestively, of the meaning of the music. The passage expresses that which it does express simply by specifying, to the alert and listening mind, that precise, sensuous, rhythmical, auditory pattern that is directly received as the nature or pattern of a human feeling or emotion, now clearly defined in sound through the ear to the mind.

No one who has not listened and heard can be presented in words with such unique and specified expression. Music can not be translated. It is never just fear or hope or exultation or love, but that precise sensuous structure of passion given in the sounding medium. As music may be solemn or gay, or rhapsodic or triumphant, so obviously enough any particular music expresses in its own particular degree, and in its absolutely determinate pattern and fullness, just that precise, determinate feeling that is externalized in its determinate form and filling of sound. Beauty of expression in general is not our present concern, however. We are only indicating at this point that fine art, in order to be such at all, is expressive, and the case of music is one of the most obvious examples of this. If a composer has no emotions to express, no vital feelings to externalize in sound, the best that he can do is to repeat more or less conventional or banal patterns, and though these may well have a smooth and even charming surface, like a violin concerto by Spohr, they remain rather æsthetic tricks and trifles than significant art, no matter how learned the musician, or how conventionally perfect his technique. For of music, as of poetry, it is always a fresh creation of form, a transmutation of the medium, that is required, if the resulting structure is to be vital or significant, if it is not to remain dead and empty sound, specifying to the ear nothing of felt significance, failing, that is, to be genuinely expressive.

Music expresses the will and the passions of human beings, feelings and emotions being its burden in a variety and precision not possible to words. Poetry expresses, though never so precisely nor with such fine and still distinct degrees of variation or nuance, a much wider range of interests and ideas, which can be denoted by words, or summoned by the musical qualities of verse, or suggested in imagery for all the senses. So color and shape and rhythm as such have also their expressiveness, not only through representation, but again, like music, in those particular sensuous kinds of specification that they are capable of, namely, those of design and color and texture and rhythmic pattern.

If the line of a hill may seem noble and strong and restful, not even pure design is inexpressive, though just how and why certain masses and shapes and configurations become significant no one has fully explained. Certain it is that the color-organ itself, even as at present constituted, stirs us to unexpected depths; and drawings and paintings and sculpture externalize to our view yearnings and meanings, and seem somehow to make immediately present to sense the attributes and ideas, and even the fundamental significance, of the universe and of human destiny. It is not safe to say much more, if there is more that could be said. But that the arts express deeply and broadly, but always determinately and uniquely, the very point of life, that they are the most precisely drawn lineaments of men's souls that we know, can not of course be questioned. To despise them totally, or to deny their expressive significance, is sheer brutality or ignorance. But especially in intellectual persons there is a tendency to minimize their precision and uniqueness of specification in expression. And this will not be overcome, of course, until men cultivate accuracy and skill in sensuous perception itself, and sound technical training in at least one of the particular arts, instead of feeding their souls so exclusively upon those ranges of experience that can be recorded in the linguistic symbolism of ordinary prose. A still further limitation or degeneracy of mind is that which deals in these linguistic symbols alone, failing to recognize through them those ultimate sensuous data or essences, to refer to which they were invented, and which are themselves the only targets that the shafts of discourse can actually hit.

In the consideration of beauty of expression, which has so far been mentioned only to define the arts and so to distinguish their nature, their function, and their beauty from that one aspect of them which is their æsthetic surface we reach an essential aspect of their fineness. Possession of æsthetic surface is the condition of their being of the nature of fine art; but this surface is not definitive of the nature or function of art in general, which is more adequately made out in terms of a technique. The technique is applied to a medium for the satisfaction of men's wants, and the creative products of technique become *fine* art as their æsthetic surface becomes satisfying to contemplation, and they themselves expressive through this surface. We turn now from the beauty of material sensuous elements and the beauty of the forms and structures into which these elements may be built, from such beauties achieved either in nature or by technical artistic creation, to the beauty of expressiveness itself.

CHAPTER XI

EXPRESSION IN THE FINE ARTS

1. Summary outline of preceding considerations; two meanings of æsthetic distinguished and justified. 2. The expressiveness of language and expression in poetry. 3. Expression in music through primary and secondary techniques. 4. Expression in painting and in sculpture. 5. Expression in architecture.

§ 1

BEFORE we embark upon the difficult subject of the beauty of expressiveness, or beauty as expression, or, still more strictly, the aspect of beauty that is constituted of the expressiveness of works of fine art, it is best perhaps to put our preceding statements into some degree of order in brief compass. We began by noticing that the æsthetic judgment, *this or that is beautiful,* records first of all the pleasant experience of contemplating the surface of our world simply for itself as the object before us, and, in thus discriminating the specific content present to our minds through the senses, finding its determinate beauties lying before us to enjoy. We also found that such beauties vary not only as content for ear or eye or taste or smell or feeling itself, but that in the sensuous content for ear or eye there are intrinsic qualitative orders, a serial range of pitches, a serial range of hues, defining the variations of the content and revealing principles of structure native to that content itself. We found further that, though in nature the æsthetic surface may be coherent to a degree and offer us, so to speak, naturally composed sensuous structures, these composed wholes are made in part of elements in the nature of which men have so far failed to discover any intrinsic ordering principles, so that human composing, while it may take over such naturally occurring forms and designs as interest it, must depend primarily upon principles of structure intrinsically present in the sensuous elements as such. And since men have before them the surface of the world for perception most vividly in the necessary tools and activities that are the means of living at all in nature, we noticed that it is upon such tools and such activities that beauty of surface is most naturally welcome, and comes to be sought and achieved in the fine arts of spatial form. But in the achievement of beauty, in the composing of beautiful surfaces, not only do we use the intrinsic orders embedded in the very nature of the sensuous elements, but also a temporal order, which, since any sense content to be present at all, must occur, and since time gives order to occurrences, is applicable to all contents, and, as felt through them, takes on a rhythm of occurrence, which is specially characteristic of such æsthetic surfaces as necessarily take an appreciable duration of time to deploy themselves before the senses, the surfaces experienced in music, dancing, acting, and poetry.

But here we have come upon the other main group of the fine arts, for when we compose consciously in either spatial or temporal structures or orders, we are artists. In the preceding chapter we noticed how beauty of æsthetic surface, while it does not define the arts as such and varies in the degree to which it is a measure of their perfection, is characteristic of all the arts called fine, though even the fine arts achieve success not merely as fulfilling intentions to produce beautiful æsthetic surfaces, but also as consciously directed technical operations. If the technique fails to produce fitting objects, these objects, however æsthetically satisfying the sensuous filling and structural form of their surface may be, fail to satisfy us or call forth unalloyed appreciation, fall short, that is, in beauty itself. But since fitness to use or conformity to familiar type is not beauty itself, it is clear that in the fine arts our aim is no longer merely practical. Since they are arts, technique, that is, applied to fulfilling intentions, some aim they must have after all, else no rational being would practise them. And since, as we have seen, the enjoyment of beauty is disinterested, this aim, so far as it can be æsthetically fulfilled, must be consummated upon an æsthetic surface, even though the beauty of that surface is not the whole aim. If, however, we are to keep clear the distinctive natures of the various arts—and this, as we have seen, can not be done in terms solely of the character of the æsthetic surface—we must find their definitions in the aim of their specific techniques. Thus apparently we must find this aim at once æsthetic and non-æsthetic, and we seem to be in a dilemma. But this difficulty is largely verbal and should be removed at once, for genuine differences in opinion and theory will give us trouble enough without adding the unnecessary confusions of ambiguous terminology.

We have used *æsthetic judgment* as meaning a judgment recording in first instance discriminated surface beauties as present to sense, and there is of course warrant for this in philosophical usage growing out of an employment of the term in its etymological signification. Æsthetic in this sense applies to what is present directly in intuition through the senses, and this is fairly indicated as sensuous surface, without regard to the beauty of such surface. But as we do characteristically find beauty here, and as in fact such surfaces are for intuition always either pleasurable or offensive, beautiful or ugly, the term æsthetic, as in the phrase æsthetic judgment, has been applied to all judgments pronouncing things beautiful in any determinate way, as attractive, charming, pleasing, for example, or as still more fully determinate and more accurately specified, not in language alone, but by the definite indication of an object pointed out in the field of perception by gesture, as having the uniquely beautiful character in question, an absolutely determinate and clearly delineated beautiful nature or quality. Hence we have used æsthetic judgment as a title for inquiries into the meaning of all such judgments of beauty or ugliness.

It is clear then that strictly surface beauty is not the full beauty of works of the fine arts or even of nature, since the surface of such objects is felt as revealing more and deeper beauty than that of this immediately present sensuous surface which is strictly called æsthetic. While this is not so plain in music, it is obvious enough in the other arts, and in music too at least the full analytical description of its specific beauties involves elements not merely sensuous or æsthetic in the narrower sense. Although it would be difficult if not impossible to keep to either of these meanings of the term æsthetic exclusively, our account so far has kept the term mainly to its thinner surface application, and until we came to the considerations of the preceding chapter, the inclusive sense of the term, as covering the whole subject matter of the beautiful was used only now and then, and without involving serious confusions. Even now when we have made out the sense in which beauty is not mere æsthetic surface, as is noticeably the case in the fine arts, which nevertheless must possess æsthetic surface in the narrow meaning, we shall not try to rule out æsthetic in its wider and deeper application. And this for the simple reason, noted previously in passing, that the bare sensuous surface, though it may be theoretically distinguished with perfect clarity—and the distinction is one of great importance—as that content which is immediately present to sense in a surface form or structure, is never present to sense alone. For senses are the avenues of intuition and perception, and it is the mind or the spirit to which any sensuous content must be present if it is to be present at all. That is, intuition and perception are single processes, involving both sense organs and the mind that uses these organs, and though we may speak of the bare sensuous surface present in intuition, this surface reveals to the mind or spirit that intuits it more than any merely sensuous elements in a unity of form. The surface, that is, must have a degree of depth to be seen or felt at all, and out of its depths comes much of what it exhibits as beauty.

It is thus clear that even as applied to the surface, the word æsthetic must include this surface quality as far down as it goes without being lost in such strictly intellectual constructions, and the grasp of such relations, as are not fully revealed upon it and hence not felt as its intrinsic objective quality, present to the mind through the avenues of sense. Where exactly this line is to be drawn we have no science to tell us. It remains for our present state of knowledge, and perhaps it must always remain, a boundary varying with the degree of the perspicacity of our sensuous perception and with a hundred other factors of training and endowment. But the two meanings of æsthetic, the thinner and the thicker, are not contradictory; if beauty is only skin-deep, that little depth may embody freshness or worn pallor, resilience or flaccidity, strength or weakness, vitality or the weariest exhaustion, youth or age, health or sickness, life or death. So the æsthetic surface holds up to view in its very form and content not only the sensuous elements as such in a structural coherence, but all that they or their structural form may summon of varied imagery immediately associated with them by the mind, all that they may reveal as technical perfection consummated in their form and texture, all that they may signify of ideas, through these elements and forms taken as transparent symbols, and all that they may express by direct and detailed specification, in sensuous media, of the passions, desires, and objective satisfactions of men. If the æsthetic surface is as such and at its thinnest only a sensuous delight, at its thickest and deepest it is the revelation in external and objective form of the last aspirations of men.

Thus the aim of each of the fine arts is that sort of expressiveness possible to its defining technique operating upon its own particular medium to produce structural wholes with necessarily sensuous surfaces; and this expressiveness consists in significant specification, the direct delineation of such elaborated and finished spatial and temporal configurations as make present to the mind its own passionate and vivid actuality, externalized in the objective determinate beauties of works of art. Our apparent dilemma is solved. The fine arts have an aim distinguished for each particular art by its medium and its technique, instead of being given in terms of the practical ends which help to define the useful arts; and this aim, namely expression, is the same in all of the fine arts, so that both terms of this designation have a clear meaning. Moreover, since this aim is accomplished and consummated upon a sensuous surface, it may properly be called æsthetic, though the adjective applies rather to the character of the surface than to the motive power that perfects it through an expressive technique. Since a particular technique may be defined, however, in terms of the kind of useful object that it is primarily employed to produce, part of the definition of a work even of *fine* art may be the name of a practically useful object. If the work turns out not to be such a useful object as the definition of the technique calls for, it is felt at once to fail, not so much of being æsthetically satisfying in the thin surface sense of the word æsthetic, as of being a work of art at all. Thus natural types and natural demands—human beings with two eyes, not one, a house that will keep out the weather—must often be conformed to, if we are to have works of fine art that are to be taken and felt as such. Merely fantastic objects, even of lovely forms, while they may be æsthetically adequate in a perfectly clear sense, are likely to fail as significant works of art.

As to the meaning of expression itself there are further confusions to be cleared away. Our overwhelming absorption in language as the vehicle of meaning, the limiting of our education so exclusively to words in books, often makes us forget that not even language can do more than refer to meanings. These meanings we are likely to take for granted as lying fully within the symbolic medium itself, and significance and knowledge as being necessarily given in words and sentences. But the least scrutiny of such a notion is enough to remind us not only that words are only approximately determinate even in their denotative reference and furthermore that they could not possibly be these meanings that they carry, but also that for further specification or determinateness in the definition of their meanings we must point finally to a case of what is meant, as embodied in an object of present perception. And here our final appeal is clearly enough to sensuous discrimination and intuition, the object of such discrimination being an articulated sensuous surface, which is thus the last word in the specification and definition of meaning as such. But for intuition such perceived surfaces possess their own specific beauty, and thus the discriminated beauties of nature and of art are meaning itself. What works of art express is simply the determinate beauty that they specify. How adequately expressive they are depends on the native physical possibilities of their medium, the perfection of the technique applied to it, and the vitality and power and skill of the artist intent upon the expression of the meaning he feels within and seeks to make explicit upon the surface of experience for the common view of all men.

The adequacy of this achieved expression depends further upon the powers of discriminating intuition in other men to grasp the meaning as externally specified. And here, at the best, expression never becomes absolutely precise and determinate, perfectly and completely specified, but is always felt to be just beyond, or within, or above,—aspired to but never reached, either by the artist or by those who contemplate his art. To suppose, however, that meanings are more clearly specified in words than in the actually present intuited sensuous surfaces of works of art, or still worse to suppose that what is really expressed in any art may be translated into perfectly explicit statements in words, is not only to miss most of the expressive beauty of any particular work of art and the character of the fine arts as such, but also to forget the special function of language, and of poetry and prose, which have expressive power not merely through the denotations of their words, but also through their sensuous character and their structural arrangement, their subtle condensations and expansions, their richness of emotional and imaginative connotation, their rhythmic feeling, their temporal rate and duration, their rapid transitions and returns, their whole discursive form and manner. The mere difference in the matter of avoiding ambiguity, and in accuracy of specification in general, between spoken and written discourse is enough to make the point clear. Not even the simplest prose narrative carries its full and precise emotional force to the mind unless the ear is functioning as well as the eye, and a reader who fails to feel with the writer will fail to produce for himself in his reading what was entrusted to the written symbols of discourse. Part of the specification they carried in the writer's mind will be lost, whether through the reader's fault or the author's inadequacy.

§ 2

In considering the beauty of expression we begin with the arts of language. But this is not because these arts alone are literally and unambiguously expressive by virtue of their linguistic medium; for linguistic denotation as such is never absolutely unambiguous, its more precise specification depending in the end always upon indicated sensuous content present to perception, such sensuous content as the non-linguistic arts deal with directly as their proper media of expression. We begin with the linguistic arts rather because in speech and in language in general the character of the sensuous medium is so slight an element of the beauty felt, because the beauty felt consists almost wholly in expressiveness. It is a beauty further below or above the presented sensuous surface than that of any of the other arts, a beauty often most highly appreciated by individuals or peoples least sensitive to the more direct surface beauties of sensuous content proper, or to the precision of significance in expression possible to the non-linguistic arts and in these non-linguistic arts more fully revealed upon their æsthetic surface as thus specifically significant, so that their artistic form is more directly expressive, even if more thinly.

If one were quite without sensitiveness to the expressiveness of the linguistic medium, any acquaintance with a foreign language would be enough to reveal it. The characteristic turns of phrase of a particular language, the feeling-tone and the emotional coloring of its very vocabulary, the qualities in things and people and life in general that it most fully and expertly carries in its own peculiar modes and fashions, and most clearly communicates, the traditional and conventional connotations of its words and phrases, through etymology and historical and contemporary usage, and its formal character, uniquely adapted to just such effects of elegance and grace or of simple and even child-like directness and warmth as fail of achievement in other languages, are, in this perfect untranslatableness, only a few of the more obvious evidences of the too easily forgotten fact that we have not even any way of measuring how much of what we take for simple denotation is, through feeling, association, habit, perception, social and individual convention, and training and character and temperament, a matter of specification not at all clearly or strictly linguistic in the more obviously symbolic sense, according to which words have specific meanings to be pointed to through other words, and finally through gesture, to indicate, as we say, exactly what they mean.

Many of these effects in expression itself appear very clearly upon the auditory surface of speech and might have been pointed out earlier as having to do primarily with the sensuous elements of sound. But they are not effects that come under the æsthetic principles of order as intrinsic to sound itself; they are very far from being purely tonal structures. And in much of even the conscious cultivation and refinement of speech the real character of its expressiveness is strangely neglected. Men, for example, being struck by some foreign elegance or refinement in pronouncing words and syllables, actually adopt these outer characteristics in their own speech, seeming to forget that in doing so on the one hand they risk the loss of native directness of communication with their fellows that a natural and homely use of voice and language gives, and on the other that even if they achieve this foreign accent perfectly, they can never control the unconscious expressiveness of tone of voice and emotional quality, which still, though now perhaps confusedly, manifest their inner selves so unmistakably to the discerning ear. A middle western American may perhaps do well to tone down such of his consonants and vowels as strike harshly on his own honest ear, out of simple courtesy to the ears of others. But to attempt deliberately an "English accent," even to achieve one to the point of absolute and indistinguishable perfection, remains at the best a histrionic success, strangely at odds with men's social hopes in a world where our deepest need is genuine self-expression and full communication with other men.

And in the realm of the histrionic itself the fundamentals here are likely to be neglected. An actor tells us often infinitely more in the tone of his voice than in the enunciation of his words, and even courtesy and breeding and kindness and generosity lie in the sound of the voice at least as much as in the phrases it may pronounce. Sound carries its own feelings more surely than words their dictionary meanings, or phrases their connotations of elegance or social refinement. Genuine æsthetic discrimination no more fails to mark directness, naturalness, and native congruity of tone production than elegance or finish or expertness or sophistication of phrase and vocabulary and "accent." And in a world where all languages and "accents" are judged beautiful or ugly either by their native users who love them or by aliens who hate them, it is a dubious advantage to substitute one for the other permanently on supposedly æsthetic grounds, since none of them is so directly and æsthetically felt as beautiful as are natural tones of voice and familiar qualities of intonation and even native locutions. Languages differ from each other in their auditory character largely in their peculiar noises, not in pure tonal quality, and of the beauties of noises men seem so far not to have achieved any fundamental or even conventionally agreed upon canons or criteria.

Perhaps this one example is as good as another, and it would be fruitless to attempt anything like an enumeration of even the typical aspects of the expressiveness of language aside from its strictly denotative symbolic function, or even the superiorities of some languages over others in the felt directness of this denotative power itself. Certainly common opinion differentiates French lucidity, Latin accuracy and elegance in condensation, a sort of domestic and convivial heartiness and a childlike honesty and familiarity in German, where even technical terms are so often agglomerations of syllables out of folk vocabulary. In Greek and Spanish and Italian there are specific varieties of power, of formal dignity, and of literary intricacy, as foreign to English as any of the characteristic traits of temperament that so strike the least observant outsider as native or national failures or successes, ethically and socially, in those who speak these different languages at home.

If there are no criteria to mark the superiority for all men of English or French or Italian or German or Spanish lyric poetry, one over another, there is at least no difficulty in noticing in each of them specific qualities which contribute to its peculiar expressiveness, whether this happens to lie in a power to evoke ideas or images or emotions less easily evoked and precisely marked in another language, or whether assonance or rhyme or rhythm occur with more or less modification of the order of words of common speech, with a correspondingly greater or less need for selection, to meet æsthetic demands, of words less current in everyday discourse, so that verse in the language, simply by being verse, possesses a specific rarity and distinction, or on the other hand is capable more naturally in this language than in another of specifying to the mind through the ear feelings of warmth and of simple familiar fireside emotions, foreign to other idioms in the more or less formal and explicit rhythms of verse structure.

Since the possibilities of variation and specification we are citing here are of even greater range than that of the denotations of words and phrases possible to a language and filling whole dictionaries, it is hopeless to attempt any account of them even through typical illustrations. But the difference between Lesbia and Mary Morison is certainly no greater than that between the peculiar expressive powers of two different languages, since the whole difference between these two loved and lovely ladies lies in the poetic linguistic specification of their charms and their souls that is our last court of appeal in defining it. Unless, indeed, we turn to the obvious superiority of Catullus to Burns or of Burns to Catullus—

these superiorities themselves being, for all important and relevant purposes, the degrees of perfection in the native expressiveness of the two languages—to apply them indirectly as estimates and specifications of the ladies. In a later chapter we shall have to revert to this subject; but for the present it must be clear that language as such is marked by expressive powers which bring to the surface of poetry most of the beauty that we find in it. The difference between Mary Morison and Lesbia is clearly enough suggested in these different syllables themselves, were there not the ever-repeated lyrics to specify further their contrasting beauties whether of faithless lips or gentle thought.

Languages have their own felicities and accuracies for bringing meanings before the mind in an almost transparent medium, and so far as this medium is attended to its auditory character is still further definitive of the meaning conveyed, more fully determinate of the ideal significance it carries. But languages also vary in their powers to summon imagery with all its variety of sensuous beauties, through symbolic denotation present to the writer, and in his intention, at least, presented to the reader or listener. It is clear that precision here requires not only the writer's control of his technique, but the control by the reader of much of this same technique, at the very least a full acquaintance with historical and conventional usages in vocabulary and phrasing. No mind pierces another mind to see the images before it; but it must penetrate the almost transparent medium of language to reach the images there mirrored. And only so much of the unseen content of the poet's lines can be discovered as is discoverable in the individual reader's storehouse of memory or by his own creative imagination, prompted to activity by the printed or spoken symbols of discourse.

Thus the specific beauties of a poem may easily be lost to an unimaginative mind, as all the values of English poetry might so easily be lost to a world where men, intent upon their own active business, should come at last to employ "business English" as their sole linguistic medium, a medium more completely foreign to the language of Shelley or of Shakespeare than theirs to that of Catullus or of Homer. The beauties of poetry would still be those identical beauties, but these beauties would simply not occur to readers of the poets, were there any readers left, as upon the syllables and lines before them. And if these beauties remain what they are in essence, that is of little interest to a world in which they are effectively prevented from occurring. For they can not appear upon the face of experience even when men concern themselves to look upon the lines that could alone evoke them, unless men's minds already hold the sensuous elements they would summon, and are capable of the imaginative response through which they must be re-created. If linguistic lore and stores of manuscripts and printed books may plausibly be said to preserve poetry itself, its beauties, even of sensuous imagery, can not so be kept in human experience. For their occurrence, minds are needed stored with the images that contemplation has engraved upon them, endowed with all the powers of imagination for reviving them as the poetry specifies, and as we shall further see, with all the specific possibilities of feeling and emotion that their beauties must also externalize, if they are to occur in their full intended character.

But this is not all that language may express in its perfection. For as poets have themselves individuality, their own special tastes, their own most vital interests, their own selection of a way of life and thought and feeling; so they select from all the possibilities of language what suits these tastes and interests, and this manner of life and thought. What they write specifies it to other men, so that, as we say, they have their own distinctive style, often unequivocally marked in a single sentence or a line of verse. Thus through language gifted men may express their particular individual selves. And as human beings are so deeply interested in their own personal concerns and attributes, and in other men as characters or individualities, so, with even very slight feeling for the niceties of style, with little specifically linguistic training or knowledge of its technique, we often learn very early and very easily that sort of expressiveness in language that is the recognizable or familiar style of an author, though we should be at a loss to point out just what it is in terms of language itself that furnishes us so unmistakable an identification. Certainly this is no more a mystery, however, than our recognition of our friends on the street, since obviously enough here too, little as we may be able to analyze it, our recognition is the distinguishing of a sensuous surface, explicitly specifying to us that one individual in all the world of human creatures who is thus himself expressed in his appearance, an appearance welcome and enjoyed and perhaps to be called beautiful in its expressiveness, even though the strictly and thinly æsthetic surface may be far from sensuously charming. Here is one of those cases where the surface is so deep that æsthetic is scarcely the word for it; but if we are to deny all beauty to the expressive appearance of a friend, then perfect expressiveness in style itself is not, merely as such, a beauty even of literature. If we have here reached the limit of the beauty of expression, however, that is not to deny such beauty altogether; and if for strictly æsthetic beauty the actual expressiveness of the surface is irrelevant, certainly expressiveness as such can not be denied the function of giving to such a surface as is in itself sensuously satisfying, most of its significance, and in works of art to measure their vital, if not their strictly æsthetic, beauty. Least of all could this function be denied to the expressive power of works of literary art, which without it would fall short of being works of fine art at all, failing, as they then would, to be even plausibly comparable to the sensuously satisfying sounds of music.

§ 3

If in early Greek drama, where these two arts were indistinguishable, as we may suppose, we have the best evidence that poetry is elementary music in the explicitly rhythmical chanting and intoning of its syllables, this same phenomenon reminds us of the equally vital point that music is itself fundamentally expressive. And if this evidence were not strong enough, we should have at least to admit, in order to give any meaning at all to Plato's condemnation of certain musical modes, that the expressiveness of music as such was clear to the intelligent mind in even those early and very simple developments of musical art. The explicitly rhythmical and tonal qualities of Greek drama, could they be given to the ear apart from the words and meanings, would be the impossible abstraction from the concrete drama itself of just the measure or amount of their expressiveness, so far as this was beyond the power of language, impossible, that is, to linguistic symbolism as such. The music is just so much expressiveness as the words could not achieve as mere meanings; yet it adds a force and a power felt and recognized as so strictly relevant to the meanings intended as to be necessary to carry them out fully. This one historical case would be evidence enough not only of the expressiveness of music, but also of its precision and aptness in accomplishing that which language as symbolic discourse fails to achieve. If music can not say what words say, it is not that music is not strictly and directly expressive, but that its expressiveness ranges over a field of emotions and feeling that language does not exhaust in its intimate details, with a fullness of power unique and characteristic in its capacity for exactitude and definiteness in marking every various nuance.

But Greek drama is not even the most striking evidence of this power, and we may with equal relevance turn from its almost mythical and at the best historically and learnedly recognized sublimity, to the vulgarly familiar music of jazz orchestras. It is perhaps fortunate for the health and vigor of the modern world that our tradition as to the exclusive powers of language to express sentiments and specify meanings, allows the properest young lady to receive an education in matters where words would be thought shocking if they even suggested what so much popular music presents unambiguously and precisely through fresh young ears to minds not yet sterilized by dogma and dullness, and bodies young and flexible in any case, but further prepared for the appreciation even of rhythmic orgies, by the expertness and subtle strength of muscles and limbs so strenuously cultivated in modern sports.

The anomalous aspect of this direct and inescapable specification in sound of feelings and emotions foreign and even repugnant to the everyday discourse of respectable America, its steady, pushing business thrift, the inflexible and crude morality of its conventional and dogmatically orthodox converse, is nowhere more striking than in the cultivation of the arts on a grand scale by wealthy Americans who endow civic museums, civic opera, and civic orchestras. To think of an audience of Boston's staid aristocrats of shipping and banking and business in general thrilling to the sensuous tonal and rhythmic specifications of the music of Verdi, not to mention modern French and Italian and Russian composers, to whose music Symphony Hall resounds week after week and year after year, would be merely amusing, if it were not evidence of such hypocrisy or ignorance or bluntness of decayed sense perception in a pretentious culture, and such significant and quite unintentionally effective education for keen ears and the open and flexible minds of young bodies. If, as has been said of Boston itself, the arts have their revenge on puritans and desert those who neglect them; it is at least more important for æsthetic theory that music, not needing words learned in schools or learned at all, to carry its meanings, but only attentive and perceptive ears, carries to the mind through such ears as hear it all those precise and elaborate specifications of feeling and emotion that it directly expresses.

No doubt the simple literalness of these observations might be mistaken for irresponsible or irrelevant indulgence in prejudiced social comment. It is therefore necessary to be a little more explicit if the point is actually to be made that music is as truly expressive as language, its field being, however, emotions and feelings instead of the qualities and characters of physical objects. Music may of course be very accurately representative over a limited range, representative of anything in the world whose character happens to be chiefly defined for us in sound,—storms, or animal noises, or bird songs, or idyllic piping shepherds, or even elevators or fire-engines or machinery. But musical composition depends for its structure and its characteristically musical effects upon relations of tones in pitch and loudness and timbre, and upon rhythm; upon melody, harmony, dynamics, and tempo, and, so far as its main classic western European developments are concerned, upon tonality as established by the forms of the major and minor scales of all the keys, though all these more regularly musical terms are merely special names for the variations in the sensuous medium of sound that we have discussed.

Melody is a temporal sequence of pitches in specified relative durations. Harmony is the whole subject of musical effects that involve combinations of pitches sounded simultaneously as in chords and chord progressions. Dynamics is a rather odd term for patterned increase and decrease in loudness. And tempo is, as we have seen, one aspect of rhythm itself. Tonality is the fact of key, depending upon an established pitch, the so-called fundamental or tonic, with a series of pitches harmonically related to it in a scale, the intervals of which are definitely fixed, and hence felt as in normal relations to the fundamental and to each other in this scale or tone series, whether major or minor. Tonality is thus a matter of convention, or rather of norms; but how fruitful and rich a convention it has been is shown in the classic developments of eighteenth and nineteenth century European music. It will also be plain enough that even so intelligible and so to speak tonally logical a convention must be learned and practised, and that much of the precision in the expressiveness of music thus depends—if it is to be apprehended at all—on trained ears, ears that distinguish pitch relations in keys, tonic and dominant and sub-dominant harmonies, modulation from one key to another, conventional elegances of all sorts, and the very numerous defined and traditionally established musical forms, set as general types of pattern or methods of construction, to which the composer limits himself, thus revealing his intention in a unified sounding structure of the sort that a technique of sound can build.

But all this preparatory knowledge is after all auditory, and to hear music as composition might naturally be expected to require ears trained to the perception of salient tonal quality and character and variation. As we should not expect an infant in arms to appreciate an epigram, so we can not expect musical innocents to recognize tonality or even specific musical rhythms, except the simplest. But this must not be taken for any lack of precision in the expressiveness of either the epigram or the music. Most of us are musically untrained, not so much tone-deaf as tone-ignorant, unfamiliar with the simplest musical transitions and with musical forms in general. We are therefore in no position to grasp the more precise tonal specifications of music; but for all that, its precision of specification is available to us in another aspect. As in literature style is the man, whom we therefore recognize in his writing, and as the merest amateur of the galleries learns to identify Corots, say, so in music style is so individually expressive that Haendel and Haydn and Bach and Mozart are no more difficult to distinguish through the ear than familiar faces through the eye. And if we sometimes make mistakes, and go so far as to address the wrong lady on the street, we are not likely to urge our error as evidence that people do not really recognize their friends by their appearances, or that the friends are not really so distinctively expressed in their appearance as to be individually recognizable, least of all that appearing human beings are not really particular individuals. If signatures are sufficient guarantees of notes and checks, musical styles should at least be believed in even by those who do not recognize in them the specification to the ear of the composer's own self, his taste, his manner, his bearing, his interests, and his powers, in that tonal region where alone, perhaps, his characteristics are for him and for us more than personally important. For this is the region where he has given them permanent articulate form and so revealed in expression the otherwise inarticulate passions of human beings, explored and mapped by the means he best knew some realm of the human soul, so that all men may now recognize its features.

If music can thus indubitably render external and make explicit to men's ears the articulation of their felt passions, and this so precisely as to constitute the individual expression of an individual human being in a recognizable musical style, it must be clear that between this personal sort of expression and the precise specification of the finest shadings given to trained perception through adequate musical technique adequately grasped in all its precision of æsthetic tonal surface, there lie all those more generally characterizable musical expressions, sorrow or exultation, boldness, weakness, gaiety, love, foreboding, anguish. Not that music is ever merely bold, or merely gay, or merely sad. The sad sweetness of one funeral march is as far removed from the dignified solemnity of another as one man's actual concrete grief from another's, or from his own on another occasion. As a mother's sorrow over a dead infant is not a man's sorrow over a dead wife, so no one musical expression expresses exactly what another does. The specification is always absolutely and uniquely itself, and though no sensuous medium ever does more than approximate an artist's intention, the precise specification possible in music is in these matters of human passion almost superhuman in its success. It is because poetry is more than words and shares the nature of music itself that Wordsworth could be so sure of its exalted function, and that we need never fear that Mr. Shaw has outdone Shakespeare.

Melody and harmony and rhythm define with an almost numerical accuracy the specific, technically achieved, expressive auditory surface of works of musical art, and the composer's notation may with some degree of exactitude symbolize his musical intentions. But a composer has in mind, of course, the actual sounding medium of all music, and this varies from instrument to instrument and with all possible variety in number and combinations of instruments. If primary musical technique is the technique that achieves—and uses musical notation to indicate the achievement—musical structure as such, there is a secondary technique for the actual presentation of this sounding æsthetic surface to the ear. This secondary technique, too often treated as primary in musical education, is instrumental, or, if the instrument is the human voice, vocal. Its function is not the actual imaginative and definitive creation of the structure, but perfect "performance," as we say. And that it is secondary is clear enough from the bare fact that without a control of the primary technique, to give a genuine grasp of the composer's expressive intention, the style of his composition, the kind of auditory surface he was creating, no amount of instrumental skill could, except by the merest accident, reproduce in even a so-called correct reading the effective structure originally created by the composer's mind and recorded in his notation.

Thus a full grasp even of notation, in all the refinements it is capable of indicating, is as requisite to reading music as a knowledge of spelling and punctuation is to following prose. And for any adequate grasp of recorded music there is the further requirement of a knowledge of the whole of primary musical technique as such, the general and special features of which are the only proper beginnings of musical training. For it is the practice of this technique that really creates or comprehends the auditory structure and specifically and in detail defines its æsthetic surface. For appreciation, at least, the secondary instrumental technique finds its consummation in sheer transparency; to disappear in the music is its whole function. Every evidence of it upon the surface is an æsthetic blemish; whereas primary musical technique is the very structure of that surface, the lineaments of the beauty intended, a grasp of it being therefore essential to perceiving the presented auditory surface in its full detail, its structural form, and its genuine and actual character. Performers are too seldom adequate enough musicians, or such self-effacing human beings, as to give us very frequent examples of this renunciation of their life-time achievement; an altogether perfect instrumental technique is too difficult of acquisition to be often demanded, and too great an accomplishment to be allowed by a human being, conscious of his painfully achieved or brilliantly talented mastery, to disappear in the mere music as indicated by the composer.

But there is a compensation in virtuosity itself; for just at the point at which musical technique in the primary sense fails of absolute determinateness in carrying out the composer's intention, a gifted performer, whose mastery is more than adequate to actual demands, may enhance the expressiveness of this intention or even modify it to advantage, as a distinguished singer may put style and even poignancy into a very ordinary melody, as well as the sensuous filling

ESTHETIC JUDGMENT

of beautiful tone peculiar to his own voice. In general, however, even ordinary composers are so much more adequate as
musicians than professional instrumentalists, that with all
their limitations in instrumental technique, their performing
of their own or of others' compositions is musically more
satisfying than that of many a brilliant instrumentalist or
conductor; though this is less so in the case of conducting,
since even barely competent orchestra conductors must
necessarily be musicians in a sense not at all applicable to
most performers upon instruments, or to singers, who are
so commonly and so notoriously lacking in musicianship.

But after all, the physical means to music insist upon
being respected. A composer who knows little of any but
one instrument often fails egregiously in writing for other
instruments. We are all familiar enough with the flat mis-
representation of musical intention so often achieved in songs
arranged for the violin, or inexpert and unmusical "arrangements" for the piano. On the other hand a great master of
some one instrument may accomplish beauties for its timbre
and within its limitations that seem mysteriously and even
superhumanly conceived, miracles of art, performed only
by a musical god. If Bach is a giant, ranging over vast instrumental territories, Chopin achieves divinity in his own
province, and we have scarcely another comparable local
deity. Thus, although instrumental technique is secondary
in music as such, and in all sound musical training, it is after
all no slight matter even for composers. Sound is produced
physically and heard through physical ears, and it must be
clear enough that while primary musical technique creates
musical structures themselves, specifies in musical terms
that which music expresses, this secondary technique of instruments, the means to presenting auditory structures

243

through ears to human minds, is not only a necessary condition for any music at all, but in the various possibilities of various instruments and the perfection of performance, a further possibility for fullness and accuracy of specification in the auditory medium. It is not only a further opportunity for the composer's specific gifts to exploit, but a chance for the performer himself to share in musically expressive creation, and thus by way of his own instrument and the perfection of his instrumental technique, to actualize for himself and other men, not only the beauties of the music composed by himself or by another, but those further beauties which express, in sounds as they are produced, his own spirit and its passionate aspirations, and so the passions and aspirations of other men.

§ 4

In painting and sculpture it is to the nature of spatial objects and qualities that expression can most obviously be given, whether on flat surfaces, which may also express depth through the devices of perspective, or in the round. But although bare representation is itself a sort of simple expression of the features, and hence of the recognized character and significance, of physical objects, including of course human bodies and particularly human faces, representation alone is the least artistically expressive aspect of even the graphic and the plastic arts. Although the technique may be skillful, the beauties involved are those given in nature as occurring there, and now imitated, instead of being beauties of structures created by a technique which makes use primarily of the native affinities and orders of the sensuous materials, shape, direction, dimensionality in general, and elements of color, employing these more or less consciously as principles under the guidance of the imagination to delineate felt meanings in beauties thus discriminately selected or composed from the more strictly elementary and æsthetic materials of art. So-called abstract design is thus the art, whether as drawing or as painting or as sculpture, that we are here primarily concerned with as the most direct and consciously expressive aspect of spatial composition.

Such expressiveness of design is clear in so marked a difference as that between a Greek key pattern and the border of a Pompeian arabesque, a difference felt directly not merely as that between straight lines and curves, but as the difference between solid, substantial firmness and a light or perhaps even irresponsible or trifling grace, depending of course upon the particular instance. The point at which such human or moral sentiments enter and are actually expressed in pure design is not easy to fix; but that these terms are quite properly used, and as literally as linguistic terms can be used, to designate what only sensuous data themselves can actually and concretely specify and make determinate, must be clear enough. Their strict applicability will at once be acknowledged by any one who has ever noticed the sensuously rich curves and heavy masses of baroque ornament, or the clear-headed refinement and definite restraint, along with unequivocal sensuous gratification, specified to the point not so much of ingenuousness as a sort of absolute and intended definiteness, in the cornices of thirteenth century Tuscan palaces, or their wrought-iron lamps, or the effectively forbidding but handsome gratings at their entrances. Or take the variety of design in wooden porch-railings of our own old southern houses, all so clearly expressive of specific variations on the common theme that we recognize when we identify them as of their own period and type. Or take the difference in effect between Hispano-Moresque plates, in their characteristic pink-brown lustre and many-lined patterns, and later Spanish plates with their dashing use of color and their boldness of design, or between either of these and Canti Galli, where linear design is present in patterns often subtle and intricate enough, but specifying a character and quality quite other than that of the Moorish elaborateness, their color too, though emphatic and striking, revealing so different an intention and spirit from the Spanish, that no one not blind could very well take one for the other. Or compare English crystal tumblers with tumblers of Venetian glass. In one, clear-cut geometry and transparent usefulness; in the other, the feeling of a substance softened and shaped, but neither purified of all sense of the colored material medium, nor ever forced into the sharp forms defined by mathematics, but left in the softer lines that are felt as closer to its own character, or even given by its own volition, which the glass-blower has somehow felt and adopted as his.

Perhaps even more clearly than that of music, the expressiveness of spatial design is that of the medium and the technique, and words fail all the more obviously to indicate what this technique, or rather these hundreds of techniques employed upon innumerable media, can specify to the eye in the way of defined qualities, composed and coherent yet elaborated complex beauties of color and shape and line, of masses and shadows and depths. They are no longer merely lovely sense-elements in purely spatial structures, possible to the intrinsically ordered spatial and colored materials which the artist feels as thus natively related, and so, capable of being composed into the forms he feels possible and appropriate to them; they are the beauties of what the structures express through the eye to the mind, of all the specifically articulated and exhibited qualities and characters that our world of objects and human bodies contains. And here again we are using words as literally as words can be used. If eyes and faces and human bodies are expressive, clearly enough they are spatially expressive; they say what words can not say, but what a sculptor may discern in them, and what sculptured design may make permanent in its own peculiar beauty; not in its copying of their whole spatial character, not even in its representing of those aspects of texture and those few selected lines and modellings that are the discerned distinction to be fixed in marble or bronze, but in its own medium felt as holding expressive possibilities, brought to the surface by technical skill, and there, in terms of spatial pattern and texture, specifying that which the artist feels as the meaning and significance suggested to him perhaps in the observed human face or body, but only actualized and presented, only clearly and definitely expressed, in the medium that can be spatially so composed into that specific beauty of expression.

In a loose and rather general way this expressiveness is commonly recognized; sculptured groups, we often say, are noble conceptions, or the pedestal of an equestrian statue itself impressively characteristic, in its proportions and its height, of the dignity and boldness and distinction of the military figure it supports. What is not so clearly recognized is precisely what it is that is expressive here and in just what sense. On the one hand the expressiveness of the actual spatial and colored medium is likely to be confused with the expressiveness of the subject of the work of art. And this involves on the other hand further confusions which, if we take them into account, further emphasize the simple æsthetic facts. A portrait may be admired for the accuracy of the likeness it bears to a particular human face and form, and we may take pleasure in the bare fact of such representative imitation. Photographs or scientific drawings of plants and flowers, whether familiar or unfamiliar, are a pleasure to contemplate, partly, it would seem, because we enjoy representation as such. But this accomplishment is not expressiveness at all, of course, but only imitation or copying. Furthermore, what is copied, say in a portrait, may itself be expressive, as an old man's bent body and wrinkled skin, or a mother's attitude, or an infant's innocent, clear eyes. And these are not the expressiveness of art either, though clearly enough it is spatial and colored æsthetic surface that is the sole objective specification, whether in an actual human being or the painted or modelled copy of one, of the pathos here of bent and wrinkled age, the tenderness of maternal love, or the innocent eagerness or sweet contentment of infancy. So that it is clear enough that actual æsthetic surface specification upon physical objects, human bodies or not, is what we call, even in life, the expression of human traits or moral sentiments, or any other quality that appears to the eye in the world about it.

The expressiveness of art, then, is no unfamiliar phenomenon so far as it is merely one case of physical objects revealing on their surface, and thus specifying, the characteristics they express. But in works of art the means to expression is consciously and technically taken as physical material of given qualities and possibilities of æsthetic surface, to be so colored and so arranged in space as to give in its own way— the way possible to spatial form and lines and colors—the specific significance that the artist feels and is thus able to express, provided his technique is adequate. What he expresses is what marble or paint can convey, never merely just what live human beings are as such; so that, whether he has a model or not, what he puts into permanent structural form or design is the significance of that design as given on an æsthetic surface, the expression of himself, of course, but also the expression of what he feels as the possibilities of his medium to specify quality, character, meaning.

What is also often forgotten is the preciseness and uniqueness, the absolute determinateness, so to say, of this expression in a work of art. This is its peculiar and individual beauty, possessed by it, to be seen upon it, to be felt in its presence, and nowhere else to be found or known, nor to be preserved in the world at all except as this particular work of art is preserved either physically or in a memory of such detailed and complete reliability as is extraordinarily rare. Here too both the purpose and the inadequacy of reproductions become patent. Not that they are mean or worthless or false; but simply that they are not the originals, and that in so many cases the reproduction misses the very point, the completely determinate beauty that is the only great artistic value of the original, whether merely by a different surface texture in a different medium, like the most perfect plaster casts of marble statues, or by such grotesquely pronounced differences of color or line, or particular details of these, as make the reproduction a caricature. As fingerprints are absolute for the police, so brush-strokes may be absolute for critical perception.

Thus it is not just thoughtfulness that Rodin's *Thinker* expresses, but a massive, painful, heavily obvious thoughtfulness, though even here in so unimaginative and unsubtle a work of art the precision of expression can not be reached by words and is actual and present in the physical spatial object itself, not to be more than barely suggested by words,

249

and of course sadly confused and blurred for our memories by the constant sight of reproductions of it, ranging from casts in the round, and good photographs at various angles, to mere bill-board exaggerations in staring black and white. In finer and more important works of art than this, the specificity, the fundamental precision of expression, goes to much greater lengths, and often defies reproduction by any one less than a great master, so that to see a famous piece of Greek sculpture or one of the preciously preserved canvases of the Italian galleries, after being familiar with it for years in even good reproductions, is a new and exciting experience, often the first experience of anything approaching its actual character, and necessarily the first experience of the full specific expressiveness of its individual and absolutely unique beauty.

In our discussion we should perhaps mention explicitly one or two even more obvious matters, which the least attention to concrete works of spatial art would have made into habitual modes of perception, so to speak, rather than theoretical æsthetic principles. One of these Lessing pointed out in the eighteenth century, a conclusion not very striking in any the least adequate æsthetic theory, since it amounted in the end to little more than the simple notion that the spatial arts do not so well or so clearly express non-spatial aspects of life and nature. That they do so indirectly, and even very vividly, is simply enough demonstrated in the expressive power of that group of writhing figures that Lessing took as his text. But poetry and music no doubt carry more easily in their moving temporal medium the significance and character of emotions and of moving events in sequence; hence also of eventful crises in men's lives and in the history of nations. On the other hand the distinctive beauties of form itself, whether of bodily grace and poise and power, or of the spreading peace of country scenes, the depths and heights and lights and shadows of wooded solitudes, the sparkling blue of smiling summer water or the dark threats of the restless, endless mass of ocean waves on a rocky shore —all these are clearly spatial in their very nature and in their specific and characteristic beauties, the natural and successful subjects of spatial and not of temporal arts, their expressiveness itself, since it is constituted in spatial terms in actuality, being therefore akin to those beauties that spatial design as such can most clearly and richly achieve, where poetry or music would fail.

There is another obvious limitation of all spatial design, not so much a matter of the intrinsic nature of the æsthetic material itself as of the fact that the structural form is altogether spatial and not temporal. A picture or a piece of sculpture is seen ideally at one glance, all its parts held together in a momentary, and also permanent unity. These parts are not spread over time in rhythmic sequence, though of course the full beauty present at last to momentary vision may not be seen until long looking upon it has made possible the genuine apprehension of its details in all their subtlety and elaboration, as held within the structure that as a whole specifies character and intention. And the frames of pictures, or the sharp outlines of sculpture, or the finished edges of pedestals, simply avow a frankly non-temporal unity and completeness, playing a definite, albeit subsidiary, rôle in the spatial arts, very different in its strict relevance to the actual æsthetic surface from that of the bindings of books, whose function is so irrelevant to literature itself that one who is devoted to their appearance is often indifferent to their content, and *vice versa*. In music the physical object carrying the notation is so far removed from the sounding surface that music is largely left unbound, and the presence of the sheets themselves is often felt as an obstacle to performance or, if the performance is one of a highly professional and fully artistic nature, as an impertinence. That pictures are painted and bounded in the simple shapes of wall spaces or made frames, limits them of course to being spatial colored patterns of their own definite dimensions, in much the same sense in which a man's own volition limits his voluntary conduct to being his own expression of himself. But as brevity gives point to speech, so any set limitation, while it confines expression, is at the same time the condition of there being expressive character at all, exactly as the physical body, though it may hamper the free spirit, is the condition and sole means of supporting spiritual life. Emotions and prospects expanding to infinity are neither defined nor human, nor are they objects or beauties for perception or intuition to grasp as significant specification, since they are not anything at all. The mind must find or make boundaries for its objects, else what it contemplates is merely its own futile strivings to encompass the whole universe with all its meaning at once, and so to encompass nothing, to draw no lines, to find no boundaries, to delimit no objects, to perceive no actually expressive surface, and hence to fail altogether to discriminate any single beauty as expressive of its own individual and absolutely specific point, no matter how rich and full the content that is focussed there.

And this brings us to another obvious consideration. As every work of art has its own significant character, what we may call the point of it as a whole—its single point that strikes us as its expressive beauty—so there are kinds of beauty, which are the kinds of point that works produced by certain techniques upon certain media may have. The point of painting as art is clearly enough, in the view of æsthetic theory, significant design on a flat surface, where of course depth may be represented by the varying direction of lines and by varying color values that give perspective. But perspective itself, while it may also be naïvely and honestly used merely for accuracy of representation, is on more clearly æsthetic grounds integral to the design itself, as its felt depth, holding its elements together in such structural relations as are not possible to flat areas felt as flat. Moreover, in the history of modern painting it is easy to see the gradually increasing consciousness of the fact that mere representation, expressive as it is of anything that natural objects and bodies may themselves express, is more strictly and artfully expressive as it uses the native possibilities of spatial and colored elements in designs that are after all, if not mathematical in the sense of the simplest geometrical forms and combinations of forms, still mathematical and geometrical in the sense of depending upon spatial character itself, those elements of shape and line and mass that we discussed in terms of their intrinsic properties of structural order, or the intrinsically ordered elements of color composition.

So landscape may become altogether unearthly and all flat and pale lavender, to express a human mood, and human bodies may be made angular and twisted and unlovely and almost inhuman, to express human fortitude or human frailty or qualities not merely personal at all, but such as externalize in paint or stone or bronze or wood the felt domination of man by his own invented civilization, or the strength and power and defiance with which his spirit meets his world, neither man nor nature nor the furnishings and machinery of his world being here represented except incidentally, but their character and significance being specified in solid spatial design by the artist who employs its intrinsic modes and configurations to give expression to what he feels as the character and meaning of things in general, or perhaps of things in some of their most special or even esoteric aspects.

If sculpture has the freedom of three literal dimensions and the fullness they offer for complex three-dimensional design, the lights and shadows of actual depths and distance, its technique also makes two special and characteristic demands that must be felt and instinctively fulfilled. In the first place the sculptor must see his work from all sides at once, since, except in special cases, it is to be so seen by others; and secondly, since everything in the round must be perceived as an object, the objective piece of sculpture must, apparently, to be felt as anything at all, be an object or a group of objects recognizable as known forms with known names, whether natural or mythical. There are no *a priori* grounds for asserting that sculpture is so limited; pure spatial three-dimensional design, altogether non-representative, might well enough be practised by a sufficiently gifted artist. But if we insist, as sculpture necessarily does, on spatial form and surface texture as the total content of the art, the forms that seem to have interested men sufficiently so far to absorb their vision and employ their whole artistic skill are those of human beings and, less often, of animals. Intricate and interesting as are the forms of flowers and trees and rocks, there are fairly obvious reasons why they should not be reproduced in sculpture except as decoration in relief, or in general as minor works of art or craft, which put flowers into jade or fruit into glass or wax.

We must admit in passing, I think, that this love of human

bodies is not so much æsthetic as simply human. But as human bodies are the very objects of all our passions in the end, their representation in perfection of physical type, as well as in all the infinite number of their significant acts and attitudes, can not fail to satisfy our æsthetic contemplation. And once the task is set of expressing in a sculptured body its full spatial character in complete detail of volume and surface, the rigorous demands upon the artist are clear. The type must not be given up, else we miss the object altogether. Variation is narrowly and stringently limited by our demand that whatever this human body express, it be first of all an adequate and vital human body, articulated by a structure of bones and muscles, and indicative of organic function. And then further, from every angle, every line of it, every curve, every aspect, from size itself to surface texture, must carry the one central point that as a whole it specifies. Within these limitations the variety of moving vital expressions of the significance of man and his bodily life—which also is his spiritual life—that have been achieved in modelling human forms to present their thousand beauties, is great enough always, we may safely suppose, to lure certain sensuously gifted individuals into sculpture as we know it historically, to find expression for their talents and to make pure abstract three-dimensional design that should be independent of all representative intent, a pale dream until some genius shall come to reveal its full expressive powers and turn it into a new and vital ideal of art and artists.

Though we must distinguish between artistic, æsthetic design as such, which depends on composing structures out of the material sensuous elements of beauty through a grasp of these defined in their intrinsic native orders of variation, and the mere taking over for the purposes of art of such forms and types and color combinations as nature offers to attentive and discriminating eyes, these two activities are not so distantly apart in reality as our distinction suggests. For after all the intrinsic orders that define the variations in the native range of colors or of spatial elements and forms are themselves natural and discovered in nature. And if nature thus gives to intellectual artistic grasp the very principles of abstract design, how much more do all the specific curves and shapes and combinations presented in nature to sight offer to the artist fresh vital materials of beauty. For subtlety and accuracy in expression in pure design itself nothing serves the artist better, nothing more surely keeps his design from degenerating into mere convention which no longer fully expresses any vital present significance, than an eye open to those natural sources of material as well as formal beauty, whence in the end the humanly created structures of art must draw their very being and so in large measure their expressive beauty.

Of the thousands of examples of this vitalizing of pure artistic design by the discriminating observation of natural forms, two will perhaps sufficiently emphasize the point and define the real meaning of the assertion: flower-painting in western art and the use of waves in Japanese prints. As typical of seventeenth century French art La Croix, in his monumental collection, includes a painted carnation sent to a lady, with a verse in which the single blossom surrenders all her charms in favor of the lady's superior excellences and begs to retain some of her own beauty in crowning the lady's hair. The expressiveness of this flower-painting might easily be duplicated, or at least equalled, by a good piece of modern German color photography. And the china painting of the later nineteenth century with its roses and pansies and violets,

AESTHETIC JUDGMENT

which were anything but photographic, grew traditionally
stale and then offensively ugly and dead in its repetition of
outworn prettiness, no longer expressive of anything at all
but the ugly and repressed spirits of ladies not so much of
leisure as of boredom. Contrast with these examples those
huge and elegant bouquets of the time of the Grand Mon-
arch, now again so fashionable as to bring absurd prices in
antique-shops, and reproduced by the thousand for the less
exacting of the élite in matters of decoration. And finally,
think of the vivid and living expressiveness of the dozens of
sorts of flower-painting practised in the first quarter of our
own century, from the fullest and richest of color designs in
flower-forms to the portrayal on canvas of the most esoteric
aspects of the beauty of flowers, directly abstracted, as it
were, from nature, and revealed within a square frame on
canvas as genuinely expressive of present day life and
feeling in a hundred different aspects of its intensity and dis-
traction and abandon.

Our other example of wave-forms in Japanese prints is
only to serve as a reminder to those who would forget man's
dependence on nature for even the beauties of expressive design in art, that the vigor and richness of design itself draws
upon natural sources, from which by long and patient observation the greatest artists have extracted beauties from
obscuring contexts, to give fresh life and meaning to design
itself. Men who have observed the imposing and dignified
growth of an acanthus plant with its polished surfaces, the
deep-cut edges of its leaves, and its whole stately design,
will think it no derogation from the classic finality of the
Corinthian order to say that its distinguishing capital drew
directly upon natural forms for its rich, carved elegance.

§ 5

In architecture itself, as distinguished from architectural ornament, which is after all expressive very much as sculpture and painting and drawing are expressive, new sorts of meaning come to light. For buildings bespeak man's domestic and social and religious life in some of its most satisfying aspects, whether of his intimate personal happiness or of the dignity and power and range of his social institutions, or his religious hopes and beliefs. Architecture is the useful and practical art of building buildings for all the purposes that buildings may serve; but it is also the fine art of expressing in these structures, made not of brick and wood and steel and stone alone, but also of the æsthetic elements of mass and line and shape and color and texture and ornamental design and sculptured decoration, just what any purely spatial design on a large scale may express, but also, and quite beyond this, such characteristics of human life and man's whole world as are involved in the primarily useful purposes of building at all.

And these are not merely characteristics associated by habit or custom or language or accident with buildings and their shapes and sizes and inner and outer arrangements, but characteristics or qualities such as domestic comfort, family intimacy, personal privacy, studious seclusion, judicial dignity, regal grandeur, social elegance, courtly pomp, all of which, and a thousand others, are more completely and explicitly specified in particular rooms of particular sizes and shapes, in particular arrangements, or in great public halls or palaces, or taverns, or towering walls, or imposing façades, or flat roofs, or great door-ways, or low windows, than is even possible to words, that can at the best name these qualities and characters loosely and indeterminately, and must, as we have so often remarked, finally indicate their specific meaning in some one determinate form by a gesture, indicating in the field of perception the quality or character meant. If we had to define lonely grandeur, or bizarre opulence, or studious quiet, in anything but other phrases, if we had finally to point to data in perception upon the surface of which such characters or qualities are discernible, we could hardly find better or more precise specifications of them than works of architecture or particular features of such works.

To object that the qualities so pointed out have a degree of determinateness in the given cases necessarily making them not identical with other determinate cases and so less broad than the total meanings of the linguistic terms involved, is after all simply to note two important and obvious logical truths; first that absolutely determinate qualitative meaning is not a function of any linguistic term, and second, that any given case of the felt quality of perceived objects is the whole meaning of any genuine application of any term to experience, this meaning being no more and no less than may be felt just here through the sense by the mind, since what else the term may mean in other applications is not its fuller and deeper meaning, but only another determinate meaning, to which, being a general term, it applies equally well. Meaning, to be really determinate, requires complete specification in æsthetic data immediately present, taken by us all to be absolutely determinate in their own nature, though our own specifications in sense, even the most nearly accurate and satisfying ones, fall short always of that absolute determinateness that we postulate as in the nature or character or quality of the object to which we apply loosely descriptive general linguistic terms.

This point has been made above, both in regard to expressiveness in general and in regard to expressiveness in the various arts; but it appears to need a very special emphasis, if we are to judge by the easy confusions prevalent. Men, and theorists particularly, prefer somehow to suppose that linguistic symbols have a meaning of their own, above and beyond the determinate characters of reality as perceived, which, as a matter of fact, they may at the best roughly indicate until gesture comes to the rescue to point out unambiguously to perception a specific case of the quality or character. And instead of allowing this to be the end, a pure qualitative datum that is articulated for discriminating sense perception, with its expressive determinate beauty there at last, these devotees of language turn their mere verbal terms—in their own theories, only, of course—into a sort of mystic substance, in which, as they insist, the natures of all the other determinate and specific characters or beauties it might indicate inhere. So that Platonism in its most fully contradictory sense, discarded by all men in their explicit logical professions, is worshipped and clung to, as if it gave significance to the world, when what it really does as so taken, is to exalt words into meanings and impute to them what is really only a mythical substance or humanly invented power, as an elucidation of such determinate qualities, in their determinate specified natures, as lie before us to be seen by any straightforwardly trained perceptive faculties for exactly what they are, the ultimate beauties of the world, specifying to us its infinitely various nature, and our own.

So far as architecture is expressive as design it differs from the other visual arts only in two main ways, size and complexity. Buildings are on a scale which is human indeed, but which meets the requirements for human beings to move, to function variously, and to congregate. And since they may congregate for purposes of all sorts, to see great spectacles, to advise and consult with each other, to put before an assembly proposals upon which the assembly acts, to sleep and eat and dwell in great numbers in close proximity to other buildings where also in great numbers they labor together, to commemorate the events or heroes of a common past, or to call upon their gods, buildings are defined in size and arrangement accordingly. They may meet the requirements of social intercourse, of business activity, of political ambition, of private life or public; and they may even be temples conforming in shape and size and character to the demands for surroundings in which to meet the deity appropriately to men's varying conceptions both of what God is and of how He is to be met in worship. Thus while a façade may, simply as a design of magnificent proportions, express various degrees and varieties of dignity or solemnity, or fail to express anything at all, except perhaps its designer's empty or conventional mind or its own lack of genuine character, there are in works of architecture inner beauties of expression, shrines and chapels within churches and cathedrals, ball-rooms and dining-rooms and studies and court-rooms and offices and throne-rooms, railway waiting-rooms, music-rooms and libraries, and so on indefinitely, any one of which may itself, in its formal proportions and its æsthetic surface, fail or succeed in specifying character and quality and significance.

But clearly enough besides the possibilities for artistic expression added by size as such and also by interiors, which are not only capable of being beautiful in themselves but are often distinctly felt as determining in part the expressiveness of the exterior as well, works of architecture, being primarily constructions to serve human purposes, are described and indicated by names signifying these purposes, and it may be asked whether architecture as such is not a merely useful art, its technical æsthetic expressiveness being only incidental to its fulfilment of useful function. This question is essentially unimportant, however, since buildings, no matter what their use, are, in being made of physical materials, also thereby made of æsthetic ones, as we have already noticed, and since, as we have also noticed, in buildings these æsthetic materials express in full specification such characters and qualities as colors, surfaces, shapes, and spatial structures of the proportions and the complexity of buildings may present to human minds through their senses, beauties characteristic not only of design in general but of architectural design as such. But the question reminds us of those conditions and limitations of architectural works that restrict them to being what they are, and in so restricting them make them capable of being specifically beautiful at all. These limits are marked of course by the purposes that architectural technique can serve, a range so great and varied, not only by the endless kinds of building that man has accomplished or may yet accomplish, but also by the tremendous influence of variety in materials of construction so far manufactured or still to be found or invented and turned to structural uses, that it seems rather an infinite field of possibilities than a restricting range of technical limitations. And we must add to all this the enormous changes and developments brought about by the knowledge of physics and applied to engineering practice.

Once the purpose and the medium have been fixed, however, any architectural work must clearly define itself to serve that purpose to the degree possible in the medium, and even the medium itself must be chosen rather for the purpose in hand than for its intrinsic expressive possibilities. We do not build houses of nothing but plaster, though plaster as a surface for walls inside or outside may be highly suitable and æsthetically effective. Use is all-important. But the defining usefulness of a structure, since it still leaves the structure a spatial one, serves as clearly as a basic type for beautiful expressiveness, as the form of the human body serves sculpture to give it the actuality of defined spatial limitations necessary to any spatial expression at all. Besides this, though the ugliest building in the world might keep rain off machinery, for example, any transparently effective functioning of a building of any sort, since it comes at once to be defined in terms of that function, also expresses, even if crudely, some of the character and quality of such functioning in its own specifications in spatial form apparent to sense, and so to some degree potentially beautiful with the beauty of expression, almost, but never quite, regardless of the æsthetic surface content.

Once having seen that the very beauty of architectural works depends in part on an expressiveness possible only by virtue of the defining character of the useful structure, we shall not fall into the error that has, more than any other, confused architecture and blurred its beauty; nor shall we commit the compensatory fallacy of defining its beauty as its use. As the fact that an object is an object, or a body a body is not the fact of its being beautiful, so the fact that a house is a house, or a bridge a bridge, or a church a church, is not the fact that the house or the bridge or the church is beautiful. But as the actuality of sensuous surface is necessary for there to be beauty upon an object at all, as a human body to be a human body, whether beautiful or not, must have two arms, two legs, two eyes, must have, that is, the recognized spatial form of a human being; so if a house is to be a beautiful one, it must first of all be a house, a structure to keep out natural elements that would interfere with man's sheltered being, his specifically domestic functioning, his private individual activities, and his social, hospitable living. So far as elements of æsthetic surface, especially purely ornamental ones, at all interfere with these activities, so far as they are unrelated to them and fully extraneous, their beauty, æsthetically satisfying as it might be in itself, can not be the beauty of this building upon which they are superimposed; for this building is itself, defined as an object at all, by the purposes it serves. The beauty of entirely extraneous ornament is simply not *its* beauty, and is the more clearly felt as foreign and irrelevant and actually negating it, the more fully the building is grasped and realized as itself. Which is not to say at all, of course, that foreign styles may not be adapted successfully, or that ornament is not beautiful, or that it fails to enhance the beauty of buildings. On the other hand, the frank fulfilment of specific purpose upon a structure, the mere making of a long clear line of protecting roof against trees on a windy slope, or the lines of firm flat foundations achieving a convenient resting place there for human feet, though the æsthetic surface achieved may be itself almost negligible, express security, comfort, peace, protection, and so give to the æsthetic surface a beauty of expression hard to distinguish from the beauty of that surface strictly taken, since it is upon it that these qualities appear. Thus we neither need to fear that use as such will corrupt beauty nor that being æsthetically and richly beautiful need interfere with use or with vital expressive beauty itself.

ÆSTHETIC JUDGMENT

The very term sky-scraper was an æsthetic reproach until, in throwing off some of their traditional and largely adventitious character, tall city buildings used the possibilities of steel to meet their aims more directly. Now that they have come in many cases to achieve a design and a manner of ornament intrinsically successful as æsthetic surface, a sky-scraper, by virtue of being just that in name, is no more surely beautiful or ugly than a spoon or a table or a chair or a cottage in the country. But clearly enough, if its form and structure specify in spatial design such characteristics as are likely to accompany even the bare fulfilment of its purpose, as for example merely permanence, strength, and magnificent cubic capacity, expressive beauty it will possess. And if, as this huge columnar type of building becomes admitted and defined in human minds, the spatial characteristics and the effects of light and shadow and color that may be fit externals of its surface, are grasped by architects, and so, successfully achieved upon its spatial actuality, it is hard to see anything here but tremendous new opportunities for an expressive beauty that through strictly æsthetic surface character transforms mere strength and poise and permanence and spaciousness into grandeur and magnificence and a rich and even overpowering sensuous æsthetic beauty such as the Shelton Hotel in New York presents in its towering lines and shadows and masses, a beauty so familiar already that it is quite conventionally admired even by those who would, like most of us perhaps, have used sky-scraper as a damning epithet not so many years ago.

When we have once admitted that buildings are not natural events but artificial structures; when we have noticed that their use defines them as works of art, and their expressiveness makes them fine art, even though it is limited to the

265

few qualities intrinsically specified by any spatial form that achieves that form by structural technique, we shall be ready more intelligently and more whole-heartedly to be ravished and enraptured with the great sensuous richness of the æsthetic surface of architectural works, the elegant and studied proportions of interiors, the subtle and various beauties of stairways and arches, recesses and vistas, wall-spaces and doorways, and the infinite possibilities for appropriate ornament, from simple lines in moldings to the exuberance of the proscenium arch in a baroque theatre, or the luxurious magnificence of its tiers of boxes. And in exteriors we shall feel the fine dignity of a severe Spanish house of tile and stucco or the gorgeous richness of an impurely Gothic Spanish cathedral in its irregularly grouped masses and towers and its astonishing variety of architectural ornament, or the delicate and intricate loveliness of a French cathedral façade, or any of the thousand varieties of the sensuous or expressive beauties of architecture, with a fullness and depth limited only by the flexibility and the grasp of our powers of apprehension. In doing so we shall also experience moods and emotions akin to those that music stirs, since, if architecture is frozen music, the freezing has held and defined beauties whose subtle and transitory presence would otherwise have been missed.

We have conventional and useful terms such as symmetry, balance, proportion, in which much of the beauty of all spatial design is supposed to consist. But these words cover such multitudes of spatial variations that emphasis upon them rather blurs than clarifies the infinitely various modes in which they appear. And architecture is in any case not unique in its dependence upon them, since they are merely the simplest and most abstract designations of the thousands of individual specific beauties which are directly felt only as their unique spatial specification is apparent to trained or gifted perception as that upon which they are present in actuality.

But there are two more points with regard to architecture that should be noticed here. The technique of this art is not one of surface design alone, but of building. A sculptured group of figures must be supported and balanced physically so as not to collapse; but its physical stability is not that of the primary technique of sculpture as defining an expressive surface, so much as a subsidiary technical requirement, almost on the level of the modes of supporting pictures in frames upon walls. In architecture, works of no matter what degree of expressive, or of more narrowly sensuous, æsthetic beauty are constructed to support themselves throughout; and it is this physically structural technique that the professional architect must master first of all, and as integral to the operative process that achieves an architectural result. So that there is a further richness in architectural beauty, the felt structural poise and sureness not exhibited fully upon the surface except to the eyes of a mind that has to some degree mastered this structural technique, though no doubt many less trained eyes and minds half unconsciously grasp its perfection and success and are more fully stirred to appreciation of the spatial appearance that thus reveals upon its surface its inner supporting efficacy and completeness, making the work more fully a single whole and more truly expressive of these characters, associated with man's most dominating impulses and most civilized and social emotions, that architecture so signally embodies and specifies.

And finally, since, when purposes are most clearly defined, the forms that achieve them become in their turn more and more defined if they are to approach perfection in achievement, certain architectural forms, fitting certain elementary purposes, are repeated to the point of becoming for men orthodox and absolute in their familiarity, so that changes in the direction of positive æsthetic delightfulness seem at first mere wanton impiety. It is not that the familiar as such is what delights us as beautiful, but that certain forms, like sloping roofs, or flat ones, come to be identified with the meaning of roof, and Chinese pagodas and roof gardens may seem simply monstrosities or "against nature" to a sufficiently provincial mind, with no reality as roofs and so no beauty as such, though their obvious æsthetic satisfactoriness may be clear enough to any unprejudiced eye and their typical and familiar forms as necessary to a beautiful roof in one part of the world as gables in another. Since all that architecture expresses is so close to the fundamental cravings of man to live or work or play or worship at all, and since in any case vast numbers of buildings of all sorts are required, as music and painting and sculpture are not, here, more than in the other arts, we are likely to allow native use and familiarity to interfere with our pleasure in what would otherwise appear to us as its beauties.

As architecture is the art of building buildings with walls and roofs and interiors, with possibilities in size and variety of form and arrangement quite beyond those of the other spatial arts, since after all any of these may be subordinate aspects or parts of its æsthetic surfaces, and as architecture expresses not only the inner life of man, the feelings and emotions connected with his privacy, his domestic life, his hearth and home, as well as with his social prestige and power, his political aspirations, and the achievements of his civilization, but also all his success in the practical conquest of nature, though it lacks the temporal rhythm of music and the depths of poetry, it may fairly be said to be the richest and surest and most complete expression in art of man's whole self and of his relations to other men and to nature. It is fair, perhaps, to think of it as the most clearly adult of the arts, its sensuous pleasures so integrated in its expression of man's permanent interests that after poetry has faded from his soul, and music has become the world of dreams no longer to be realized and only sparingly to be indulged in, architecture still keeps its firm hold upon him, its intricate subtlety and its infinite variety, within a secure and substantial firmness, a permanent source of full æsthetic pleasure, as well as an infinitely expanding one, to which all the powers of his mind may more and more fully respond to find satisfaction and beauty as they grasp its outward sensuous richness, penetrate its inner strength, and realize its integral and humanly expressive perfection.

CHAPTER XII

THE COMBINED ARTS AND PROSE

1. The complexity of the combined arts, especially of the arts of the theatre. 2. Characteristic individuality of works of any of the combined arts. 3. Specific nature of these arts as varying with the predominance of one or another of the subsidiary constituents. 4. Illustrations: opera, verse with music in songs; summary statement. 5. Prose fiction as illustrating the combined character of literary art. 6. The linguistic medium and its linguistic structure; the underlying non-linguistic sensuous media and their non-linguistic structure. 7. The fundamental power of prose as art.

§ 1

IN a general treatment of æsthetics it would be inappropriate, as in a limited space it would be impossible, to attempt any full account of the arts, either as historically developed or as technically differentiated and characterized. But for any comprehension of the nature of expressive beauty, illustrations are required from the characteristic major arts, which have been treated separately one after another because expression in each of them is determined both by the peculiar technique and by the special medium of each, in other words by the kinds of æsthetic material of which its structures are composed and the way in which these elements are operated upon to form them, as well as by the artist's intention. Though this intention might conceivably take on external expressive form in various arts, the expression actually and determinately effected in one could not in the nature of the case be identically the same as its determinate specification in another. Moreover the arts are, so to speak, not pure. When we judge their works beautiful, we are not recording, except in rare and very simple, special cases, the beauty of one sort only of elementary æsthetic material.

This is obvious in the spatial arts, which use shape, space-relations, textures, and colors all at once, and often in structures not built entirely on principles native to these materials, to serve the artist as his sole guide to coherence and design. For in all these arts, types and forms are sometimes offered or even prescribed by nature or tradition or use, and expression thus comes about in terms congenial to æsthetic structures at least in part so determined. In the linguistic arts the composite character both as to elements and as to principles of structure is still more obvious, and even in music, rhythm, either as constituent elements or as more general form, is as important to strictly æsthetic beauty and expressiveness as purely tonal elements. Not only do the principles of structure as determined in the native orders of pitch, loudness and softness, and timbre, offer varying modes of combination themselves, but there is further the difference between sequence and simultaneity in combining tones, melodic structure as well as harmonic, that is, and there is of course the inner feeling and intention of the composer to modify all these structural possibilities. Thus even in music, the most strictly æsthetic of the arts, there is great complexity and variety both of constituent elements, or æsthetic materials, and of structural principles; and the expressive artistic intention may be more or less compatible with its medium, and so turn music away from its tonal paths, to strive for effects verging on those of poetry or drama or still more distant arts.

And this variety in the nature of elementary constituents, the complexity of structural principles, working in harmony or opposition, arising from the differing intrinsic orders of the various kinds of elements, the requirements of different specific techniques, the demands of established types and useful aims conditioning some of the forms employed, the drive of the artist's own expressive intent insisting on specification to the utmost possible degree of determinateness compatible with any actual medium, and the imposition of orders not intrinsic to the nature of the elements—all this complexity is vastly increased when the structure built is, say, an opera, when, in general, we are considering the so-called mixed or combined arts, those that employ not only æsthetic elements and structural principles themselves of divergent natures, but also finished, structural, expressive wholes of the various arts as constituents in their larger and more complex wholes, works of art having their own peculiar complex techniques and their own specific and unique expressive aims.

Here belong traditionally and characteristically the arts of the theatre; but, as we have noticed, most of the arts are from the point of view of æsthetic material and structural modes, also mixed arts. And since the judgments that record our experiences of beauty are so largely applied to these mixed works of art, since also the beauties of nature are mixed beauties in much the same sense, as we saw early in our account of the æsthetic surface of our world, it is clear that for any semblance of completeness even in a general survey, we must notice, if not the precise nature of these combined or mixed arts and of all the minor arts that enter into them so significantly, at least the general directions and tendencies in them, and so the nature of their kinds of æsthetic and expressive beauty.

It is only in examples that this can be made really clear, since every work of art is individual and unique, and only so capable of being expressive at all and to be called a work of some one nameable and characterizable art. But we may notice at least the way in which the combined arts range from the immediacy of music to the strictly transparent symbolism of language, as their character is more or less dominated by that of the arts of which they are combinations, or that of the æsthetic elements or the structural principles of these arts, their own specific character as expressive modes or varieties of beauty being further determined by possibilities not present to their varying elements or to the structural principles of their combination, except as these principles take into account effective fusion and the expressiveness possible and peculiar to their complex character, a character not that of the subsidiary constituent arts, but their own. The theatre uses dancing, spatial design, color and light, as it also uses poetry, and prose, and music; but the theatre speaks in its own terms as theatre, and architecture itself may be a minor element here, and so employed, moreover, for theatrical purposes and significance, as to transform its character and give it a determinate beauty as in and of a moving chain of events, quite beyond the powers of literal architectural design, not to be distinguished as architecture at all except by a separate analysis of its purely subsidiary structure. Its proper function is served, and hence its artistic character is grasped, only as directly constituting one aspect of a beauty through and through theatrical, and expressive only in the theatrical terms in which it appears.

In all these arts of the theatre it is at first sight difficult to find any clear conception of grouping or arrangement or classification, and the historical development of opera, for example, tells us little of its æsthetic principles as a developed artistic form. But our analysis of surface beauty and types of strictly æsthetic structure offers us a clue that brings some order into this apparent chaos and indicates on fairly sure æsthetic grounds the general sorts of beauty to be expected in the combined arts. Our analysis also indicates the determination of the character of their specific beauties through emphasis now on one now on another type of structure, the preponderance of one sort of æsthetic material over another, the predominance of one particular art over others, in the character of the whole, and the subordination of all subsidiary technique and all subsidiary materials through a structure achieved as the expression possible to the complex art itself, in its own terms, and specifying in these terms what it would be otherwise impossible to present to sense as exhibiting the one central point or significance.

But first let us notice the genuine complexity that faces us here. The stage itself, or if not a stage proper, the achievement anywhere of a spectacle for an audience, involves architectural design and arrangement to suit this new determining condition. And as all architecture has an internal filling, exits, entrances, suitable spaces, furniture, hangings, and even utensils and implements, so the stage requires its properties, works of any number of minor arts and crafts, and even representations or suggestions of natural outdoor surroundings or weather conditions. And within, it may use paintings and sculpture and decorative design, incidentally complete in themselves and integrally significant in the whole. But the performance may involve all the temporal arts as well. If so, it employs them both as completed subsidiary wholes, songs, dances, poems, and in their characteristic elements, tonal qualities, rhythm, transparent linguistic symbols for denotation, and poetry and prose for all that poetry and prose may achieve as single arts, as well as for their share in the functioning of all the elements and structural patterns, to give expression to the significance of the movement, gesture, and speech of human bodies in a plotted whole of emotionally charged action, presented as spectacular pattern or as representation or as both, to eyes and ears and minds capable of grasping a defining artistic intention, thus uniquely revealed in all its determinateness of expressive specification.

What with costume as historically rich in association, or as purely decorative, or as emotionally significant, the conventional movements of bodies and gestures as directly but also subtly denotative, the dance as pantomime or as pure spatially patterned rhythm, music as emotional coloring or dominating rhythmical structure or even symbolic denotation, as in Wagnerian motifs, poetry in all its possibilities for thought and emotion and imagery and sounding æsthetic surface, the human voice with its fullness of defined intention in words and accent, and its depths of vital emotional power in pure tonal quality, the immediate surroundings of this action in stage properties and decoration, in lighting and color and design, and its outer encompassing or confronting auditorium and audience, felt as participating not in the drama itself, but in the full proportions of its spatial completeness and in the emotional significance of its actualized presentation, with music sharing in all possible degrees of integration, from accompanying emotionally touched decoration or interlude, to such full participation as sets rate and rhythm, or propounds and specifies the emotional themes exhibited in the whole performance, a musical conductor actually dominating the scene with his baton—with all this, and as much more as any one who has ever been to the theatre may easily add, we do seem faced with a complexity not to be analyzed to any advantage. For no one knows what possibilities it may hold for the future, and in the past it has so varied in expressive intention, structural form, and sensuous content, that we might go on almost indefinitely in the mere enumeration and definition of types of theatrical art, from ballet and tableau and vaudeville, to farce and comedy, or historical pageant, or tragedy itself, or perhaps to oratorio or cantata or opera, with little to add to our general comprehension but a long list of names of combined forms of art. Sometimes these are so unmusical as problem plays, with a text hardly even dramatic in form or style, and only emotionally effective and expressive so far as the problem is lost in the vitality of characters and in social situations clearly depicted in themselves, with definite human significance as events or conduct quite apart from any thesis that the play is expounding.

§ 2

From Aristotle to modern manuals of play-writing or short-story composition, we are told of course that there are three elements to be considered in narrative or in dramatic composition, plot, character, and setting. And there are analyses of dramatic or of narrative structure that point out such obvious necessities as unity of one sort or another, though it turns out that this may be achieved in many ways, and that even as technically achieved to perfection, it may be the merest external framework, useless to dramatic art, since it is often only a specious unity, not clearly demanded by vital expressive intention, and hence actually irrelevant. But it would be absurd here to attempt to outline the technique of dramatic composition, even if there were any acceptable or clearly distinguishable single technique involved. The very point of our account is rather that all the arts of the theatre involve numerous subsidiary techniques, as determined by the media employed. Their distinguishing feature is the coherent unity achieved in actual presentation in terms only very loosely to be called the terms of other arts, since the expressive aim in view requires such a combination of these under a dominating expressive intention as transforms their terms into those of the theatre, the formidable strength of the steel and stone of architecture, for example, being abstracted, so to speak, and even increased in effect, as thick masses of dull color, produced by stage-lighting upon burlap hangings.

And it is not mere representation here that gives the effect intended, though that may often play a very great part in the rich and stirring emotional connotation, but sheer design. In some purified theatrical world we might very well suggest the terrors of even so famous a building as Macbeth's castle at Inverness by purely spatial arrangements of colored shapes and shadows, more effectively than by any recognizably architectural structure. This is in fact only one example of what has actually been attempted in our own time with important results. What it indicates for general æsthetics is the literal truth of the statement above, that the very terms of the subsidiary arts, as employed in the combined arts, are transformed by the aim of the particular composition, and whether there is or is not any accurate type-name for this composition itself—tragedy, light-opera, farce, comedy of manners, miracle-play—the individual composition, the work of art as a case of complex or combined art, must have, in order to be clearly anything at all, its own transforming intention and expressiveness, its emotional tone, its specific character, its point, in short, upon which every subsidiary constituent, from æsthetically elementary patches of color, or single sounds or shapes, through all the structural possibilities to completed artistic wholes of the major or minor arts, must be focussed in a felt perspective which so transforms them all as to make them appear, separately taken or actually removed from this complex set of technically achieved and expressively dominated structural relations, tawdry, ugly, pointless, and deformed.

So even, or perhaps most of all, of bodily movement and speech. As stage jewels, exhibited upon a human throat that is to be seen from distant tiers of boxes, should be large rather than precious, thus achieving specified splendor or richness in the æsthetic medium of sparkling color upon a physical substance quite irrelevant except as it furnishes this required æsthetic material, the flashing light and color itself; so for theatrical purposes exaggeratedly clear enunciation, rates of speech slower or more rapid than those of ordinary life, rhetorical effectiveness, poetical richness or extravagance, bodily movements more swift or more agile, more emphasized and more formal, and costume out of place at the grandest of grand balls or the most regal of garden parties, may be only the surest terms in which to carry out the theatrically unified and determinate emotional and conceptual specifications of a performance. And masks and wigs and even puppets may serve here better than human countenances or human bodies. We should expect, indeed, that quite literal realism on the stage would fail, though of course no one need be so ignorant or so rash as to deny its past triumphs or its future possibilities.

It is such specific possibilities, all-important as actual works of art, that creative minds realize for us. It is the part of general theory simply to notice that there are no prescriptions to be made except those that lie in the nature of the sensuous elements, the structural limitations, or rather the structural possibilities, of the less complex arts themselves, and the vital creative powers of the imaginations of men, intent on expressing felt significance in æsthetic terms. So simple a consideration as this of the necessary subordination and transformation of artistic terms in all the arts of the theatre, would answer those narrowly literary critics that speak of the bombastic rhetoric of Shakespeare as if his plays were not genuine works of theatrical art, only so to be properly comprehended. Lines from *Othello* may be quoted, out of their context, that would condemn any poet of rhetorical absurdity and fustian; but in the terror of those tense scenes poetry would become pale anti-climax, were its terms not carried out as dramatic text to dramatic action, where, since we have no drums or brass or cymbals to employ, words must outdo themselves in all the brazen trumpetings of rhetoric, unquotable outside its stage frame-work and its desperate emotional context of sweeping human passions, hurling themselves abortively upon their object in a theatrically inevitable sequence and sum of significant dramatic events and action. In all of the combined arts we may notice further how one sort of element or another, one sort of structure or another, through emphasis upon it due to the direction of an artist's native gift and training, or his general inclinations, or his special intention in a given case, comes to predominate, and thus to characterize his work as primarily poetical, or primarily dramatic, or primarily musical, or as pantomime rather than ballet, or interpretation and representation rather than creation, or spectacle rather than dramatic action, or as sheer ideas in discourse instead of full emotional movement in bodily and vocal animation.

§ 3

To begin with the dance. There are two tendencies even here, one that leads to formal pattern achieved in difficult bodily movements, conventionalized and named in a whole special vocabulary,—*pas de quatre, pas pointe, pas allongé, entrechat, battement*—perpetuated in schools of ballet-dancing, and appreciated only by one who realizes something of the possibilities of the technique and the strict limitations of its conventional execution. And there is the freer, unorthodox ballet, tending towards pantomime and representation, and so, were speech added, to representative dramatic performance. And dramatic performance, to be at its best, never gives up the expressiveness possible to patterned rhythmical bodily movement, though actors often neglect this fundamentally powerful element of their art. Indeed they may so turn to speech as their medium as to suggest that the reading of a play is as good as a performance of it, a suggestion not to be taken too seriously, however, since, as merely read, a play is not presented in those theatrical terms which alone can give the intended æsthetic specification literally and directly to vision as well as hearing; especially, of course, to the listening ear, not merely to the mind through print, imaginative and flexible as that mind may be. If one's own reading is preferable to a bad performance, at least such an imagined play is not quite fully or literally played.

Even more than in music, the art of the theatre, through its subsidiary technique of acting, allows artists in this technique of performance to transform a mediocre and perhaps vague conception into a distinguished and intense one, fully animated by the body, the voice, and the controlling mind of the actor or the director, to a determinate specification in immediate æsthetic terms of a point not felt by the writer of the lines in any such fullness or vigor or significance. The familiar reverse process by which great plays may be ruined, or foreign plays domesticated, or brilliant plays dulled in presentation hardly needs to be mentioned. Our point here is simply that the primary technique of the theatre, like that of music, is not merely the subsidiary technique of performance, of the actor's art. So that two points follow, as in the case of music. On the one hand the general technique must be grasped by all the participants, whether actors, decorators, costumers, or stage-directors, if the presentation is to be focussed upon the achievement of that temporal and spatial specification that is its perfection. On the other hand, the author of the play, while he need not be either a stage decorator or an actor or a director, must feel and imagine and compose in terms of all these subsidiary techniques, as well as that of the literary form—also subsidiary—that he uses.

For the theatre is relentless, more clearly than any other art, in its domination of all its constituent elements and constituent arts, which it presents only in its own theatrical perspective, from which, if they are separated, they fall to pieces as worthless rubbish, like stage-jewels or stage costumes from an old actor's chest. The poet must be not solely poet when he composes for the stage. He must see and hear his words, picture his images, feel his rhythms, as issuing from actors' lips before an audience in a theatre facing a stage; else they may fall flat and exhibit sheer impotence upon an æsthetic surface empty of beauty even for those who come to hear and see in all good faith, as a lovely and delicate face and complexion, under stage illumination, may be only pale and indistinctly featured and uninteresting to the view of spectators. To achieve beauty upon the stage even the human face requires such emphasis of color and line, needs, that is, to be presented in such æsthetic terms, as in life would be exaggeration or caricature or the stark ugliness of physical deformity. Here again, however, we must remember other possibilities such as the realism of Duse, actually blushing upon the stage, to the despair of actors less astonishingly gifted with intense feeling to summon to their effects, and not only the wonder and admiration of native and foreign audiences, but a model of the actor's art in the eyes of the most hardened and the most discerning critics. But such so-called realism does not fall out of a theatrical conception or an emotional tone. It is simply that a gifted actor may use even his most everyday natural movements on the stage so long as he chooses them under the full guidance of the point of a play to see that they are terms in which the art of the theatre may achieve its specific intention in the given case.

As we pass from the pure, rhythmical, and even traditional patterns of ballet to the full richness of dramatic action with gesture and bodily movement subordinated to the rhythms of poetic speech, with its burden of suggested images and clearly denoted ideas, we pass also from fully rhythmical, and in that sense musical, art to art in which the predominating medium is more and more linguistic and symbolic. The extreme would be not even prose plays on a real stage, where at least some spatially patterned rhythms and some actual tonal elements must survive, but plays in books, only a step removed from the dialogue of novels, where all of the characteristically and directly given visual and auditory surface would have disappeared, with its theatrical and architectural restrictions on the one hand, and its full sensuous volume on the other. And the indefinitely great variety of authentic expressive possibilities that lie between, or beyond, in other directions and other sorts of combinations, needs only a passing remark. If rhythmic and tonal qualities predominate, the principles of musical structure become more important. Opera is usually thought of as a form of musical rather than dramatic art, though even the music of operas, given in concert, is felt to be truly dramatic. But opera clearly suffers from over-complexity. If it sustains itself as beautiful spectacle without losing the rigor of its strictly musical structure, so much can not be said for it as moving drama. For here, apparently, one technique and one expressive intention conflicts with another, the explicitly measured rhythms of a musical score largely failing to allow the more irregular and subtle rhythms of emotional acting and language to exhibit their native tempo and character, and the elaborateness of color and spatial design, which may in general tone harmonize with the music well enough, often failing to suit the dramatic fable, or *vice versa*.

§ 4

At least it must be said that, as we are most familiar with it, so-called grand opera is so *very* grand in decoration, in spatial and colored elements of setting and costume, as well as in the complex richness of its music including the tremendous technique of its vocal performance, that either of these aspects is enough to occupy fully the perceptive grasp of a spectator. The beauties that are actualized at all are distinguished and separated as those of musical compositions or of changing spatial designs in color, or they may be more truly representative beauties. The dramatic aspect is only too likely to be lost in caricature or parody or nonsense. At any rate, even the music dramas of Wagner stand higher as music than as drama proper, and although there is no doubt of the immensity of the opportunities in this sort of combined art, perhaps this immensity is rather too much for human beings. Opera, as we hear it, and see it, and pay for it, is fairly barbaric in the way in which it overwhelms us with very slightly integrated sensuous splendors and distractions; and it is very modern and civilized indeed in the way in which it provides for exhibiting the vocal technique and personal charm of the actor-singers, the plutocratic standing of members of the audience, and the ingenuity of costumers for both. If it is sometimes very beautiful in parts as a successful subordination of elements and of whole works of subsidiary arts in one defined and significant whole, it must after all be said to fail, since it pretends, at least, to be an art of the theatre, in which human action and humanly moving events are portrayed. And it is very doubtful indeed whether either opera singers or their audiences experience any very full or very fine appreciation even of operatic music, since as music it is often, at least in large part, a matter of vocal virtuosity, or, on the other hand, an extremely complex musical structure not even perceived in its complete tonal æsthetic surface except by very thoroughly trained or gifted musicians, who would alone be able to appreciate the actual beauty of its specification of quality and character and significance. The orchestra score itself may be quite lost on a typical opera audience, or it may, for those of musical capacities and competence, be all that the opera really offers that is to be dignified by the term art at all.

So simple and almost natural a combination of two arts in one as verse and music in songs is a more familiar and perhaps more useful illustration of the nature and tendencies of the combined arts. Here, as clearly as in any case, however complex, we recognize the unity of the whole as one of mood and intention. The tonal and rhythmical definiteness of the music must be the specification in these terms of the kind of thing the song as words or verses says and means. We may take for clarity a simple folk-song, sung by a child, with no instrumental accompaniment, no other harmonizing voices, no idea in the singer's mind of the words separated from the music or the music without the words, the one absolutely demanding the other as in the song itself, learned from a mother as just a song. In our recognizing of the fitness of the character and quality of the tonal composition as a whole, here a simple melody, to the verses, we are acknowledging the oneness of the expression, its single point as a work of art. And this fitness is more than merely that of the character of one whole to another, for the tune in its literal temporal progress must carry the same mood and intention, or the changes in mood, which the verses alone express only so far as such expressiveness lies in the power of words. Taken with the words in the song itself, the music carries this expressiveness out, at once further specifying and defining and deepening and completing an expression not itself, because not fully determinate, except as words and music are part of each other. The rhythm of the verse is formalized and measured and emphasized by the more explicit rhythm of the notes; its rising and falling feeling and meaning are heightened and deepened, or at least not contradicted, in the purer tonal medium of melody, by movements in pitch and loudness and timbre, or quality of voice. Its significant syllables are never lost and are often made more significant in musical stresses. Its rapid or slow changes are made more explicitly slow or rapid in actual musical measure, in beats and their mathematically simple divisions; its whole intention, if not in its conceptual aspect, at least in its lyrical feeling, is carried out more fully and more precisely as well as more richly. Both mere music and mere poetry disappear as such. While as component arts they lose, perhaps, the one its purity of tonal character, the other its subtlety of factual denotation, they become together a song, with a quality, a character, and a meaning peculiar to the art of song and impossible to either of the subsidiary arts that go to make it what it is.

Thus words and music can not be arbitrarily fitted to each other, as the commonly inept translations of foreign songs so often remind us. If the song is not composed as such, both words in the music and music in the words of one mind with a single intention, at least to set verses to music, or to furnish a musical score with words, requires full grasp of the given specified feeling and significance of the one or of the other by whoever is to put upon music such a denotative linguistic burden as it will carry to an æsthetically determinate emotional completion, or upon lines of verse such tonal structure and measured rhythm as will make them a single whole, deeper and richer and more determinate, perhaps, than poetry itself. While musicians use speech habitually, poets unfortunately are often little acquainted with elementary musical technique. Thus in our day it is usually musicians that set poems to music, as we say; and songs are written as if they were strictly and solely musical compositions, the words perhaps not inappropriately set, since they are taken as found by one who at least understands them as language, but the music composed not so much to carry them as to use them to its own sophisticated musical purposes in a composition, where, along with the melody, harmony enters, with its further tonal structure, the elements chosen and the structure perfected almost wholly for their characteristically musical effect.

Thus the combination is dominated by one of its elements which might, theoretically at least, have remained subsidiary, as we may suppose it did in Greek choruses, where the whole structure was certainly no more dictated by musical form than by strictly poetic rhythms. The combination was neither music nor poetry in the narrow sense of either term, but a poetry so explicitly musical as to be sensuously richer and emotionally deeper than poetry would otherwise be, or a music taking on a whole range of linguistic denotation otherwise definitely beyond its powers of expression. Not that this gives us the character of the Greek chorus, which remains still a rich mine for exploration, or at least a rich field for speculation; but that the Greek chorus would seem to be, in one of its aspects, an actual example of the amalgamation of two arts in a unity not dominated by either one of them, but achieving specific character of its own out of the characteristic materials and forms of component arts. Perhaps, too, the demands of musical form in its present elaborate stage of development make the creation of songs, pure and simple, in the sense in which we have used them as illustrating the æsthetic principles of the combined arts, unnatural or even impossible. Even the *Lied* of the great nineteenth century composers is primarily a musical form. It uses words, of course, often those of famous poets, but one almost feels that this dramatic content fails to be sung except as the singer calls upon his dramatic and even theatrical gifts and powers rather than upon his purely musical competence. It might even be said that such *Lieder* are dramatic performances, not songs at all. But that fact would not vitiate the principle illustrated above in a form of combined art which is not dramatic but simply lyrical, songs of children, songs of simple people, or those songs whose music the very spirit of Burns adopted as its own, his new words being so natively akin in feeling and meaning as to become the music's own.

What we have said of the combined arts may be very briefly summarized. First of all they are themselves. They speak in their own terms, whether those terms are the characteristic materials or the finished products of the more nearly simple or purer, less mixed arts. And hence the elements and structures of these arts are so transformed, as components in a larger whole, as to be, if taken separately, neither satisfying nor beautiful, and very possibly deformed and ugly. Secondly, the complexity of any combined art may be so great as to fail of accomplishment, in which case it falls apart before our eyes, and the perfection of the mere fragments caught by perception is rather an indication of the failure of the whole to transform these for its specific intended effect, than an indication of its success; for no single work of art can ever be a mere sum of lesser ones, but only their fusion and transformation into aspects of its own unique and singular beauty. But thirdly, such failures can not dictate to creative spirits, whose powers no mere theorist need attempt to delimit. And fourthly, then, all manner of combinations may be possible, their beauties being primarily rhythmical or symbolic, temporal or spatial, plastic or static, musical or sculptural or architectural, as the artist's sensuous perception, creative powers, and spiritual affinities, whether native or the results of training, lead him to allow one or another sort of æsthetic material or structural form, or one or another of the arts themselves, to lend to his works of combined art a beauty and character more or less removed from the effective beauties of these less mixed arts.

§ 5

In prose fiction we come upon an art in the sense of technical method and medium to achieve expression, and of course also prose may present an auditory æsthetic surface; but our common phrase, *literature and the arts*, indicates plainly enough that the status of literature, if literature is among the arts at all, is peculiar there, and it may seem odd to introduce at this point in an essay on æsthetics a characterization of literature, which, though it is an art in the clear sense just noted, is so slightly æsthetic in the narrow sense of the term. While prose sentences and prose styles have their own peculiar beauty, novels and stories and essays, which we may take as typical, are hardly enjoyed sufficiently as technically achieved auditory surfaces to account for the high place of prose literature in men's estimation, much less for its enormous popularity with all civilized peoples. And more than this, novels are not even intended for reading aloud, so that as the actual discourses that they are, they have no immediately present sensuous surface character at all, and so no strictly æsthetic beauty. Neither script nor print is the surface of discourse, but only a very familiar symbolic notation, employed and hence taught, primarily less for the purposes of literary enjoyment than as a means to practical communication. Thus prose discourse itself has no visual surface; and silently read prose, though it may often involve some auditory imagery, certainly does not require and need not achieve, as poetry of course does, a full and directly sensuous specification of any sort in order to be appreciated as the intelligible and, as we all sometimes surely feel, the beautifully expressive thing that it is.

If prose is æsthetically satisfactory, it is so on the grounds given to define, or at least roughly to describe, the æsthetic experience in our first few chapters; prose discourse is certainly as truly as coffee or as sculpture disinterestedly attended to in absorbed contemplation, indulged in for its own sake, and with positive and enduring pleasure. What seems to be lacking to it, considered as æsthetic surface quality, is any immediately presented characteristic sensuous content, and without this it would seem to be a mystery that it can be contemplated at all, if it is yet to remain objective in any clear sense, so that its beauty shall be its own quality and character, and not merely that of our intellectual and imaginative activity. What we have already said about language, however, solves this difficulty; for the peculiarity of language as a medium is its universal range of denotation, its own symbolic nature being such that what one man means another man may know from his words, because words in discourse have meanings long since assigned to them, and learned by all those who use speech instead of gesture or some other sign language. And these meanings are learned in rich experiential contexts, which language also inevitably carries.

§ 6

Now it is obviously these meanings in relations indicated by the formal structure of a language, its grammar and syntax, together with all its other conventional, sometimes latent, modes of connection, of transition and subordination, juxtaposition, and word order in general, stress, accent, phrasing, and intonation, all of which may be carried out in the printed or written notation of systematic symbolism—it is these meanings that are presented to us in discourse, and almost directly, for written or spoken discourse is almost transparent to educated ears and eyes. These meanings are in large part, as we have already seen, ultimately æsthetic data, not so fully specified by linguistic symbols as by actual sensuous and particular æsthetic surfaces, but called up by the imagination, or, in their connections and relations, grasped by the intellect. In the one case they are recognized sensuous content, in the other a changing structural scheme, within which a world is held together not essentially or qualitatively different in its form and structure, or in its movement, from the actual physical world, which appears to sense, but whose structure after all is itself for human knowledge just such a discursive logical scheme of ordered relations. Thus prose fiction has in the main no strictly æsthetic material peculiar to itself, its medium being spoken or written symbols instead of actual, æsthetically appreciable and enjoyed surface, except, of course, so far as spoken discourse shares in the rhythmic and tonal character so important in poetry, and in music its explicit and characteristic elementary nature, immediately present to mind as auditory form and content.

Our characteristic and common enjoyment of prose is not only of its sound. Even when the sound is comparatively important, meaning is infinitely more so; and this meaning, although it is ultimately determinate only as imagined sensuous content, is not limited to the images of any one sense, nor its relational structure guided mainly by principles of order native to any one sort of æsthetic material. Words may in fact indicate, even though relatively indeterminately, any sense content whatever, as well as any relational idea; even the precise character of a particular work of art that words can name, as well as any event or series of events, any emotional climax, or other change of emotion, any character of art or life or nature.

It is not fanciful, then, to consider prose fiction as one of the combined arts, with the added complexity that its own peculiar medium, instead of being sensuous or æsthetic, is symbolic and even logical. As so considered prose fiction is characteristic of literature in general. It is ideas, as well as sensuous data, or objects, or events, that literature refers to through its symbolism; and though its range is universal, its specification is never fully determinate. It is a peculiar creative flow that carries us along over all sorts of æsthetic material, discerned through its almost transparent linguistic symbolism as in significant relations which make of the terms a genuinely coherent world. This world is different from the world of life only in being clearly bounded, separated from the universal context of nature by a distinct beginning and end beyond which it does not reach at all, and in being composed of select and perspicuous material also clearly outlined in explicit temporal and spatial relations, which, instead of being embedded in a confusing and overwhelming matrix of other relations and events, as the realities of nature and of life are obscured in the moving universe of all reality, stand out clear and emphatic and consistent and whole and independent, a bounded and ordered unity, an anagram of life and nature, a humanly composed whole, exactly what we call a work of art, and a work of fine art, since its sole aim is its own achieved definite and unique expressiveness,

not practical communication or any other ulterior sort of usefulness or purpose.

Thus if every art must have its own peculiar, strictly and
fully æsthetic medium to achieve expression upon such a
unique sort of surface, prose must be considered either not
an art at all or not very fully an art. For it uses a symbolism
for medium which is itself only slightly and incidentally
æsthetic, scarcely at all so in such intelligent and rapid reading as may yet follow and grasp almost all of what a novel
expresses either for its author or to its readers. Not that the
symbolic medium is literally or completely transparent;
both as print and as sounding syllables it has sensuous character in order to be seen or heard at all, and it would be false
to deny beauty to this character. Mathematical symbolic
form itself is not devoid of appearance, and as the adoption
of Arabic numerals made possible much of mathematical
progress in ideas, so languages crystallize thought. We may
go so far as to think a dog an animal of three letters because
a three-lettered word is all that we habitually notice in reading of him, or like those hackneyed provincials, so often
used to illustrate the point, we may identify a sound with
a meaning and think people barbarous and uncivilized who
call bread *pain*, when it is really bread. All of us no doubt
give to our world and its objects some of the character of
the names they bear. A rose, if it might smell as sweet by
another name, would only smell *like* a rose, and not quite
be one, to a mind trained exclusively through language and
in language.

As this is true of names and single words, it is still truer
of linguistic orders; so much so, that in the last resort great
thinkers have put upon the real world the structures of logic,
and upon logic itself the structures of language, as if physi-

cal things were grammatical objects and subjects by nature, and sense qualities really verbal adjectives and grammatical predicates. If the art of prose is not so to confuse us, we must admit that much of its success in expression, and hence its true perfection and beauty, is not in its own sounds or order, or in their strictly auditory structure, but in their calling to mind of such qualities as our imaginations recognize in full sensuous and æsthetic specification, put into such order and relations as are possible to the natures of physical objects in the world, the natures of passions in human souls, and the natures of such events and crises as come about when these souls confront each other in this physical world, the true medium of prose being thus all the qualities and relations of all things.

Not that literature merely represents the world of life and nature, but that, being primarily denotative and symbolic, and structurally systematic, it builds a significant expressive arrangement out of such elements as it selects in such order and coherence as it is capable of. This coherent, ordered whole is fiction, romantic or fanciful or realistic, but still fiction, by virtue merely of the selection of what excludes all that is not thus selected, put into a structure built by mind and imagination, not by history itself in the natural course of events. The history that men write in books, so far as it is fine structural prose and logically sequential treatment, beginning at one point and ending at another, is of course an artistic structure, not a natural one, and rather a variety of fiction than a sort of science.

If we think of the linguistic symbolic medium of prose as peculiar to the art of prose, and as the full medium it employs, instead of thinking of its medium and structure as mixed, and of prose itself as a combined art using all the possible sorts of ideal and imagined qualities and characters which it indirectly presents through these never fully transparent symbols, then it is a single unmixed art, but decidedly a lesser art æsthetically, since this symbolic medium is so thin and poor, tonally and rhythmically, so elaborate but also so wavering and various in different voices and to variously acute and variously trained ears, as to have no clearly felt or fully grasped principles, its structure depending instead upon inaudible and latent categorical determinations, and on logical and conventional principles not auditory at all, and often not capable of being auditorily conveyed, but only grasped through a painfully learned and then unconsciously appropriated dogmatism of referential systematization, plentifully enough illustrated in the mere existence of homonyms.

But in realizing the preponderance of meaning in the beauty of literary composition, and treating it as an art whose æsthetic material lies mainly just beyond the semi-transparent surface of its symbolic technical medium, we must be careful not to seem to be denying the refined and sophisticated beauties of words in sentences and paragraphs, not an altogether different sort of beauty from that called economy or elegance in mathematical symbolism and its structures. But in literature this beauty is far more subtle and complex and personal and even arbitrary than mathematical elegance, so that, as we noticed above, the hearing of a single sentence of an author's writing, even when we do not very attentively follow to grasp its import, may positively mark for us an author's identity in his style. It is very often forgotten, however, that it is not merely sound in such a case, but diction and sentence structure that we say we hear, when really we are, to a definite degree, conceptually and not sensuously grasping the diction, taking it directly as the meaning that it has, and taking the sentence-structure as an order of ideas rather than an order of words, an order not possibly auditory, except so far as the meanings underneath the words may in certain special cases have auditory reference, when, that is, the meanings themselves are sounds.

No one who has written sentences or paragraphs is likely to forget the very flexible but very insistent demands of the bare sounds of words in connection, if they are to convey meaning economically and at the same time precisely, and yet not offend the ear. Scientific reports themselves make rigorous demands in this respect, and at the best may achieve a kind of beauty in transparency not very different from that of the subsidiary technique of performance of a 'cellist like Casals, all of his performer's art disappearing in the heard musical composition. But pure transparency is not rich æsthetic content, and scientists as scientists do not write prose. As their ideal is mathematically precise generalization, so their medium ideally approaches mathematical symbolism, not the medium of verbal language, whether presented as history, or as the more imaginative fiction of narrative, or of psychological analysis.

The point that we have been making may now perhaps be accurately and clearly stated. If prose is to be considered a more or less unmixed tonal temporal art, its peculiar medium is systematic symbolic verbal language, and this medium is æsthetically, for the ear, subject only to very ill-defined and very flexible principles of tonal and rhythmical structure. Its bare elementary æsthetic auditory material is far poorer and less intelligibly or intrinsically ordered than the tonal and rhythmic elements of poetry, not to mention music. But since this medium is always more or less transparent, instead of being an ultimately given and arresting æsthetic surface, it may be considered the medium only of a secondary and subsidiary technique. In that case the primary æsthetic medium, upon which the imaginative creative technique of the author's mind operates, is not language as such but all that the linguistic symbols refer to in æsthetic and moral content, and structural and dynamic relations, established not among words and sentences but within this imaginatively rich field of content itself. So considered, prose is a mixed art, its subsidiary technique being linguistic and symbolic and formal, its genuine underlying æsthetic surface, contemplated through this semi-transparent medium, being composed of the widest range of elements of all æsthetic varieties, in structures built on all sorts of principles, but finally held together less through the æsthetic principles familiar in the other arts than through the vaguely felt or entirely unknown principles of moving nature, various felt emotional and vital spiritual demands, and conscious or half-conscious imaginative affinities and connections, realized in the author's mind and brought to light more or less explicitly in his finished writings.

Without at all minimizing the subtleties and difficulties and perfections of the peculiar symbolic technique of literature, we must, in order to account for its tremendous expressive power and beauty, admit its complex combining nature, where all the elements of all the other arts, and all the vast range of elements and meanings that the other arts do not so easily operate upon, or can not operate upon at all, are used to construct its works.

Hence the temptation to turn prose and even fiction to so-called moral purposes of instruction or persuasion, as if it were a nobler function to persuade men of some human dogma or to offer them in a mildly pleasurable, but indirect and hence blurred and confusing form, such information about the world as science gives us more economically and more accurately, than to present to them the pure possibilities of human life in the natural world and in the society of men. Didactic and propagandist fiction, taken as fiction, is just so much less effective and perfect literary art as it is successful in its teaching or its persuasion, since either of these two motives may at the best not seriously interfere with clear imaginative vision and structure. As instruction and moral persuasion, such fiction may be valuable for educating children, or for teaching or persuading those adults whose minds shrink from the hard clarity of facts, or from so much of undiluted or unsweetened truth as men may actually have achieved or mistakenly feel that they possess.

§ 7

But we have still to notice the outstanding artistic value of literature, perhaps properly to be called its intrinsic and peculiar beauty, which lies in the fullness and range of its expressiveness, its function being thus moral in the old-fashioned sense of the word, humanly significant, that is. The elementary and particular qualities and characters, both of nature itself and of human nature, are more or less within the content or at least the possible grasp of all human minds. Hence the creative genius of rich and powerful minds, using these particular elements as materials, may build such structures as characterize and specify for us otherwise undreamt depths and complexities of emotion and circumstance and events. Here we may contemplate more fully than in any of the other arts the vast possibilities of life, of human passion and human emotion, the weakness or pathos or tragedy of human character, the sweetness of human spirits or their baseness, the graciousness and generosity and rich delight possible to social intercourse, the extravagances of love, the tawdry or thrilling external glory of war, as well as its waste and violence and sordidness, the horrors of natural calamities, the rigors or desperation of poverty, the power and strength and greatness as well as the small meanness of human beings, and all the thousand relations that men bear to each other and to society and physical nature, whether in Russian villages, or French courts, or Italian cities, or English country houses, or mid-west American towns.

For modern life, as music seems able still with its strict æsthetic surface to reveal to us and specify those emotions and feelings that we know or aspire to in our hurried complex activities; as architecture, more than ever necessary to all the functioning of business and society, is still vitally expressive of so many characteristic aspects of our whole civilization; so in our time literature, most of all prose itself, expresses for us, in reasonable compass and an intelligible order, the general and the particular possibilities of human life over a range and to a depth that make it peculiarly satisfying. It not only meets our demand for contemplation in a world too rapidly moving and too complex to be grasped in its whole actuality, but expands our vision and enlarges our sympathies, and allows us like gods to view all things natural and human *sub specie æternitatis.* Whatever the æsthetic nature of prose fiction, its vital and its vast expressiveness distinguish it as beautiful with the beauty of great art.

CHAPTER XIII

EXPRESSIVENESS IN NATURE AND SYMBOLISM IN ART

1. The possibilities for expression in nature. 2. The nature of symbolism. 3. The confused intention of the symbolist in poetry. 4. Direct expressiveness of natural phenomena; æsthetic types. 5. Dependence of expression upon the observer and consequent variations in natural expressive beauty.

§ 1

THE beauties of the fine arts have been felt by many theorists to be the only noble and spiritual beauties, and the general underlying principle of such a view is plain enough. Since the arts are works of mind and spirit, carried out in such natural material as is itself only physical stuff, beauty being wrought upon it by human imaginative intention, working through an appropriate technique of operation and thus externalizing in defined form and structure a mental or spiritual content, this beauty of works of art has been felt quite naturally to be humanly significant and expressive as nature could not be. And if men's minds are taken to be not merely God's works, but his highest works, their spirits sharing in his divinity, the works of these minds may be even divinely expressive. What may easily be forgotten here is that all physical materials, in being sensuously perceptible, have as their surfaces strictly æsthetic content. Hence to use physical materials is to use those æsthetic materials, texture, color, and the rest, that such physical materials inevitably carry with them and bear upon their face. Furthermore, and this is still more to the point, any finished work of art has still a sensuously perceived surface itself, the surface of physical stuff or of events as present to mind through the senses, so that its own qualities must of necessity be such sensuous æsthetic qualities as the surface of physical nature presents, its beauties, therefore, the beauties of natural sensuous elements, in structures which at the most rearrange these elements to form specific designed æsthetic surfaces, acceptable to human beings in contemplation, and intuited by them as beautiful. As the sheen of silk fabrics is still the work of worms, or of those forces or substances in nature that give us dyes and lustres, so the beauty of music is only the beauty of a structure of such sounds as are produced by physical contacts of various sorts of resonant bodies; and more of the beauty of the classic works of Greek art lies in the beauty of native Greek marbles than we always choose to remember.

But further than this, the structures, temporal or spatial, in which works of art become the individual bounded wholes that they are, as well as the intrinsic relations that define tonal or colored or other specific sorts of sensuous elements, and so are the necessarily observed principles or even laws of their possible combinations, are found in nature too, whether as what we call the objective character or quality of the elements, or as the less known but equally natural and established principles of human sensing, human perceiving, human intuiting, or even human feeling and knowing. Human apprehension is as natural a fact or process as any other.

Thus we may, if we like, call the æsthetic surface of the natural world, as perceived by us and felt to be satisfying, only accidentally and not intentionally beautiful. Certainly this surface is not artistically beautiful, for the distinction between art and nature is clear enough, and there would be no theoretical justification for blurring it. But since the accidents of nature are integral to nature's own course of events, accidental, as applied to natural beauty, might just as well be called inevitable or necessary. The fact that events ever appear to occur accidentally is due, as we may suppose, to our ignorance, not to any irregularity or arbitrariness or contingency in them, subject as they are to the one foundation of all regularity, all order, and all intelligibility, namely nature itself. For even men's own activities of sense perception and knowledge are within this natural world, which is discovered, definitely felt and perceived as character and quality, and then operated upon by men, only so far as men discern its own intrinsic properties, its orderly habits of change and motion, and also, of course, its æsthetic possibilities. If the beauty of art is sensuous at all, it is nature that furnishes both its materials and its structural principles. And if men operate artificially upon materials to construct consciously intended and expressive works of human art, these materials themselves, together with the structures that they might take on in the natural course of events, would seem to offer all the essentials for such beauty as art itself exhibits.

The beauties of nature, then, while they are defined as those not involving nature's supreme achievement—if the phrase has any meaning—that is, not involving those special complexities of structure and function in human beings that operate consciously through the techniques of the arts, offer all the possibilities that there are of beautiful sensuous elements, all the possible kinds of structure native to these elements, as well as all the spatial and temporal possibilities for variety and for combination that could be imposed upon them by men as artists. They may involve besides, all those elements and principles of structure of which men still remain ignorant, and they may occur on a scale quite beyond men's powers. As nature offers us color and light and shapes and perspective, color harmonies and even musical sounds, so she offers us such refined and sophisticated forms as animal and human bodies, among which sculpture finds its models and patterns. The greatest artists may go to nature not only for elementary forms to refresh and vivify their art, but for modes of combination more complex than any they yet grasp, and for completed beauties, involving not only such complex or at least unknown principles of combination, but also such varieties of sensuous material, smells and tastes and textures and noises, as conscious human art has as yet no clear use of, since their orders and their natures are so vaguely felt, if felt at all, as to be beyond man's assimilation in his own designed compositions.

So much was suggested early in our discussion of the content of æsthetic judgment. What we need now to add is the sense in which natural beauty is also definitely expressive, and hence, though often obscurely, often also fully and clearly beautiful, exactly as art may be beautiful.

If mountain storms are not human or divine wrath, if black clouds do not intentionally threaten destruction to trees and animals and wayfarers, these same storms and clouds do literally in their actual appearance exhibit such violence and power as human wrath itself only mildly displays; and the destruction incident to their occurrence is often humanly and morally portentous to a degree beyond the powers of human armies bent on the destruction of an enemy. If to express is to give outward sensuous and formal specification to meanings, characters, qualities, and significant activities, then floods present us, if not with the fear they inspire, at least with fearfulness itself. Trees, if only figuratively patient, are literally sturdy and lasting; if they do not consciously suffer winter's cold, they do last it out; and it must be plain enough that whether our terms are figurative or literal here begins to become a question. A white lily is not morally pure, since it is not morally characterizable at all; but it would be hard to find just what the meaning of moral purity is, if we can not picture it or think of it in any æsthetic terms whatever.

Moral qualities indeed, as strictly defined, are highly abstract. Their determinate natures, however, as characterizing human beings in specific acts, or as being specific human traits, are concrete but complex specifications, never more clearly or fully grasped than in such terms as equally clearly specify and indicate qualities and characters appearing in their elements, or as complex wholes, upon the face of nature, like the fragility of flowers, the strength of oaks, the physical if not the moral reliability of rocks like Gibraltar, the power and swiftness of lightning, as if it never hesitated in choosing or in striking its objective, the restlessness—or must we say only the unresting or unarrested motion?—of ocean waves, the serenity, literal or figurative, depending on which of two languages we are using, of the day or of the heavens themselves. In the end there are no literal expressions of spiritual truths, so that whatever we say of man's soul might be said in the same terms of natural objects and appearances in some of their various aspects. Nature's actual surface in its æsthetic particulars thus gives us the last terms in our definitions of even the most humanly or the most divinely significant meanings. For strictly orthodox religious thought this is not so; but it will be noticed that it is at least as characteristic of religion that bread and wine may literally become spiritual nourishment, as that the spirit of God only shines through the brightness of the sun, and that his voice is not the thunder, but only the animating resonance within it.

Thus simple and direct representation in art may still be expressive, since so much of what could be expressed by men, so much of what they could even want to express, is to be specified and defined most clearly in those natural appearances that representative art as such is concerned to reproduce in other media that are more permanent or, as the substance of a work of art, more easily possessed and preserved, to be present when we choose, instead of only at nature's uncontrolled bidding in the order of its course.

§ 2

But there are those who still insist that nature, instead of being beautiful and expressive in the various aspects of its æsthetic surface as such, is only so if taken symbolically. And symbolism even in art refers not to the use of such a necessarily symbolic medium as language, but to this further inclination to see in the character of what is æsthetically present an intimation of something else of another character, or to see in nature only faint, though sometimes supposedly unmistakable, signs of God. For any clear mind, however, it is difficult to see how there could be relevance in such symbols at all, did they not bear upon their æsthetic surface some of the actual nature or character that they are taken to symbolize.

Such arbitrary symbolism as that of mathematics or of discourse in sounding syllables and words is no problem.

If we choose one æsthetic element, say a certain sound, such as that of the word cat, to mean always the nature of one of those domestic creatures with which we are all so familiar, or the sound of the word four, or a visual spatial æsthetic configuration such as an I and a V, or four dots upon a die, or four hearts on a playing card, or the Arabic numeral, to mean that number which we learn as two times two, or as the number of the quarters of an apple, or of a dollar, or of the great winds, or the number of sides of a square or a diamond, —this is the simple and comprehensible establishment of a one-to-one relation. As the symbol means the object or the quality or the number, so the object or quality or number, if it is to be indicated by us in discourse, must call up the symbol in our minds, which we then employ unambiguously to give our meaning. But such symbolism is man-made, and with time and practise transparent and unmysterious. The symbolism of nature and of art is quite another matter, a matter ultimately vague and mystical even where it is justifiable at all, since that which the symbol is to be related to in our minds can not in the very nature of the case enter them or be present except just as itself. It may be accompanied with all that one may demand of vague or intense feeling, but if it is more than its own æsthetic appearance, a symbol at all, that is, and not a mere mark, it remains a meaningless abstraction such as divinity without sensuous attributes or logical structure, a perfect nothingness, or such as moral or spiritual qualities, non-æsthetic altogether, and hence utterly indeterminate and as thoroughly meaningless as words can be. If it has an arbitrarily fixed signification, the symbol is no longer a peculiar sort of artistic device, but simply a private language, the advantages of which for art are dubious enough; and in any case such symbolism is not worth discussing here, since it is at its best a special case of that symbolism that we have already discussed as the medium peculiar to discourse.

In its rather less justifiable employment, not in nature or the representation of nature's forms, but as peculiar to such works of art as follow their own laws of design in their own medium, and attempt thus to be purely and artistically expressive, symbolism is again a striving for what can not be given in æsthetic terms. It is therefore also a striving for what can not be given at all. A symbolist, feeling the inadequacy of linguistic or other conventional symbols, traditional or mythological, but always rigorously determinate as well in their own sensuous æsthetic form as in that which they symbolize, whether men or gods or astrological or magical or alchemical powers or entities,—such a symbolist in art turns to a symbolic correlation of his own, its significance to be discovered by others only through attention to his context, often with needless labor and even pain, though in the case of a genius the esoteric correlation may enrich the beauty of his mainly non-symbolic art, as faintly suggested clouds might enhance a portrait.

§ 3

But it must be confessed that in most cases the characteristic symbolist seems not fully conscious of the necessary limitations of symbolism as such, thinking instead to have found the expression in æsthetic symbolic terms of the absolutely inexpressible. His success, if he achieves it, often negates his attempt. Instead of inventing new symbols, or genuine symbols at all, he has discovered real, or imaginatively possible, or highly forced and artificial, similarities or identities, such as that between the æsthetic spatial and colored appearance or sounding surface he employs and its meanings, or similarities among images called up by the strictly conventional and commonly used words and phrases and forms of language itself, these images in turn at the best figuring and specifying, in their literal æsthetic aspects, qualities and characteristics identical with those of such moral or human or divine actualities or artistic creations as he is presenting the nature of in art. A symbol, if it is not perfectly conventional like words or numerals, is only suggestive of anything at all beyond its own æsthetic appearance so far as it naturally resembles this that it symbolizes or is associated with in human minds. So a white flower may symbolize purity, a red one sin, or a blue one some unrealized and uncreated romantic ideal of beauty in strangeness. But this is simply the use of literary figures instead of what is usually called symbolism in art. In the latter the significance of the given symbol is secret or occult. It lies deeper than words or images by just so much as it is either purely arbitrary and individual in the author, and hence opaque and at odds with the very purposes of discourse, or else genuinely unintelligible because its deeper meaning is simply not to be discerned at all. No doubt it is this indeterminateness, or some feeling of striving for what he has not attained or can not attain, an immediate and fairly definite as well as commonplace experience, that the author takes for esoteric and important significance, instead of recognizing it and presenting it in the medium he is using.

The poetry of Blake illustrates both sorts of symbolism. The inexpressible was what Blake strove to express; but clearly the inexpressible is always lost so far as expression is achieved. Take so characteristic a poem as the lines about inexpressible love, which would seem to be a warning against symbolism in art as well as in nature, a poetic version of the account of symbolism just given:

> "Never seek to tell thy love,
> Love that never told can be;
> For the gentle wind doth move
> Silently, invisibly."

Here, so far as the mystery is presented at all, it is in just such terms, the silence and invisibility of the wind, as indicate a familiar phenomenon. In the last stanza the traveller may have departed silently, but the effectiveness of his silent fascination, its true quality, since it is by definition not æsthetically, and so not at all, perceptible, is made clear to us by naming a silent and invisible natural power. We are satisfied with its description simply because naming the wind calls up such images of effective power as we recognize in the wind's silence and invisibility only through acquaintance with its visible if not also its noisy effects. But this is hardly symbolism at all. Instead of using the wind as symbolic of the power meant, wind is felt at once as similar to any silent power, and gentle wind to a power like that of felt love. And this is only the poetic expressiveness possible to natural phenomena used in art, an expressiveness in which such art presents the æsthetic character of these natural phenomena through the intelligible, unambiguous, and perfectly conventional symbolism of the language that evokes their images and so their qualities and powers.

It is in Blake's elaborately esoteric works that the arbitrary and often fruitless sort of symbolism is to be found. And here the beauty of his poetry is so uncertain that we call him prophet, as he called himself, and if we are so inclined, lose ourselves with him, not in the æsthetic or expressive delights of poetry or art, but in the mystical raptures of religious feeling. Even this feeling is sensuous and æsthetic so far as it goes, and it is called up by vaguely sensuous and confused imagery. Nor does it reach God or those supernatural realms that Blake no doubt intended to delineate to us; for even Blake could not leave the sensuous space-time world to reach the transcendental and ineffable regions of his aspirations, without departing this life altogether. As for such arbitrary and crudely esoteric symbolism as is sometimes imputed to Ibsen, for example, arguments against such attribution would rest most solidly upon all the evidence that may be summoned to prove him a creative dramatist, conscious of the function of language, and employing its directly conventional symbolism, unclouded by such vagaries as impotence takes solace in, or those spirits for whom nature as well as the materials and forms of art are too clear to seem significant. For both art and nature may express only what men can see or feel or hear or know as natural organic beings functioning in a natural world, which may itself be beautiful or beautified by them as art.

§ 4

But it is not true of course that this world is a mere collection of meaningless materials. Its own ways bring about physical and organic variations and definitions of shape and size and aspect that become familiar to man, and recognized by their appearance as objects interesting to him, because they serve his needs or please his senses or his comprehending mind. They are in any case significant, both variously and definitely. For these objects come to mean more than just their appearance, and to be connected in men's minds with their functions in the economy of human life, as well as with all the other objects, activities, and eventualities related to them. If their sensuous surface and their form is not positively offensive on strict æsthetic grounds, its value, even for disinterested contemplation, is not merely that of this not unpleasing surface content, but all the associated images and feelings that are involved in the recognition of it as what it is and what it means in our world, functioning as it does, and integrally related as it is, in our lives and interests. Thus its friendly and familiar aspect is pleasant to perception itself even when we are not interested in its use, as an antique chair in a museum looks comfortable or dignified or appropriate as well as æsthetically distinguished in design and finish. So far as these human qualities are defined for us in how it looks, so far they are expressed by its form and appearance in general, making that form more richly and vitally beautiful.

But natural as well as manufactured objects become thus familiarly acceptable to sense, and they too may express in their appearance the friendly or sustaining functions that they serve. Water is marvelously colored in sunlight, and wonderfully smooth in texture, sparkling in fountains, or shining in pools, or flowing in streams; but it is also cooling to bathe in and refreshing to drink, and hence these qualities are signified by it when we recognize it. Gasoline may look as smooth, and oil-wells may gush as magnificently; but if we recognize them by their odor or any other mark for what they are, they fail to give us the sense of life and freshness and friendliness of water. As in art expressiveness is a great part of its vitality and fulness of beauty, so much of nature has more of expressive beauty upon its surface than would appear to the eye of a mind innocent of all experience except that of bare sense perception. Not that the strictly and narrowly æsthetic beauty is increased in such cases, or that the strictly and narrowly æsthetic lack of beauty is not felt; but that the æsthetically satisfying surface, seen for example as the surface of water, is grasped in intuition as expressive of refreshment and coolness, its beauty therefore deeper and more voluminous and stirring than its merely æsthetic surface loveliness, however beautiful the surface may happen to be.

Moreover, as in sculpture we demand a humanly possible anatomy or some perspicuous comment on familiar forms, if we are to grasp the object at all, so that it can be held in attention to be beautiful to contemplation, so in nature we are limited, in what we can feel to be beautiful, to what we can readily perceive as something in itself. And our training in perception and knowledge makes more easily available for appreciation such forms as are at least familiar enough to be grasped at once as some specific type of thing. It is not that we love the familiar as such, nor that all familiar appearances are beautiful—what is more familiar than ugly city streets or ugly human bodies in ugly clothes?—but that for easy and pleasant perception of objects at all, there must be specification under some type or other already known, whether established in nature or in imagination. Hence the importance of structural and functional natural perfections, or at least conformity to type, if any beauty is to supervene upon natural objects, which are commonly and often necessarily viewed not as mere sensuous surfaces, but as the sensuous surfaces of familiar sorts of things.

Besides these natural types there are also æsthetic types, properly speaking. If some natural features are more pleasing to perception than others, such features may be enlarged or stressed, and a type come into vogue which thus makes much of some natural æsthetic beauties while it minimizes other aspects, which, though equally prominent in nature, are in themselves intrinsically less satisfying to purely æsthetic contemplation. Large eyes, long pointed fingers, or the elongated limbs and bodies of El Greco's figures, are clear enough illustrations, and there are countless others, of course. Such æsthetically rationalized types may then in turn become familiar in art, and even replace more ingenuously expressive ones, to which they are æsthetically superior. Through long familiarity in works of art they may come to be taken as equally or more fully representative; as long familiar, symbolic syllables are sometimes taken to be closer to the nature of things than actual representations. Even artificial æsthetic types, if they are successful, may become vital by their own partly symbolic expressiveness. But the dangers here are clear enough. Smooth and perfect æsthetic beauty achieved at the expense of any recognizably natural appearance may grow very flat and weak by losing that sort of vital beauty that is the expressiveness of natural objects; and such natural objects more truly exhibit the beauty of nature, even though as art, based upon strictly and narrowly æsthetic principles, they may be of a less satisfying perfection. A masterpiece of art based solely upon æsthetic principles, and developed solely by the conscious mastery of æsthetic means, in the achievement of an æsthetically perfect surface, may sometimes stand weak and dead in its pallid beauty beside the more vital and expressive beauties of natural objects, fine human bodies, leaping tigers, or such simple, familiar, typical forms as we all see on every hand.

Thus art not only draws from nature elements and forms to employ in its own expressive constructions, but it is from nature that it learns the very meaning of vitality, without which no art is fully beautiful and expressive. For it is from nature that the sole fountain of vitality issues, that is, life itself, whose forms, even when they possess only the faintest strictly æsthetic beauty of sensuous elements or structural form, may be moving and beautiful in their sheer expressiveness. On the other hand, we must remember that to be beautiful a form must be grasped in vision, and so far as natural forms are too blurred or too complex to be so grasped, they fail of beauty altogether. Hence artists may achieve by simplification and formal arrangements that actually violate natural forms, not only strictly æsthetic surface beauty, but such beauty of expression as comes from design. Pure design may make of a mere horse a sculptured steed for a god, and of the human body a form of superhuman strength and poise, or of such a grace or loveliness or dignity or repose as lies beyond that of human bodies in the flesh.

§ 5

But the artistic expressiveness of sculpture we have already discussed. Our point here is the expressiveness of natural beauty, which depends on several factors that we have not yet considered.

One of the most important of these is human perception itself. Gift or training in the technique and materials of art results often in a sensitiveness to naturally produced æsthetic effects, as well as in habits of perception which are æsthetically, instead of practically or morally, directed. Weeds look ugly to a farmer or a rancher who has spent time and effort year after year to rid his fields of them, and one does not argue with him that they are beautiful. Straight rows of corn or beans, with clean brown earth between, are on this level a designed and intended and expressive beauty as much finer than tangled fields of natural growth, as in another sphere the clean-cut expressive beauty of a sculptured Chinese horse is superior to any living horse in the world. But if one attends habitually not to ranching, but to color and form, the sloping ranch lands with sheets of yellow mustard are lovely, informal, decorative designs, or the dried dead mustard weed along the crests of hills to the east late in an August afternoon makes a shining intricate lacework, edging the fat, rolling contours of velvet yellow stubble with a delicate gleaming loveliness that fades, as the sun sinks, into a faint spidery skeleton of beauty against the blue still shining beyond. The desert valley which is parched and barren and ugly may gleam with beauty to the eye that looks at its appearance directly and distinguishes its shapes and lights and shadows and colors. And as artistic training and sense discrimination find beauties in barrenness and ugly weeds, so religious training or a superstitious turn of mind may blind us to much of the æsthetic character of what is before us and make us see fertile tilled fields or rich meadows, regardless of light or shape or form or color, as beautiful works of God's beneficence, or stormy seas as ugly and horrible with his wrath. At least it must be recognized that in nature beauties may be distinguished by æsthetically trained or gifted perception which are not present to the dull or the unskilled. It is the imaginative and expert artist that finds in nature before his eyes those ravishing beauties that so many of us miss, this or that specific effect, lost to the indiscriminate altogether, and only faintly and incompletely seen by those of us who are unskilful enough to let our vision wander into blurring complexities or extensions of the scene, instead of marking those boundaries with the eye that emphasize the discriminate beauty by framing it as a coherent and distinctly structural whole, with its own particular material and formal and expressive quality and character.

Furthermore, we are free to view æsthetically only such aspects of nature as do not overwhelm us as dangers or obstructions to our own activities and purposes in such wise as effectively to preclude disinterested contemplation. Early peoples, though they knew nature's external features and habits in a way quite foreign to modern life, which is so thoroughly protected against them by a greater scientific knowledge of nature's inner substance and its more microscopic habits, felt it as a more personal and a more inscrutable enemy, whose countenance was not often good to look upon. The appreciation of nature as beautiful in itself, especially of inanimate nature, as evidenced in art, seems to be of a comparatively late date, and landscape painting is a modern art. It seems not unlikely that men came to feel beauty in nature's more imposing aspects with the growth of freedom of thought, which gave to natural life and this world a value that it lacked in the middle ages in Europe, as well as with the growth of such technical mastery of the production of necessities as freed them somewhat from risk of starvation, and of such mastery of natural obstacles as ships and railroads and telegraph wires achieve. If mountains are passed over in a day on a luxurious train, where we sit in idleness, we may easily contemplate their æsthetic aspects with disinterested pleasure and find the Alps beautiful, which to early travellers were hideous, shapeless masses, barring a man's easy passage to some desired destination important to his practical welfare.

Thus clearly the aspect that nature wears differs in its beauty to different epochs and to men of different training.

ÆSTHETIC JUDGMENT

If green is the proper and familiar color of fertile lands, burnt California hills may look merely desolate and ugly, their fine rigor and austerity of line and form lost for a view of them which seeks greenness by habit and training, or a more familiar and intimate scale in magnitude. And as we shall see later, judgments with reference to the same æsthetic content may honestly and even necessarily differ in recording, the one beauty, the other ugliness, as the felt objective character of an experienced place or thing, which is thus as truly beautiful to one man as it is ugly to another, without involving any mysterious contradiction either in nature or in the nature of beauty. But these considerations as to the factors which make nature expressive and beautiful lead us to questions of the validity and meaning of æsthetic judgments in general, and to the basis in æsthetic theory of the principles of criticism, to which we shall turn in the following chapter.

CHAPTER XIV

CRITICISM

1. Responsible criticism begins in direct appreciation as recorded in æsthetic judgment. 2. Æsthetic criticism as suggested or explicit evaluation according to standards; the nature of standards. 3. Criticism as æsthetic analysis and as explanation through technical structure. 4. Criticism as translation and as personal appreciation. 5. Requisites and significance of critical competence.

§ 1

So far we have been surveying and illustrating the content recorded in what we have called æsthetic judgments. But all that we have considered here, aside from giving the general character of such judgments as differing from other sorts of judgment, and as marked by referring in first instance to the datum or content directly discriminated by perception, or its echoes in imagination or thought, and felt as delightful and called beautiful, are after all only typical illustrations. For all experience is æsthetic on its surface as being the experience of elementary qualities or complexes of qualities in relation. To give more than a number of typical illustrations would be to survey in theory all that the whole world offers to be surveyed. But not everything is beautiful, and what is most characteristically beautiful and so recorded in judgment, what is strikingly and fully and importantly beautiful, so that judgments referring to it are of any great interest, is limited to such complex unities of visual and auditory elements as the fine arts define and specify in their works, or as nature offers to perception in configurations and natural compositions appreciated as beautiful only so far as we can mark them off by the discriminating and unifying activities of apprehension itself.

In such natural beauties sensuous elements may occur and structural principles be sensuously bodied forth which the technique of art does not as yet command, either in all their variety or in all their modes of combination. Thus while natural beauty may be intense and genuinely felt, the actual nature of its structure, so far as that is not equally exhibited in works of art, is felt rather as a vague compulsion or fascination in its order, or as an intimation of further depths of significance so uncertain and vague that it is scarcely to be discussed further in intelligible terms. So far as æsthetic theory is of any use to us at all, it is in what little clarity it may introduce into our knowledge about the meaning of æsthetic judgments. Since vagueness can not as such be made clear, these vaguely felt beauties, no matter how intense or significant they may really be or be thought to be, are not fruitful subject matter. We have mentioned them, admitted them as beautiful, noticed their great potentialities and powers and their wide distribution, their ubiquity in fact, and beyond this our theoretical account of them can hardly be expected to go.

Æsthetic judgments as records evidently contain, as that to which they refer and that which they record, so much of the sensuous surface of the world as in actual experience strikes upon our discriminating perception and summons a response in which the delight we feel is our sense of the beauty of the object. We have run over the elements or materials that are characteristically beautiful and capable of structural composition by virtue of the intrinsic orders that define them as variations in an ordered range, of sounds or colors chiefly, and we have further noticed the beauty to be found in temporal and spatial arrangement as applied to these elementary materials. We have found, moreover, that in art these strictly æsthetic beauties, though necessary, occur rather as the specification of an artist's particular intention, so that the vitality of beauty is largely its expressive intent. We have been careful, too, to observe the complete integration of this expression, which becomes fully specific in just those sensuous elements in the controlled and composed structures that constitute the æsthetic surface of works of fine art. Beauty is unique and individual always, as the beauty of this or that particular entity that has it. Æsthetic judgment as record points first of all to this simple fact, that here or there at this or that time some specific particular beauty was manifest on the face of the experienced world to a mind. Here criticism begins, and without this starting point in direct perception and felt appreciation, criticism is ungrounded, unreliable, and perhaps dishonest, if not altogether irrelevant and meaningless.

A scholar may tell us when a picture was painted, and where, and by whom, and even what materials the artist used. He may say what the subject is and what the position and shape and size and color of every detail in it; he may even trace its design and indicate the excellence of its technique. But he is not a safe guide to its æsthetic value unless that value has been felt by him in really delightful æsthetic contemplation of the picture, so that its point as art and its beauty as æsthetic surface, the one the soul of the other, and hence manifest only in the sensuous content which is its actual æsthetic body, are plain to him. This feeling of delight, the point of the picture as art, is the focus of a perspective, from which alone its details of quality and character and structure appear as the constituent aspects of its beauty. This is its unique beauty and its unique value, and criticism that has not viewed it as in this perspective of delighted grasp of it as a whole, can never be trusted to be relevant, much less authoritative. Only from this point of vantage will the critic be fully aware of the limitations of his words about it or of their aptness in indicating its various aspects. Words can in first instance never describe any specific beauty except that composed of words themselves, which they actually repeat. They can only indicate in linguistic symbols the occurrence that was the critic's own experience of beauty. On this basis alone can he proceed to any further authentic description or analysis of æsthetic materials or structure, or of artistic expression, in any given case.

Thus dramatic criticism of a current play tells us the place and the date of the performance as well as the name of the play. We are to suppose that the critic saw that particular performance and records his actual full appreciation of it. When we read a book-review, we take it that the reviewer who signs it has read the book with his mind, and realized it fully in his imagination, not merely used its name or its author or its subject matter as an occasion for expressing himself on some other subject suggested by it. The fact that professional reviewers are so often too pressed for time to read many pages of the books that they discuss is one of the marks of journalism, part of what we mean when we use the word derogatorily of any writing. But that professional book-reviews are likely to be bright, entertaining journalism instead of the criticism that we sometimes hunger for, has nothing to do with the fact that criticism, if it is to be of the least relevance or importance, that is, if it is really to be criticism at all, must be grounded in the full and direct discernment and appreciation of the literary or artistic point and beauty of that which it purports to criticize, or of the intended point and beauty not achieved, but actually suggested in a still inadequate technique. Only by such direct apprehension of failure or of excellence could criticism be expected to point out the best that men have thought and known in the world; and even Arnold's moralistic view of art and life and letters is based on so much of the stubborn necessities of the critic's situation.

But criticism that did no more than point to objects that were beautiful in the critic's eyes would serve a slighter function than it is capable of, though this function itself is likely to be thought even less important than it is. Some supposed or self-elected critics are of course incompetent, and their impressions of the values of what they discuss are mere psychological data to know the critics by if they are by any chance worth knowing. But if a critic has discriminating perception, training in the technique of any of the arts, a normal or more than normal sensitiveness to the sensuous and structural and expressive aspects of æsthetic surfaces, and a mind stored with the beauties that have been achieved in the past so that their varying degrees of intensity may set a standard by which to measure the degree of some present beauty, his mere statement that here or there a play is being given that is worth seeing, or that in this or that exhibit there is a fine drawing, or that some young author or some recent novel has distinction, may be the performing of most of what Arnold defined criticism to be. Certainly such a critic would serve a function in society not unlike that of any expert who selects for others, say in schools or universities, what they shall attend to with pains, and finally master, to become competent in this special field themselves. But the critic is of course pointing out final values, not mere means to future accomplishment.

§ 2

Criticism, however, does not end here, as the mere record that there is beauty in this or that corner of the world if we choose to go and look for it there. Even in the bare record that this or that is beautiful there is often suggested, if not logically implied, a superiority over something else. Criticism does not merely record the fact that something or other has æsthetic value. Value itself is so largely a matter of degree that the critical record often hints, or carefully specifies, that the object of its comment has this or that relative value. Criticism is full of words and phrases like distinguished, very fine, incomparably rich, fairly secure, easily adequate, and so on indefinitely to all the cautious comparatives and care-free superlatives of the language. And these phrases suggest comparison and hence standards, the most vexed subject in critical theory, as in the theory of value in general, a subject not to be settled offhand, of course, but one which at least some views in modern value theory seem to have clarified and simplified to an appreciable degree. On the basis of our earlier analysis, at any rate, the definition of standards offers no great difficulty for theory, though their application in practice is likely to be so naïvely dogmatic or so nearly unconscious, or so subtle and sophisticated and various, that here, as elsewhere, a theoretical grasp of even very clear general principles is no guide at all to the intricate elaborations of practice. Criticism is in this sense an art no more learned when one has understood this special one of its functions, namely, evaluating according to standards, than the physician's art is learned when one has understood the general function of surgery as distinguished from that of internal medicine or of dentistry or diagnosis. What standards are is not hard to say in general, and we can even give particular examples. But it must not be supposed that to do this is to give an account of the technique of criticism or hints for its practice. It is merely suggesting and naming, and as well as may be defining, one of its major functions.

If a man of sensuous bent and swift perceptive powers has experienced many beauties, he has some knowledge of the richness and intensity and volume of these, the felt magnitude of their beauty, as well as of their purity, the absence in them of irrelevant or distracting elements, and their degree of coherence in structural unity, as compared with one another. If then he calls a work of art intensely beautiful, or richly beautiful, or purely beautiful, or structurally coherent and complete, or vitally expressive, he means not that it is absolutely so, but that as compared with other works of art of like or related sorts, it belongs high in the scale as being more intense than some others, or more coherently held together for perception, or more strictly æsthetic, or more fully and determinately expressive. And his standards can only be the degrees of intensity, richness, purity, coherence, adequacy of expression, that he has experienced and has been interested and attentive enough to retain in memory for present comparison. Thus only other works of art in their specific qualities and the degrees of these can possibly furnish the standards really applicable in æsthetic criticism. More strictly the standards are the degrees, not the qualities. But often it is hard enough to name quality or character itself, without any accurate indication of degree at all, and once a designation for any quality or character has been found, this name is likely to be set up as that of one of the standards of literary or æsthetic criticism, its sole validity as standard, however, consisting in its own intrinsic æsthetic value as felt when it occurs. Aristotle named unity, as achieved in different specified ways, and called it an essential character of tragedy, and innumerable critics through centuries were thus enabled to pronounce upon a drama as soon as they discovered the sense in which it could be said to achieve unity or fail to do so. As might be supposed, their judgments were often so forced and artificial that, if they were taken seriously, they would rule out as worthless most of the great achievements in all drama except that of ancient Greece, from which Aristotle derived his notions, or imitations of Greek drama, so many of which have not stood more genuine æsthetic or critical tests.

The application of standards is a dangerous or trivial practice in criticism in general excepting as these are standards in the sense of degrees of beauty, or of its aspects. Any work of art of any degree of felt beauty is after all valuable to just that degree, whether it measures up to the degree of other works of art or not. And it is less or more valuable or adequate as art only so far as it is strictly comparable in æsthetic quality or qualities. Since most works of art that are beautiful in any full sense are so complex, and also so specific and so definitely unique, both in their mode of combining æsthetic elements in a structure to which these elements become fully integral, and in the specific intention of the artist which they express, and which the medium of his technique will carry as its own, standards of comparison must be very cautiously applied. It may even be the case that less rich, less intense beauty than a critic of great experience would highly prize is all that a less sensuously gifted and less experienced mind can feel at all; and all standards fail except as we adopt the principle that the more valid judgment, since it is the more complete record, is that of the mind that distinguishes all the quality and detail and structural form that another mind does, and appreciates it fully and as expressive, but also recognizes further what this other mind either can not see or can not so apprehend as to feel its beauty. Thus a sort of reverse test of a critic is not to be despised. The fully competent musical critic, for example, is one who does not fail to appreciate a hurdy-gurdy or jazz, though he finds more to be desired, more complexity and richness, more subtle modes of coherence and emphasis, more kinds of rhythm, and the expression of some fraction of the limitless emotional possibilities that these slighter instruments and forms of music never even broach. When, as in all great art, unique beauty is achieved, calling for a response that absorbs the whole attention of a human mind and resounds through the whole human organism, comparison is futile and standards fail, though the critic's function does not.

§ 3

For genuine and æsthetically adequate criticism does not merely record cases of beauty or evaluate the degrees of these beauties by the standards that the critic has at his disposal. Criticism is engaged rather in discriminating the aspects of one whole and single beauty and putting into words this real analysis. Such analysis is not the dismembering of a work of art before our eyes, making of its parts separate fragments which in the beauty of the whole they are not. For this beauty is not theirs but that of the composition in which they function as aspects. Critical analysis of art reveals the mode of integration of these genuinely æsthetic constituents, the way in which sensuous elements are held in structural form, and the way in which structural form takes on expressiveness in æsthetic surface specification. Since the process by which this is performed is partly the native effectiveness of the æsthetic materials themselves in combination, but very largely the technique of the art, the critic's discussion will almost surely turn to more or less technical considerations, and his analysis may lead him on to the still more perilous and difficult field of explanation.

As explanation, criticism attempts to say, so far as that is at all possible, how the specific beauty in question is achieved, the means to this, the media, the technical operations, the contributory function of details. And here it is still clearer that a critic, like any discriminating lover of beauty, must have some mastery of technique itself, if he is to know even his subject matter. One does not know what Art is unless one knows an art. Art as such and in general is a mere abstraction; to know it is to know a word to conjure with, no doubt, but it is little more. To know an art is to know not only its æsthetic materials and forms and possibilities of expression, but the physical material upon which these æsthetic materials appear as surface, the practical operations which alone achieve its structural forms in actuality, and the native and intrinsic potentialities of the sensuous medium for so functioning, for bearing upon its surface the specification of intention, which is the expressiveness of the work of art achieved.

A discerning and brilliant critic of the theatre sees the actual presented spectacle as produced by its own theatrical means in its own terms. Not that he misses its effects, but that they are not bare, unconditioned effects for him, much less mysterious ones, no matter how surprising or even overwhelming. The gradually increasing intensity of a scene is perhaps the artfully contrived and intended change in rate and tempo of speech, the increased sharpness of outline and perhaps also swiftness of bodily movement. These are of course felt by all the audience; they are what is actually there to feel; but they are not grasped fully as what they are, or rather they are not seen to be the constituent conditioning details of quality and structure upon whose actuality as presented the intensity supervenes, summoned by them as they work together for the intended effect. What is experienced may be taken for some inexplicable, esoteric, or mysterious expressiveness direct from the dramatist's soul instead of from the actors' bodies, an expressiveness achieved by spirit itself, instead of an artificially and technically produced expressiveness of the rhythm of sound elements or the patterns of motion and gesture. If the drama comes upon the stage at all, its point and style and meaning projected thence upon an audience, instead of being lost in incoherent and distracting movements in a merely traditional stage environment, accompanied by the recitation of the dramatist's lines, which are now quite irrelevant to the scene—if the drama is to appear to the audience at all, then gesture and dress and tone of voice and lighting and stage properties, being its only body and actuality, are what a discerning critic, fully appreciative of the art of the theatre, will see as composing it.

He would no more be offended by seeing the details that go to make up the presentation before his eyes, no matter how subsidiary they are, than a Chinese audience is offended by seeing the actual manipulation of stage properties going cn in full view, or than a lover would be offended at distinguishing the specific and purely sensuous shade of blue in eyes which may shine no less truly with love for being physical, bodily members seen to be moist oval surfaces that make up in part a precious face. The lover does not as a lover mention these details, perhaps, but when he speaks as poet, or as an admirer who would justify his love to other men, or make it convincing to the object of his affections, there is no limit to the specification of contributory detail, sensuous elements and particular features, that he enumerates. If criticism seems so often overloaded with technical details, and too much concerned with technical achievement, it is usually because we who read it have not realized that technique is the creative process itself, the spirit's intentions reaching expression and definition only in physical media, physically operated upon in a fashion no more foreign or irrelevant to artistic æsthetic expression, than emotion itself is foreign to what we call its bodily manifestations. From the critic's point of view it would be simpler in both cases to speak of actual substance and nature. Art lives in its technique and its media as fully as the spirit lives in the functioning of its own body, without which, so far as we know, it is simply nothing at all.

§ 4

But if critics often dwell on the technical perfections and deficiencies of art, in attempting to account for its beauty, or to describe that beauty in its genuinely æsthetic aspects, or to justify their own appreciation and their high estimate of it, even here criticism has not exhausted its possibilities. For critics, in realizing that their own record, no matter how honest or accurate, may not be representative of other men's experience, are only realizing that where they have found beauties others may fail to find them. Thus their evaluations will not be acceptable; their æsthetic analysis will be unconvincing, and their attempts at explanation through an account of technical processes and technical achievement will be meaningless, or at least beside the point, since all of what this is to describe or explain, though it was actually present to the critic, is a character or quality or meaning that will not have been present at all, perhaps, to others. Failing of any full opportunity to educate others in perception and technical training necessary to a spontaneous and ready appreciation of artistic beauty, the critic's task is now to make the blind see and the deaf hear; and this miracle he sets about to perform, sometimes indeed by prayer and exhortation or command or bullying, but more intelligently by such methods as are rationally employed by other teachers of the defective. That is, so far as may be, he translates from the language of sculptured form, or design in color, or musical composition, or architectural fitness and expressiveness, into terms familiar to those whom he is to convince, as a teacher of the blind translates visual character into the terms of touch. The medium of critics is of course the symbolic one of language, which, as we have seen, is sufficiently transparent to reveal beneath its verbal surface such æsthetic content and such artistic expressive intention as may be achieved in any sensuous medium, in any sort of æsthetic materials, through any kind of structure.

As touch alone never gives the actual visual terms of the experience of those possessed of sight, so language never quite fully or specifically succeeds in this translation into terms of linguistic symbols and their meanings; but its rendering need not be so vague or indeterminate as to fail completely. For a man who is deaf to the tonal and structural qualities of a particular work of musical art, for example, need not be deaf to all music; and the composition whose beauty the critic is extolling and recommending will have something in common with such simpler music as this less ready or less trained listener is familiar with and appreciates. A child may be displeased and bored with music only slightly complex; but if he is convinced by words that such music uses the very melody that sounds beautiful to him alone or sung by a voice, he may easily learn to hear at least this aspect of the beauty of the more complex music, and gradually come to appreciate more fully the more developed and difficult composition in which it is a contributing factor. So, if we are informed on mere authority that the rhythmic delights of jazz are themselves only one element in music of quite another sort, which contains much else besides, and in which we have missed even the rhythms, through lack of penetrating perception of the whole sensuous volume and richness, we may at least admit an appreciative critic's estimate of the music we can not clearly hear or have not yet fully heard. And so of all the arts. Criticism may present to us in linguistic terms and their meanings such an array of indisputably lovely elements and forms, and such a coherent character, and such expressiveness, all as the description of a work of art that is altogether non-linguistic, that we may be convinced of its æsthetic value, through thus indirectly becoming acquainted with its character, and then turn to itself to discover upon its own surface its properly unique objective nature and beauty, which has thus been given to us in a rough, but more or less intelligible, translation.

Mixed with this there is another aspect of criticism, the expression in language of the critic's own feelings of delight in a beauty he has recognized and felt. By sheer contagion he may produce in us vicariously some of the enjoyment and appreciation proper to such works of art as we either have not or can not ourselves discriminate in their specific quality and detail and expressive point. This last sort of criticism is perhaps most popular of all and most dangerous to genuine, direct appreciation, if it is not merely part of such more adequate translation, analysis, and explanation as lead to direct appreciation and direct recording judgment. Whole audiences may be thrilled by the brilliant lecturer on Latin poetry or Greek drama or Egyptian antiquities, or on current literature and art. But what they are thrilled with may be only the lecturer's communicated enthusiasm, a feeling possibly authentic and appropriate to the work of art in question, and in that sense genuine, or a feeling aroused by qualities and emotions in him entirely irrelevant to his purported subject matter; as also whole nations may read, with the greatest appreciation of the author and his work, so-called stories of art or of literature, or even stories of science or of philosophy, so foreign to the spirit and achievement of artists or scientists or philosophers as to make those who read them only more impatient than ever with the exacting demands of literature, science, and the arts themselves. If a little learning, though pleasant, really is dangerous, a little vicarious appreciation, supposedly of art, may perhaps be pronounced at least as dangerous as a stimulating drug, which we take to our good or our harm as it is intelligently or unintelligently administered. Its effects, at any rate, can be known only empirically in their ensuing occurrence, and perhaps they should be carefully observed, if culture is not to become still more of a by-word than it is already.

§ 5

If our whole subject were not limited to æsthetic judgment, but included judgments and criticism of other sorts as well, we should have now to consider the vast field of influences and prejudices conditioning criticism and appreciation. A nation of pioneers may demand expression in pioneer themes and all that is significant to pioneers. Or a drab, poverty-stricken nation may appreciate as truly beautiful only the luxuries of glittering wealth, as heaven itself for some purposes must be heated by the fires we think of as appropriate to hell. If there were no other example of the genuine relativity of taste to all sorts and conditions of life, and hence the actual relativity of all æsthetic judgment, dress alone, which illustrates so much else in æsthetic theory, would be a sufficient testimony. One who denies it its beauty altogether is not only blind to the beauty of dress itself, but to the possibilities of color and design in general, to the whole province of costume in the theatre, the draperies of Greek sculpture, and the paintings of human beings clothed. If the beauty of dress, like the miraculous in events, is relegated to a distant past, the inconsistency is no less flagrant. Those who deny the beauties of the passing mode, a beauty than which none could be more strictly relative to even the bare surface character of social conditions and of living in general, must miss beauties of inventive expressiveness, of style, whether strictly personal or not, and beauties of the merely chic, which it would be hard to deny explicitly, since they are so obviously and so sensitively appreciated, most of all by the discriminating expert, but very greatly by men at large, as well as by women. But though it is clear enough that what suits one time and one place, and is there and then seen as beautiful, may fail of beauty elsewhere or at another time; that what one nation likes another may not; that appreciation of beauty, which is one of the conditioning factors of its presence, varies with history, with geographical situation, with the peculiarities of peoples, with interest and training and possibilities for leisure, and so on indefinitely, the theoretical questions involved here are not those of æsthetic judgment as such or of primarily æsthetic criticism, much less of general æsthetic theory.

So far as men have senses alike, so far as they are capable through training or native endowment, of the same sort of discriminating perception of the surface of their world in its various aspects, so far as arts are cultivated at all, so far the beauties of nature and of art are available to all men with normal faculties, if only they do not lose in so-called practical activity, and interested action in general, acuteness and freshness of perception. So far, of course, as they do not cultivate discriminating perceptive activities, so far as they stifle and deaden and finally kill their feelings and emotions, and thus lose interest in free human expression altogether, and so far as they limit themselves to the technique of some one art or of no arts at all, so far do they lose the richness of their sense of beauty, or the sense of beauty itself. How deeply or fully or variously, or how coherently or expressively or vitally beautiful any beauty will actually be, in its appearance to any man, depends on all the conditions of bodily and mental endowment, social relations and interests, personal prejudices, and training and knowledge in general; but most of all of course on sensuous gift, perceptive training, and full human flexibility of the imagination and the emotions.

Critics will speak for as much of the truth and for as many men throughout the ages as they are capable of by virtue of these same qualifications. Discriminating perception and emotional richness of nature will be the condition of their having any criticism to make. Expressive powers in their own linguistic medium will be the technically efficacious means of their making it, and the grasp and power of their intellects will determine the genuine significance of their judgments. Our distrust of critics and of experts in art and literature is something of an anomaly in a country so attentive to experts on sport and business, of whom we demand technical details and a minute acquaintance with their subject matter that any scholar might envy in his own field, and from whom we suffer a technical jargon that would be called unendurable in any other field. But in this same country, while every man is a business man and at least an amateur athlete, of necessity acquainted sufficiently in these realms to appreciate the expertness of experts, few of us are even amateurs of art. Thus charlatanism is widespread in the regions of æsthetic judgment and of art itself, and when a really competent critic appears, he is no more trusted, and is even less appreciated, than the entertaining journalist whose human feelings, at least, are patently sound, and whose wit and spirit are themselves satisfying to other men, though his judgment of books or plays or music or art may be sadly to seek. But all this borders on another topic. The critic performs a social function, and critics vary in competence and character with the varying interests and degrees of knowledge and of civilization that characterize a whole society. But so also of art and artists, who may themselves be critics, and it is to the function of art in life and of the artist in society that we now turn.

CHAPTER XV

ART IN LIFE AND ARTISTS IN SOCIETY

1. The finality of æsthetic value as the ethical justification of artistic activity. 2. The function of æsthetic surface in actual living. 3. The qualifications of the individual artist and the value of art and artists to society. 4. The application of æsthetic criteria to all values; the artist as critic.

§ 1

THERE is a clear sense in which æsthetic value is final and ultimate, since the possession of it is the possession of what is good in itself. It is not merely one of the means to living well, but part of the actual content of the good life, or rather one aspect of the nature or character of the very goodness of that life. It would be easy, too, to make out a case not only to show that what has æsthetic value is the model or type of everything that is finally valuable at all, but also to show how all value is literally æsthetic just so far as it is fully and genuinely value in the strictest sense of the word. Means are only valuable with the actual value attributed to their real ends; and this attribution, if it is valid, always involves the situation in which the end-value is directly and immediately experienced. But all such direct and immediate experience is clearly enough of a sensuous or imaginative surface of some sort, which is either constituted of an elementary æsthetic datum, or else is itself a more complex æsthetic structure, directly appreciated in contemplation. Thus all that is valuable in itself, and hence also all that may lend value to what is only derivatively valuable, is æsthetic in the narrow and well-defined sense of the word æsthetic, though not of course in its deeper and more specific sense, which applies to beauty as such, or more particularly to the beauty of art, which is more than æsthetic in the thinner surface sense of the word.

If all value is æsthetic, not all value is artistic. The beauty of art is a specific kind of beauty, involving on the one hand the achievement of æsthetic surface, but on the other the fulfilment of intention by technical artistic means, and so the expression of meanings. In the case of the beauty of objects which are also useful, there is involved, besides all this, the perfection of a form dictated within the general limits defined by their useful function, by their particular and specific purpose. If æsthetic value is the type of all value, or even the essential defining character of value as such, it does not therefore follow that the beauty of art, which is only one kind of æsthetic value, defines the nature of value in general, nor that all value, because it is ultimately immediate and hence æsthetic in the narrow sense, is also artistic.

If fine art is ultimately and absolutely valuable in so far as it achieves a directly satisfying æsthetic surface, it also involves practical activity carried on partly or wholly in the interest of useful ends, and always for the sake of expressiveness. Since such activity might be employed upon other materials to other ends, whether in other fine arts or for practical purposes, the final value of the æsthetic surface of any particular work of art is only one of the potentialities of the technical materials and operative energy used up in its production. Hence there always remains the question as to whether, in an actual world where we must eat and sleep if we are to live to enjoy, the devotion of any given material wealth, or any particular human powers and strength, to artistic activity and the production of particular objects of fine art is justified, and in general when and how far and in what circumstances this is the case.

Fine art, though its æsthetic value, and therefore its value in general, is unquestionable, being as it is an actual, positive addition to the good of men, an enriching of the world they live in, the absolute creation of æsthetic value, is also to be judged as a luxury, which may often be too expensive in the world, because it uses materials and human energy that might indirectly, as means, serve to produce values other than those of works of fine art; though in the end we might very possibly be forced to concede that all value is properly to be called æsthetic. So also the function that artists perform in society is to be admitted at once, on the best grounds that there are, as valuable; but how many members, or which particular members, of a society ought to be devoted entirely to art, how much of the world's materials and wealth in general these men should control and use, is still a social question, not to be decided solely on the grounds of the absoluteness of the æsthetic value that such men create. Since our concern is with æsthetics, we need not consider this very broad question further than to acknowledge its pertinence and its ethical finality. Fortunately, in the most important cases of all, we may comfort ourselves that it is answered in the right way by the individual propensities of such gifted artists as answer it by their refusal to consider it, governed, one may suppose, by the natural necessities of their nature that drive them on to the only sort of life they can even conceive for themselves, in the production of creative art that feeds other men's spirits as well as their own.

What seems appropriate for us to consider here may be put under four more or less strictly æsthetic heads: the broad scope of æsthetic value in all satisfactory living, the æsthetic qualifications of men who may properly be devoted to the creation of such value in works of fine art, the specific æsthetic value of these works of art in individual personal life and in society, and finally the sense in which the ethical criteria, by means of which alone the relative value of art and artists in a social order is to be judged, are themselves of a nature not in the end to be distinguished from that of rigorously æsthetic criteria. As critics of the fine arts must have some of the special qualifications of artists and some training in artistic technique, so critics of society, and reformers, if they are to be at all adequate to their self-appointed social tasks, must employ ultimately æsthetic criteria. It is only as artists, or at least as æsthetically discriminating minds, that they judge society with any show of adequacy or justice, or imagine for it new rules or regulations, or new institutions, or a whole new social order, such as could be supposed to be good by any thinking man, either as contributory to a better world for men to live in, or as the actual definition or description in concrete social terms of the nature of such a better world.

§ 2

What we have already said of æsthetic judgment makes it plain that the face of the whole world that we live in, as it appears to men who are attentive to it and discriminate its actually presented surface aspects, is what æsthetic judgment refers to as its meaning. Thus life as it is present to us, things as they actually appear and as they are seen to stand in functional relations to us and to one another, the whole recognizable furniture of the earth as well as of the heavens, is first and last æsthetically viewed, if it is viewed at all. Of course this whole æsthetic surface is very often either neglected so far as possible, or only implicitly recorded for us in a systematic symbolic notation, where familiar words or consistent scientific formulas are all we ask and all we have of it, or, as is much more commonly the case, in a context partly sensuous, partly scientific, but very largely made up of prejudices, social dogmas, particular personal ambitions, idiosyncratic imagery and ideas, all of which are guarded and kept intact as if they were sacred possessions of more worth than a clear and direct view of the actual aspects of men's life and their world, which is always pressing in upon their senses. Instead of seeing cities and streets with physical buildings that shut out the light while they shelter the body, but also confine the spirit in a prison of routine, we shut our eyes and dwell on notions, or phrases merely, like industrial progress and national power and business efficiency, all of them vague imagined contents, made interesting and absorbing to a great extent only as they are vitalized into a dream of luxury and wealth and power for ourselves in such a largely hypothetical or imagined world.

Or perhaps our ideals are traditionally or conventionally higher:—service to men, social justice, garden cities, happy communities of workers, with municipal bathing beaches and community choruses, or civic centers architecturally expressive of social concord, where libraries and opera houses and the motion pictures of the future are to delight all men. But in the first place the terms of all these dreams are mostly pleasant images of sense, so that any adequate fulfilment of them must be seen in æsthetic terms. And secondly, dreams are socially worth having only if their terms and structures are such as reality may furnish to build its actual structures in the world of actual life. It is the æsthetic content and surface of a real present world that surrounds us. It is this actual world that either realistically satisfies us in contemplation when we are at work in it upon our own business, or else makes us more drab in spirit and content, the more we feed our mind's eye upon it, or more hopelessly inept if we neglect its actual features, in our preference for imagined or half-imagined structures of another sort of life than is possible to men. And even this other inner dream-life, if it is to be satisfactory at all, can only be the work of creative imagination, working with æsthetic materials to form æsthetic dream-structures. Thus our whole actual world, which after all contains also our ideal worlds, is æsthetic, its surface sensuously perceived or imagined, and enjoyed, or else not known at all for what it is, and real life thus falsified or foregone in dull, half-conscious bodily functioning, or sterile, abstract thinking, or in irrational and trivial dreams that fade with the years.

Nor do we often realize how much of our purely human social relations are æsthetic in their content, and how fully our judgment of human beings rests upon æsthetic grounds. Forgetting that it is the given surface from which alone we can derive such judgments, we neglect æsthetic data, or attempt to, and fail to grasp the actualities of men about us. No doubt in doing so we are governed by supposedly deeper or higher motives, which—though mysteriously—are to help make our judgments better and sounder, as we try to neglect the actual data by which they must at least subconsciously be governed all along. If we judge with any degree of correctness, it is thus rather in spite of our moral principles and our social and personal prejudices than with the appropriate

conscious attention to what is offered on the surface of bodily
life to go by.   Not that the surface is completely, or too
often obviously, revealing, but that it is all we have.   And
if æsthetic surface is to be despised, or if it is simply to be
forgotten that we are in any case aware of it and always
dominated by it more or less, and to just the degree to which
we are dominated by actuality instead of inherited or induced
dogmas and fables and linguistic habits and patterns, at least
it is clear that it is present, and present as the nature of men
and the world and society.   A realist must take account of it
by all the discrimination and attentive pains that he is capable
of exercising, applied to the only content given to his view,
the actual surface immediately present on every hand, out
of which, either as it stands or by transformations worked
upon it, his world is made, appearing to him beautiful or
ugly, and so by virtue of its æsthetic surface good or bad
to live in.

§ 3

But if all of us see our world only so far as we are willing
to look, and see it more richly and more accurately as we
train our perception in use and discrimination, not all of us
are adapted by native endowment to devote ourselves to
creative art.   Here as elsewhere aptitude and training determine skill and success; and though some technical skill in
at least one of the arts is requisite for any full appreciation
of artistic beauty, and so an obviously desirable part of any
education, and a necessary part of any adequate one in a civilized world, a life-long occupation with the rigorous and
exacting demands of artistic technique is no doubt most
wisely undertaken, in view of an ideal social or moral economy, by such sensuously gifted natures as may achieve in
art what will satisfy themselves and contribute to others at

least such expert work as is acceptable, or such instruction as is necessary, if the arts are to live at all. For great art, of course, there is demanded of the artist greatness, whatever the term may mean; and since the vitality and importance of art lies so largely in expressiveness, not even the greatest sensuous endowment, together with the best training and the achievement of a perfect technique, can be expected to give external æsthetic form to anything finer or nobler, more intense or more significant, than lies within the grasp and the emotional range of the artist himself. Not only must he have discriminating sensuous powers, specific aptitude, and technical expertness, but he must have a generous endowment in the way of human emotional capacity and what we may call ideas, in order to express and specify through his technical operations, upon the æsthetic surfaces of his works, meanings that are of depth and scope enough to be worth other men's contemplation, and satisfying to their minds.

As there are no prescriptions for the achievement of great beauty, so there are no rules for discovering potentially great artists, although a native sensuous gift may well be cultivated by a training in the various techniques of the arts as a necessary means to artistically adequate expression for even the greatest genius; and it is obvious that competent journeymen of the arts, though not great men, or even really artists in any full creative sense, function as the mediators, by way of education and critical appreciation, between genuine artists as well as their works, and society, which without them might undervalue or mistakenly estimate its greatest benefactors, as well as miss the distinction and fullness of the beauty of their works. For it is only as artists' productions, in their distinctive character and individual expressiveness, are brought to men's appreciative attention, that artists become men's benefactors at all, to contribute then so largely to the richness and satisfaction of their lives. If genius is something of a myth, superiority of mind in given directions is not. Nor are the vastly superior powers of certain men the least doubtful, whether of vital energy, or sensuous discrimination, or intellectual grasp, or emotional breadth and depth of sympathy.

It is of course only such men that are even to be called geniuses in art or in any other human realm. They are so rare too, in all ages, that perhaps, in the light of their uniquely valuable function, society does not yet do enough for them. While rich communities sometimes pay them large fees in money and prestige, once they are recognized, scarcely anywhere are they really allowed such freedom of conception and expression, even in art, much less in manner of life, early in their development, as would give to the world through their unhampered activities what after all the world most values, though it usually feels no desire for or satisfaction in what is offered it at any given time. The gifted artist is just such a mind as goes beyond other men in his own field and creates such beauties as they do not in general appreciate until long afterwards. It is more usually lesser artists, though not for that reason despicable ones, of course, that achieve fame and wealth in their early lives; and it is the greatest artists who, as we all know, wait so many years for recognition, and perhaps die before it comes. And this will always be so in the very nature of the case, unless we come to cherish the arts more universally and in their own actuality, use our powers of discrimination and judgment upon them as fully as may be, and, where these fail, trust to critics and experts, the adequacy and validity of whose judgments, in turn, we may be in a position to estimate through our own lesser gifts and training. If we can have trusted and respected referees in sport, surely a society realistically educated in the arts, acquainted with their actual modes and manners, and with their past achievements, might enjoy the more mature benefits of sound critical opinion in the field of art itself, whose works would seem to be a more integral and lasting element in civilization than even those athletic sports to which we now devote so great a part of our wealth, our energies, and even our educational enterprises.

But what, on the basis of our discussion so far, is this mature and lasting good that art brings into life? The answer is too simple and too obvious to be at all convincing, for all that art brings to life may be put in one word; if it is successful, what art furnishes men's world with is beauty, which a serious-minded people may think of at the best as a pleasant luxury instead of a necessity, an expense, not an investment, if we must put it in our most vulgar terms. This is like condemning art as legislatures condemn universities, whose presidents in answer use the same vulgar terms. Even in these terms it is not hard to make out our case for art. We may do so merely by remarking the traditional and common application of great wealth to the acquiring of works of art, as all that wealth in the end can be spent upon, all that it is good for, if it is to buy immediately and intrinsically valuable objects instead of mere means to further wealth, or more indirect means to the welfare of others, or those expensive evidences of itself that capture the attention of men and give it prestige and power in their eyes. But we may do much better not to rely on such arguments but to seek the evidence of clear thinking, to meditate upon the true satisfactions of life, that is, until beauty comes into its own proper place in our estimation. Persuasion is not the province of æsthetics, and the question here is in any case one of value in general and of relative values in society, not a question of æsthetic theory only. But it may have become clear in the course of our survey that æsthetic considerations are considerations as to the immediate and often ultimate nature of the actual qualitative world in which we live. When this quality is at its most satisfactory, the world is beautiful; and since the creation of beauty is the aim of art, and since the achievement of artists is the beauty of their works, there is some ground at least for admitting the great actual value of both artists and their works to all men everywhere.

§ 4

Another consideration enforces this point and carries it much further. It is after all æsthetic criteria that are final in judging the values of all things, including even that of social usages and laws, and of forms of society in general. And it is direct æsthetic attention that most realistically and surely discerns the features of society as it is. The artist as artist is innocent of ulterior purposes and looks upon the world to see it as it actually appears. And such judgments as he gives us as a critic, as well as such accounts of it as his own artistic medium may express and present to us, are likely to upset our habitual notions of its character, constituted as these notions so largely are of social and religious prejudices, pseudo-science, personal inclinations, and dogmatic conceptions, instilled by conventional education and training. It is the artist's very innocence that is so disconcerting here, like that of a child who fails to see reason in an unreasonable order of things, until he is initiated into the mysteries of adult economic fears, religious dogmas, and social superstitions. So the artist fails to see the ugly aspects of our world and our society as beautiful, or its beautiful ones as ugly. But unlike the child, who is gradually tamed into conformity, he fails here permanently, refusing to falsify his own sure, trained perception to suit such esoteric fancies or palpable delusions as are thrust upon him on all sides, refusing to be initiated into a view of life and the world that denies those very appearances that he apprehends so clearly, in the interest of an abstract and often foolish or imaginatively inadequate construction which purports to account for them as merely superficial, and hence somehow unimportant aspects of a reality handed down by the fathers, or built up by patriotic or industrious and ambitious sons.

Radical reformers themselves also often lack the artist's innocent and direct perception of actual beauty and ugliness for the same reason as conservative businessmen or politicians. For their attention is likely to be focussed less on genuine appearances, which are the sole indications of any possible underlying reality, than on their own theoretical explanation of a state of things that does not even exist, but merely exemplifies their theories, and so in actuality needs no remedy, or upon some one, single, objectionable aspect of civilization which can not sanely be removed, unless it has been fully grasped as one aspect of the form and character and quality of the larger complex whole of which it is an element. When such critics and reformers do turn their attention to the form and features of this whole, they succeed in working it over towards a better one, only so far as they have clearly present to mind the content of that better world, a content viewed in the imagination under a structural form, and with a filling which, so far as it is defined at all, is defined in æsthetic data as the vision of a greater perfection.

There are obvious, crying evils which men may mitigate without too long hesitating over the further effects or ulterior transformations involved, but once a critic or a prophet or a reformer turns to the future, his dreams themselves are æsthetic structures, made out of such elements as he may have discovered in his discriminating perception of the æsthetic surface of the actually appearing world.

More than this, the society he dreams of and works towards will not be adequate to any full human living, or rationally to be desired by other men, or a satisfactory consummation if achieved, unless the dreamer has dreamt of beauty in it, and of art and artists, the function of art in life and of artists in society being of prime importance to men's happiness in any circumstances.

When we come to the ethical and social standards themselves by which we attempt to measure the satisfactoriness of a society, actual or imagined, these too, like all standards, turn out to be qualities, or degrees of qualities. Obviously, of good qualities and characteristics, the degree is to be heightened; but what are these qualities and characteristics, and what is our test of their goodness? Æsthetic vision again, direct feeling of their intrinsic satisfactoriness, which is so difficult to distinguish from beauty that the great thinkers have named it always in æsthetic terms, justice itself being only a sort of harmony. And in judging specific details these æsthetic categories are equally important. If the rich were forced to look upon the squalor and suffering of the poor, they could not endure it, as the officials of great corporations can not allow themselves to dwell even in imagination on the actually appearing misery or the sordid ugliness of the surroundings of men at the bottom of the great edifices of industry, and still remain content with the scheme that necessitates such sights. It is in their ultimately felt æsthetic quality that men all find such sights revolting and unendurable, and it is this ugliness that tells us unconditionally that they must be removed if any of us are to live even tolerably free from anguish in the world.

Hence the real strength of the democratic principle, which simply reminds us that we live in a world with other men, but with *all* other men, the various aspects of whose lives and surroundings we can not forever conceal, since in our dependence upon them they must come to our attention and finally be exhibited to us as integral aspects of our own life and world. If we are to be happy in a world as it really lies before us and about us in its actual appearance, that appearance can not remain unsatisfactory to contemplate, that is, æsthetically unsatisfactory,—condemned in the bare honesty of recording æsthetic judgments. If poverty and disease bore a pleasant aspect to discriminating perception, if injustice were æsthetically and directly satisfying to experience, and to dwell upon, what would there be to condemn it in any rational creature's eyes? For it is only in the embodiment in concrete æsthetic data of such abstractions as injustice and suffering and poverty, only their appearing in the world as unmistakably marked for aversion in a direct æsthetic view, that makes them unsatisfactory and ugly and bad. Thus it is finally æsthetic criteria that allow us to make those ethical and moral evaluations that we agree upon sooner or later; and it is æsthetic discernment that is required both to see the evils of the world and to picture a better one from which they can be said to have been removed—not merely changed for other or worse evils—just so far as this new world itself is positively valuable in beauty.

But such criticism or such social constructive thinking and

imagining as either condemns or rejects or praises and elevates artists and their function in society, will judge artists not only as the makers of art, but as men. In their sensuous and emotional vitality such men as artists almost inevitably are, may do things in life neither æsthetically nor morally praiseworthy. The criticism that this activity calls down upon their heads, whatever their merits or failures, and whatever the competence of the criticism, is not of course criticism of art, nor even of artists as such, nor has it any place in æsthetic theory, though in much purported art criticism it has been dragged in or substituted for æsthetic judgment itself. It would be an absurd mistake to confuse moral shortcomings with æsthetic ones, even though the ultimate criteria both in morals and in scientific theory are themselves æsthetic standards. Beauty is as such a pure good, whatever it is the beauty of, and whoever may be its author; and beauty transforms the surface of what might be in itself merely unclean or unchaste or unholy, into what may be still unlovely in itself, and yet so hold our eyes to its beautiful surface that it seems purified of its evil, as actually happens in a work of art, where it is just this surface that specifies the whole beauty and significance of the object.

The authors of artistic beauty, being men, may also of course be bad men, except in just this authorship, in so much of their activity, that is, as satisfactorily fulfills their artist's function. And what they do here is so absolutely valuable, their function as artists is so precious, that society may perhaps wisely forgive them for their æsthetically irrelevant sins, especially since what we think of as sins in such men are so much oftener the natural and innocent expression of that vitality and power that makes them artists of significance. In a fully civilized society which allowed free rein to the expression of natural human instincts, or at least tried to provide for such expression as the basis of its polity, these so-called sins might turn out to be childlike innocence, or inventive gaiety. Artists need not be allowed to steal or murder; but these are not the crimes of which they are likely to be accused as characteristic failings. In a world where we are just discovering how antiquated and inhuman most of our social institutions are, and how discordant with the necessary or even possible nature of men, and hence how inimical to their happiness, we can afford to be indulgent to any one or anything in the world of which in any sure sense we can affirm great positive human value. This we can do in the case of art and artists, and if society must have high priests at all, we might well substitute great artists as at least better candidates for the temple than the philosophers whom Plato would have made kings.

CHAPTER XVI

ÆSTHETIC JUDGMENT AND KNOWLEDGE
IN GENERAL

1. Æsthetic theory a general summary of particular æsthetic judgments. 2. The natural antipathy between
scientists and artists in purpose and procedure. 3. Determinate pluralism in æsthetics. 4. Further alienation between scientists and artists through inadequate critical
theory and practice. 5. The conflict to be meliorated by
genuine acquaintance with the arts and by æsthetic theory
based on such acquaintance.

§ 1

In examining the nature of æsthetic judgment we have all
along been discussing æsthetic surface and the beauties of the
arts as the content referred to in assertions. Æsthetic judgments, like all other judgments, are statements purporting to
be true. We have seen too, how, from the simple elementary judgments which are bare records of the experiencing
of beauty, there are developed in fuller æsthetic criticism,
judgments of evaluation according to standards, themselves
furnished by æsthetic discrimination and taste; then, in still
more fully developed criticism, æsthetic analysis and also
explanation in terms of technical processes employed and
technical details contributory to the effect or point. Finally
there is appreciative criticism, depending on all these varieties of æsthetic judgment, and going beyond them all in
attempting through linguistic forms to reproduce the sort of
beauty here recorded in its general nature, though never

exactly in its own definite and determinate content, and reinforcing this by an account or communication of the feelings aroused in the critic himself, feelings appropriate to the work of art commented upon, and so, if successfully communicated to a reader of the criticism, inducing in him a mood properly receptive of the special sort of beauty of this work of art, which he may thus indirectly and derivatively appreciate and enjoy, his vicarious valuing and evaluation of it again to be recorded in his own æsthetic judgments. How strong these derivative feelings of value are, as well as our faith in them, is shown by the fact that our taste is often formed at least as much through our confidence in the authenticity of feeling and judgment of parents and friends and teachers, who recount to us the beauties they have known, as by our own actual first-hand æsthetic experiences.

Beyond, and usually also implicitly within, all these particular kinds of æsthetic and critical judgment, there is a body of principles, which is of course sound only so far as it is the generalization of specific first-hand judgments in more abstract and inclusive judgments. If these are made explicit, they are the formal statement of the principles, their full meaning contained in all the specific judgments of which they are a sort of framework or pattern, into which any one of these specific judgments accurately fits.

If a particular shade of red appeared gay and bright and pleasant to see on some one occasion, we make the simple record of this fact in a judgment asserting that that specific red was in this small but determinate fashion beautiful. Then the experience is repeated, perhaps, and we further discover that red in general, in a large range of its possibilities of variation, is characteristically warm, and in this way emotionally satisfying or even comforting. We experience the beauties of other specific colors, and generalize still further to the effect that colors have always a particular emotional tone to contribute to visual surfaces, and so also to design and composition. But so analogously of other sensuous elements. We finally come to say in a broader and more abstract but equally sound judgment, that sensuous elements experienced separately or in compositions are in general materials of beauty, both sensuous and to some degree expressive. So on to form as such, and more satisfying structural expressive beauty, to the particular arts, and their special kinds of æsthetic surface and expressiveness, and then to other sorts of expressiveness and other more complex arts, and finally to a clear consciousness of the general nature and the varieties of beauty, and of judgments, particular and concrete or general and abstract, recording beauties found.

Æsthetic theory itself is thus seen to be nothing but a system of related abstract judgments, whose concrete meaning lies in particular æsthetic judgments, out of which its generalizations have emerged. Here then we are faced with a body of knowledge covering a field of experience, not too well defined, but obviously offering genuine concrete data to check generalization and allow it to take on the form of rationally established theory, if not of verified scientific doctrine. Æsthetics is an intellectual enterprise, apparently to be included as part of learning and knowledge in general, its abstract content, however, drawn from the species of judgment that learned and serious scholars are likely to frown upon as not judgment at all, but a sort of emotional gesture, expressing individual feeling or personal taste, and only accidentally in the form of logical discourse in words. What is worse, the verifying and controlling data of æsthetic theory lie in the field of art and of perceptual discrimination in general, where it is the relatively unstable and only vaguely defined distinctions of sensuous experience, along with its burden of accompanying feeling, integral to the apprehended object, that are the last criteria of accuracy and truth.

§ 2

Hence, although beauty and the arts have always received the devoted services of artists, and so of some of the greatest of human lives, and though some of the most distinguished men of history who have not themselves been artists, have occupied themselves with critical appreciation, the rest of the articulate world, especially professed scholars and scientists, has given to the arts and æsthetics, or to Art, as they are likely to call it, little but lip-service. It is as if serious devotion to knowledge and truth were more or less independent of the arts and of æsthetic experience itself, as if indeed æsthetic judgment were a mere personal concern. In a region where even distinguished experts in criticism differ so conspicuously in their pronouncements, a scholar of traditional mold can hardly be expected to take these experts or their subject matter too seriously. For truth must be what is so, and hence singly what it is. It can not be contained, or always more and more closely approximated, in a motley variety of opinions exhibiting not mere disagreement but contradiction at all points, and this not only in theoretical conclusions, but in observed facts, along with such a use of terms in varying and conflicting meanings as is alone enough to be completely confusing. If truth is to be found in some one of these many expert opinions, the scholar is at a loss to know in which of them; for in his own intellectual field, while there may be ignorance among laymen and wide differences in informed opinion, such ignorance and such differences are, at least in science, always more or less temporary. In other fields not so strictly scientific, they are usually susceptible of removal, or at least of rational statement and rational discussion, on some common basis. At any rate they are never taken as ultimately mere arbitrary irresponsible assertions or irresolvable contradictory confusions. Thus art and science, or truth and beauty, are, though not in their own nature, still in men's minds, violently divorced.

No doubt both artists themselves as well as æsthetic critics are largely responsible for this, and it is easy to see why they should be; but scientists and scholars are responsible too. In his modes of apprehension, as well as in his interests, the genuine artist is not primarily intellectual but sensuous. He lives very largely in perception and feeling, and in the sensuous expression of feeling. He is successful when his work specifies in its own terms what he finds to be his felt intention; for obviously no intention is fully determinate except as it passes through technical operations into a sensuous objective form. We are all of us intimately acquainted with this technical fact in talking and writing. What we mean becomes clear, becomes definitely what it is at all, to ourselves or to others, only as it gets actually said in words. Since the artist is often not saying anything in words, since what he expresses in his own medium becomes finally clear and specifically determinate in non-linguistic terms, his meaning simply could not be recognized in determinate form except as sure feeling carries him along in his work to a completion, which is the revelation to himself as well as the exhibition to others of just what he does mean, constituted fully and finally before our eyes or ears upon what we have called an æsthetic surface, felt as expressive as well as sensuously apprehended. Even if the medium is language, the specific determinate significance of a work of art is not what could be extracted or abstracted from a poem or from prose as the so-called sense of it, such an abstract, logical, systematic relation of terms in discourse as the intellectually minded insist upon as its actual import and value. For it is the subtle rhythmic and tonal qualities of the linguistic medium, together with the whole vast but determinate denotation and connotation of the varied æsthetic content seen through this medium, this latter content in turn articulated and organically coherent in the structure of creative imagination, that the literary artist really gives us.

With such particularization as it stands, and without such an impossible summation as practical or theoretical convenience seems almost to demand, intellect as much, especially scientifically trained or scholarly intellect, is dissatisfied and irritated and merely exhausted in being so widely deployed. Knowledge and truth attempt to be one single coherent whole, as simply, and hence as abstractly, systematic as possible, their comprehensiveness being due to just such abstract simplification and generalization. Hence the very habits and tendencies and ideals of the rigorous, though perhaps narrowly, intellectual mind tend in the opposite direction from the habits of the artistic mind or those of the appreciative observer.

§ 3

In art and in æsthetic appreciation we are both discovering and composing always new varieties of beauty, the unique determinations in detail of all the possible sorts of æsthetic elements, all the different modes in which these can be operated upon and built into structures, and all the possible kinds of individual structures so built up. These, if they are successfully perfected, specify in determinate æsthetic detail what is only felt by the artist; and such æsthetic specification is not quite seen or heard or defined in any terms, until the artist's work is finished. His whole activity and effort is carried out at the bidding of an insistent, dominating inner urge, always ready to correct his movements if they begin to miss its point and intention, a controlling force that governs his work from first to last, when finally this feeling itself becomes a determinate meaning in clear external form. Such a completed formal surface may be lovely in its mere sensuous quality, but more significant art is often less easily acceptable on that score; for the easier forms of beauty can not often be accurately or fully expressive of important artistic ideas and meanings. The æsthetic specification of these last, however, is always beautiful with the vital beauty of achieved expression, and so far as the æsthetic elements and the formal structure are integral to this expression, beautiful throughout. This is all that there is of what is sometimes called intellectual beauty. Intellectual beauty is not the mysterious and awful spirit or the Unseen Power of Shelley's poem, but the actual lustre in the sky, a determinate specification upon an æsthetic surface of directly appreciated significance, whether the surface is that of nature or of art.

Beauties are ultimately plural and individual, discrete differences in the world's aspect, not its whole and single being, which is neither possibly present to sense, nor very convincing or clear to intellect, if it is even conceivable. What scientists and scholars seek, on the other hand, is abstract, systematic unity. It is true that unity is a category applicable to all works of art, a canon of all criticism, and a demand of all logic. But this unity as such is not a relatively systematic whole; much less is it the Universal Whole.

ESTHETIC JUDGMENT

That would be making of its mere distinguishing separateness its actual character and form and nature, which is of course a rich, full, structural whole. The unity is merely the fact of its being a single entity, not its structural coherent character. It is the unity that is the distinction of one concept from another in logic, the mere distinction of this from that, which is necessary to articulate thinking. It is the unity that designates any surface or object a particular object of contemplation, its parts, if it is not absolutely simple, as scarcely anything is, coherent within the unit by virtue of the object's own special inner structure. The unity of the unit, its being one, is an achievement under structural principles, but the bare oneness itself is not constituted of these nor does it exemplify them. Its being one is only its own separate distinctness from all else as the particular work of art that it is. It is only this sort of unity, so often confused with the coherence which in all genuine compositions is incident to its achievement, that the critical canon demands. So that it must be plain that this is a very elementary demand indeed, no more that of art than of logic as such, or of any discriminating perception that is to have any objective content whatever.

If our references to Plato have seemed so often intended to discredit his theories, it is because on this central point Plato and the Platonists were themselves mistaken, and so gave countenance to a misleading doctrine espoused by many lesser minds. Nowhere has the specific sensitiveness to particular and various beauties been more fully realized, if we may judge by its expression, than in some of Plato's famous passages. But such variety being incomprehensible in one unifying and unified idea, Plato felt its imputation of inadequacy to any conceptual grasp of the world as a single intelligible whole, and he felt this, it may be supposed, in direct proportion to the degree of his vital feeling of the æsthetic charm, which he therefore interpreted as seduction, of the many and various beauties, each absolutely particular and determinately individual, of the sense world, a world whose rich and variegated surface he distrusted, because it held men absorbed in æsthetic contemplation at the expense of civic patriotic activities. Rather than be lost intellectually and morally in this powerfully seductive variety, Plato denied its genuine reality in favor of a One, Invisible and Intangible. And this One of his was so authentically mystical that his professed followers in later ages were the great mystics of history, denying in the end, and inevitably, any valid knowledge except the pure vision of Transcendental Oneness, which even they failed to achieve as men, since its achievement is the denial of articulate thought and the negation of living human consciousness.

In our discussion of color, and again in our account of the expressive beauty of architecture, the logical theory involved in a pluralistic view of beauty, a view that finds it always to be unique and particular in its individuality, was hinted at. We can not properly, in a survey of æsthetic theory, fully justify, much less carefully expound, this or any other logical theory. But we ought to stop long enough to say that the theory has been expounded and justified in the careful work of modern logicians, and that it is not the outworn and discredited nominalism of the Schools, or of the empiricists of modern philosophy. Moreover, its foundations were laid by Kant, who insisted as fully upon the ideal of complete specification of infinite detailed particulars in the achievement of knowledge of what he called the phenomenal world, as upon the ideal of a single, necessary, completed *whole* of knowledge. Both ideals were, he insisted, plainly beyond the scope of fully significant rational demonstration on the one hand, and of empirical realization in a specification over the whole range of actuality on the other.

Now scholars and scientists are not pluralists in method; they pursue above all else a systematic abstract completeness. Artists on the other hand always discover and create and specify in full sensuous detail and particular individuality new determinate surface beauties; and the two kinds of mind are thus definitely, and apparently fundamentally, at odds. The scholar or scientist is never content to leave particulars and details as they stand; he must group them under categories, reveal them as instances of general principles, or at least list them in a catalogue with systematically arranged headings. He is interested in details very often just because they do fit his general account of a subject matter of a given sort, and he explains away, so far as he can, every aspect of things that would appear to be unique and unclassifiable. Variation itself is not satisfactory to him until he has stated a law of variation and a measure of its degrees. But an artist seeks just that specific and peculiar variation in elements, forms, and structures that will externalize his own individual feeling, in an expression of it distinguished by exactly the individualizing difference that it achieves as a uniquely expressive work of art.

§ 4

But this aspect of the activity and thinking of artists, irritating and obnoxious as it may be to the typical scholarly mind, is not all that serves to alienate them and their works, as well as criticism of art, so completely from the full sympathetic comprehension of intellectually active and honestly inquiring students. For the specification of detail as such is after all an admitted element in the methodology of science in the classic terms of such an intellectualist as Kant himself. And æsthetic theory, as distinguished from its subject matter, and from criticism of the appreciative type, is as general and abstract and systematic in method and intention as any other sort of theory. What more completely effects this alienation of science and art in the flesh, and at the same time lowers art and artists in the eyes of strictly intellectual workers, is another aspect of their thought and their expression of it, namely the strikingly divergent accounts of creative artistic activity and of completed works of art, which are also infected with an ambiguous, loose terminology, and the contradictory evaluations of art and artists pronounced by artists themselves and by æsthetic critics.

In part, as we saw early in our general treatment of æsthetic judgment, such valuing and such evaluations must differ, so far as they are honest, straightforward judgments at all, just as greatly as men differ in their specific response, by reason of gift and endowment or through training, to works of art in their presence. Men differ in what they actually perceive, and in the feeling stirred in them by their apprehension of æsthetic surfaces of particular sorts. If a man has suffered long from jaundice in his early years, yellow may become biologically offensive to him, and hence naturally and directly apprehended as ugly. Such cases are common. The apprehending subject may even know that it is only for this reason that yellow looks ugly to him; but since the response to it in himself, when the sole object of his conscious attention is the yellow he sees, is the felt opposite of delight, he attributes this quality to all that occupies his consciousness at the time, and ugliness is thus the objective character of the intuited, visual yellow surface. If this is an illusion, it is only such an illusion as we all suffer if we see objects even with definite spatial character and boundaries. For actually occurring objects are always changing, always only slow events, their imputed character being thus attributed, as the nature of its own independent being, to what is after all only an arbitrarily, or rather humanly and naturally, discriminated and separate, and perhaps static, entity. And this nature is also necessarily static in the sense in which quality or character or logical concept is static, that is, defined as what it is and as no other character or nature, not susceptible therefore of change any more than a geometrical definition throughout the demonstration in which it is being employed.

Thus genuine æsthetic judgments are relative to the subject making them, and not only to his perceptive training and gift, but to his readiness and flexibility and depth of emotional response as well. When these little studied specifically human factors enter into a situation which is itself as objective and natural as any other, such theory as refuses to take them into account for the sake of simplicity, and the supposed avoidance of personal or arbitrary or subjective confusions, inevitably falsifies its account of the matter, and, so far as it penetrates into the actual phenomena, inevitably finds difficulties and inconsistencies. The clearest, most honest æsthetic judgments, if taken to apply to the object of apprehension alone, instead of to this object as in an established natural relation to a perceiving and feeling mind, will appear contradictory. And artists and critics themselves so often neglect this fact that their developed critical pronouncements, going beyond the simple fact of the primary æsthetic record of their experience of beauty in an object, suggest nothing but confusion to outside disinterested, scientific, or even merely rational, inquiry.

Furthermore, training and orientation of mind in general are determined by infinitely various conditions of time and place, history and tradition, physical and social surroundings, national and personal interests, and too many other factors to attempt to list them here. Not only do individual æsthetic judgments differ widely, therefore, but æsthetic judgment as in one locality instead of another, in Italy instead of Finland, in Greece instead of America, in the seventeenth or eighteenth instead of the nineteenth century, in war or peace, in famine and flood or in times of plenty. Any change in any condition possibly affecting the content and activity of men's minds may also change men's appreciation of objects æsthetically viewed, and difference in æsthetic judgments of what we call the same object are not the exception but the rule. But none of this makes accurate æsthetic theory arbitrary or non-objective; it only makes it difficult. And it has so far left it extraordinarily incomplete and unsatisfactory to scholarly minds.

We hardly need remind ourselves by illustration of such historical and empirical differences. Current judgments of present day art are enough to convince us of their genuine existence. And if these are too close to ourselves to be believed authentically and necessarily divergent, we have only to turn to some of the innumerable examples in the history of art and criticism,—the vogue of Dickens, its decline, and the rehabilitation of his works once more; the eighteenth century opinion of Shakespeare, the omission of El Greco from even very thorough manuals of art history, the tremendous popularity and the violent condemnation of Raphael and his works. Even objects of nature, as we have already noted, are equally loved and hated, and so actually and genuinely found beautiful or ugly, by different men at different times in different circumstances. It is no wonder that æsthetic judgment, and the generalizations of it in systematic æsthetic theory, present a welter of contradiction as to facts, and a confusion in theory, to the scholar, himself so little gifted or trained in sensuous discrimination and appreciation as to have no familiar experiences to account for such divergence and such confusion.

We should of course discount the violent and irresponsible utterances of incompetents, not only among artists and æsthetic critics and theorists, but also among scholars themselves. There will naturally be those whose own intellectual endeavors are so exciting and absorbing, and seem so significant, that their methods and results will seem to them the only methods and results worth applying or achieving. They will forget their constant employment of quite other methods, especially their purely sensory discriminations, and perhaps finally cease from such sensory activities, so far as possible, as being unworthy of their intellecual or scientific calling. And in doing so they will fail to see how dangerous this may be for their genuine success. Symbolic language or mathematically formulated statements will appear to them to contain all the true meanings that there are, all the knowledge that minds can achieve. But since in the end, or rather in the beginning, the whole range of content that they purport to have included and summed up in their generalizations and abstractions is strictly æsthetic, in neglecting and undervaluing æsthetic discrimination and æsthetic data, they will become meaninglessly abstract. Their results will be, if not false, at least not so inclusive and not so accurate as their own ideal demands.

When such thinkers do turn their attention to art and beauty, they are only too likely to dispose of it as being as unimportant to men in general as it has become to them in their narrow preoccupations, or else they will come to think that it has essentially only such value and meaning as they can translate into their own abstract terms or force into their generalizations. But these generalizations have so neglected the vast field of æsthetic data, in their actual insistent particularity, that they are not at all fitted to give any account of them. Such thinkers may go so far as to abstract what they call the logical content of a poem, for example, as what it is attempting to express, and they sometimes even commit the childish fallacy of literary interpretations of music or painting or sculpture, as if such an interpretation could be anything more than a suggestion of the general sort of emotional content and significance of these arts. In the end, much of the foolish criticism of art that we read is their own work, or done under their guidance, or under the influence of their methods, and the history of language as a symbolic discursive medium, with an account of changes in vowel sounds and particulars of spelling and syntax has sometimes actually been substituted for the reading and study of literature, as if it could take its place, or were of greater importance.

But there are difficulties on the other side. Artists, forgetting that they have expressed themselves and their intentions and meanings fully and even ultimately upon the æsthetic surfaces that they create, attempt impatiently to convey this untranslatable significance to ears and minds unfitted to grasp it as it stands revealed here, but putting it into the intellectual and linguistic terms that such minds can apprehend and accept. And here they are false to them-

selves and their works, unless they happen also to be intellectually trained, and not only clear-headed and generally
informed and possessed of substantial philosophical powers,
but also skilful in the medium of words. If artists do not
need to be mathematicians or philosophers to be true artists,
they do need all these varieties of training and knowledge to
be teachers or critics. If they and all the other critics were
so trained and so informed, there would be a great falling
off in inaccurate terminology, inconsistent statement, and
irrelevant contradiction in methods of teaching, estimates of
artistic success, and evaluations of works of art. The point
might be further illustrated, but the single example of the
use of the term rhythm to mean so many different things,
and its indiscriminate application to spatial form as such,
which we noticed in our discussion of that subject, will be
enough to remind us of the kind of obstacle that artists and
æsthetic critics themselves, as well as theorists, put in the way
of other men's appreciating their value and their true function.

§ 5

It is only general and widespread education in art itself,
including of course a grasp of its primary technique, that is,
the elementary principles of composition in sensuous elements of any sort, as well as training in sensuous perception
and discrimination, that will furnish an honest and intelligent appreciation of art, or establish the place of æsthetic
judgment in knowledge in general. Some such account of
the nature and principles of æsthetic judgment as we have
been attempting here may be of service, not of course to
make men into artists, but to aid artists, however slightly,
towards an adequate intellectual grasp of their own function
and the nature of their works. And such an attempt may

also be of some avail in persuading the intellectually and linguistically minded to take æsthetic judgments seriously, as furnishing important knowledge, and constituting an intellectual realm of their own, to be neglected only at the risk of missing all the meanings and all the human intentions that are not and can not be made evident anywhere else. But of course no such survey can possibly give to any one the discriminating sensuous perception to find or to see works of art in their actuality. That is to be acquired only through some amount of technical artistic training. This may serve, then, as an apology for even so thin and summary a treatment of the subject; but before we leave it altogether, in what is at best so incomplete and unscientific an outline of its manifestations, there is one more consideration that ought not to be omitted even here.

We have been engaged with theoretical questions, and the purpose of all theory is the intellectual grasp of our world or of some of its aspects, so that we may be more at home in it. Æsthetics is not a rigorously defined field. In one sense it treats of all the world as the world offers a surface to immediate sensuous apprehension, a surface upon which beauty sometimes supervenes. But beauty appears and is actual only as there is some one for it to appear to, since the beauty of objects is not an independently constituted, sensuously and formally expressive surface, but the felt satisfactory quality and point of such a surface. Thus, like all value, æsthetic value occurs as a quality or essence in apprehension, in discriminating perception that deepens into a particular sort of delightful response; and this specific sort of delight, being found only in the apprehension of objects upon which full attention is focussed, so that they are the complete content of consciousness at the time, is imputed to them as their own objective quality, a quality which we found early in our discussion to be as truly objective as any other. It is determined in natural circumstances by the properties of things as well as by the properties of minds or bodies that see these things as so qualified, by physical conditions, in other words. The actual situation is one in which a connection is established through physical, which we must remember includes physiological, media. What happens is simply a natural event, as all happenings are. But some natural events, involving human bodies and brains, are accompanied by appearances, and beauty itself is in and of a specific appearance as its uniquely valuable quality.

Thus æsthetic theory is a branch of the general theory of value. It may also be true that æsthetic theory, in surveying beauties, is an account not only of one type of value, but of the essential nature of all value. If this is so, æsthetics has a high place in the realm of knowledge in general, since what it treats of is the creation and assessment of value as such, and since value is by definition the character or quality of all that is important to men, whether as artists, or as theorists, or simply as moral beings.

INDEX

INDEX

372

INDEX

beginning in direct perception and appreciation, 320; place of technical details in, 329; as translation of beauty into linguistic terms, 329-332; relation of critic's own enthusiasm to, 331; requisites to competence in, 332-335; uses, 352; inadequate methodology, 361

Critics, function in society, 322

Cross rhythms, 160-161

Dalcroze, Jacques, 148

Dancers, appreciation of rhythm by, 163-164

Dancing, 275, 280; origins, 51-53; content, 78; correlation with sound, 113; rhythm of, 155; art of, 163

Darkness of color, 97

Day-dreams, 13, 32, 35; primitive, 50

Decoration, a mixed art, 99

Democratic principle, strength of, 349

Depth, 131

Design, theories of, 130; pure expression in, 245; spatial expression in, 246, 254; and nature, 255

Detail, discrimination in, 11, 40; specification of, an element in scientific methodology, 362

Determinate nature of beauty, 8-10

Diatonic scale, 91

Dickens, 364

Dimensionality, 129-133

Discrimination, of surface qualities, 11, 30-44; lack of, 36; in criticism, 334

Disease, æsthetic unsatisfactoriness of, 349

Drama, temporal arts involved, 275

Drama, Greek, poetry and music, 235

Dramatic action, 282

Dramatic composition, 276

Dramatic criticism, 321, 327

Dramatic unity, 325

Dress, beauty of, 333

Duse, Eleonora, 282

Dynamics in music, 238

Einfuehlung, theory of, 126

Elements, beauty of, 138-144

El Greco, 364

Ellis, Havelock, 164

Emerson, on sense discrimination, 37

Emotional capacity, necessary to artist, 343

Emotions, free expression of, 52; expression through sound, 78; expressed in music and poetry, 250; and the stage, 279

English poetry, 170

Events subject to nature, 302

Every-day life, 40-44

Exaggeration on the stage, 278

Expressiveness, beauty of, 81, 218, 219, 224; in words, 226; in individuals, 234; in music, 235

Extension, principle of, 73

Façades, 146

Fear, 54

Fiction, 289, 294; didactic and propagandist, 298; as a great art, 299

Fine art. See Art

Flower painting, 256

Flowers, beauty enriched by fragrance, 65; in sculpture, 254

Flux in nature, 7

Forms, in primitive art, 53; beauties, 251. See also Spatial form

Fragrance, of flowers, 65; of air, 178

Fry, Roger, 149

Function a primary requisite in useful arts, 187

Funeral dirge, 49

Funerals, 44

Garden, subtleties, 179

Generalization of æsthetic judgments, 353

Genius, 344

Geometrical order, 73

Geometrical rigor of our judgments of space, 117

Geometrical shapes, 126-127; contrasted with sense objects, 118; beauty, 133

Gesture, 275

Gothic architecture, 125

Grand opera, 283

Graphic art, primitive, 50-51, 53

Greek art and Greek marbles, 301

Greek chorus, 287

Greek drama, rhythmical and tonal qualities, 235; unity in, 325

Greek key pattern, 245

INDEX

Greek poetry, 170
Greek sculpture and architecture, restoration to original colored appearance, 142

Harmony, 238, 241
Heroic figures, 189
Hispano-Moresque art, 245
Historical changes in æsthetic judgments, 364
History, 294
Hogarth's fallacy of independent objectivity, 124-126
Hues, 96, 114; complementary, 100; order, 143
Human activities, directed, 182
Human bodies, as instruments of sound, 79; spatial character of, 131; expression, 247, 255, 263, 275
Human character, judgment, 38, 341
Human life, possibilities of, expressed in literature, 299
Human minds, God's highest works, 300
Human point of view, 125

Ibsen, 310
Ictus, 171
Idea of Beauty (mythical abstraction), 119
Ideals, importance of æsthetic surface to, 340
Ideas, as part of artist's equipment, 343
Imagination and poetry, 232
Incense, 65
Independent activity, fallacy of, 123-126
Indiscriminateness, 36, 40
Indolence, as a quality of æsthetic judgment, 13
Industrial arts, 44, 76; preparation of materials and tools, 185; value of function, 186; preserve useful techniques, 203
Inexpressible, The, 307, 308
Innocence of vision, 182
Insanity, 2
Instrumental technique, 242
Instrumentalists, adequacy as musicians, 243
Intellectual beauty, 358
Intelligible structure, lack of in tastes and odors, 63
Intensity, in music, 94-95

Intrinsic order in æsthetic materials, 68-71, 105-108, 127, 130
Intuition, 223

Japanese prints, wave-forms, 256, 257
Jazz, 164, 236, 331
Journeymen of the arts, 343
Judgment, limited knowledge of, 2

Kant, 360

La Croix, 256
Language, technical control of, in poetry, 204; as vehicle of meaning, 225; beauty of expression, 227; auditory character, 230; felicities and accuracies, 232; symbols, 260; universal range of denotation, 290; crystallizes thought, 293; translation of beauty into, 329-332; inadequacy for interpreting art, 365-366
Latin poetry, 170
Length, 135
Leonardo da Vinci, classification of types, 124, 136
Lessing, æsthetic theory, 250
Lieder, 287
Life, literature expresses possibilities of, 298; æsthetic surface, 299
Lightness of color, 97, 111
Lines, intrinsic order, 68, 73; Hogarth's classification, 124; as elementary material for spatial composition, 129
Literary composition, 295
Literature, and the arts, 289; moral function, 298
Locality, effect on æsthetic judgment, 364
Loudness, in music, 94

Marbles, Greek, 301
Mathematical objects, beauty, 27
Mathematical structure, 127
Mathematicians, æsthetic appreciation, 120
Mathematics, symbolism in, 293, 305
Meaning, vehicles of, 225, 259
Melody, 238, 241
Men, neglect of sense discrimination, 37
Mind, God's highest work, 300
Miniatures, 189

INDEX

Moral function of literature, 298
Moral qualities, 304
Mural decoration, 146
Music, origins, 51, 53; emotional responses to, 54; only a part of audible beauty, 82; rhythmic elaborateness, 156; æsthetic value, 184; the temporal art *par excellence*, 193; sounding surface, 202, 241; abuse of technique, 207; emotional expressiveness, 214, 240; in Greek drama, 235; jazz, 236; technique, 241; and the drama, 275; expressiveness, 250, 285; structural possibilities, 271; instruction in appreciation of, 250; opera, 283; tonal and rhythmical qualities, 285
Musical compositions, 159
Musical conductor, 243, 276; rhythmic motions, 155
Musical notation, 156
Musical scale, 88-91, 141, 238
Musicians, composers and instrumentalists, 243
Mysticism, debt to Plato, 360

Narrative composition, 276
Natural forms, æsthetic effect through use of, 194
Nature, as the inspiration of primitive art, 50, 55; beauties of, 67; profusion confounding apprehension, 180; and art, 194, 302; and design, 256; accidentally beautiful, 301; expressive beauty, 303, 313
Neutral colors, 98, 103
Noise, as distinguished from tones, 81
Notation, 241
Novels, 289

Octave, 88-91
Odors, 60-68, 178; blending with sound, form and color, 64, 67
Onomatopœia, 202
Opera, complex structure, 283
Orchestra conductor, rhythmic motions of, 155; as musician, 243
Orchestra score, 284
Order, of spatial forms, 122; thought of, in spatial terms, 134
Organ tones, 65
Ornament, primitive forms, 47; concealing function, 189; beauty of extraneous, 264

Ostwald, Wilhelm, color notation, 98-104
Overtones, 92-94

Painting, a mixed art, 99; æsthetic surface, 200; expression in, 244, 253
Palate, perception by, 59
Partials, 92
Patterns, 47; spatial, 146; rhythmic, 151-162
Pendulum, 86
Perception, 57, 223, 314; limited knowledge of, 2; term, 20
Perfumers, as artists, 63
Perspective, 74, 253
Philosophers, appreciation of rhythm by, 164
Photographic representation, false conception of art as, 56, 248
Photography, as a fine art, 198
Pigments, as distinguished from colors, 103
Pitch, musical, 72, 82-91, 93, 114, 238
Plane shapes, 130
Plato, 235; on sense discrimination, 37; on music and gymnastics, 164; conception of unity, 359
Platonic fallacies, 118-123
Platonism, 260
Play, reading of a, 280
Playwright's technique, 281
Plot in dramatic composition, 276
Pluralism in æsthetics, 357-361; justified by modern logicians, 360; antipathetic to scientists, 361
Poet, qualifications, 204; and the stage, 281
Poetry, stanza forms, 159; rhythm in, 166-173; printed with indication of tempo, 168; æsthetic value, 184; as an auditory art, 193, 204; sounding surface, 202; linguistic medium, 204; as an art, 206; tonal and rhythmical possibilities, 214; style, 234; in Greek drama, 235; expressiveness of, 250; and the drama, 275; set to music, 286; Greek, 287; of Blake, 308
Points of a line, 130
Pompeian arabesque, 245
Portraits, miniatures and heroic figures, 189
Portraiture, 198

INDEX

INDEX